Peter Godfrey
Father of New Zealand Choral Music

PETER GODFREY

Father of New Zealand Choral Music
An oral history

ELIZABETH SALMON

m

Dedicated to Peter Godfrey and
my dear husband, Tom Salmon

A catalogue record for this book is available
from the National Library of New Zealand.

ISBN 978-0-9941065-8-2

Cover: Peter Godfrey as a King's College chorister, 1930s.
Back cover: Peter Godfrey conducting in Auckland, 1970s.
Both images from Peter Godfrey's private collection.

Cover design: Mākaro Press
Book design and typesetting: Paul Stewart
Editors: Mary McCallum & Paul Stewart

Printed by Wakefields Digital,
Wellington, New Zealand.
First published in 2015.

Mākaro Press
PO Box 41-032 Eastbourne 5047
makaropress@gmail.com
makaropress.co.nz

pp 29-31

Contents

Foreword

Sir David Willcocks CBE MC
British choral conductor, organist and composer

I HAVE KNOWN PETER GODFREY SINCE OUR DAYS AS STUDENTS AT KING'S College, Cambridge, in the 1940s. He and I were close friends at Cambridge, and afterwards when he was working at Uppingham School and Marlborough College and I was organist at Salisbury and Worcester Cathedrals.

When, in 1958, Peter announced that he was moving to Auckland as a lecturer in music and organist at St Mary's Cathedral, I was one of the many friends who doubted whether it was the right move. But what a tremendous success he has made of his career, his choirs achieving standards of first-class choral singing.

Peter has done more than anyone else in New Zealand to inspire young conductors and singers, and to raise the standard of choral singing throughout the country. I have personally witnessed many of Peter's choirs, and in particular have been impressed by the Auckland Dorian Choir, and the New Zealand Youth Choir, which has won many international awards.

Peter has contributed hugely to the musical life of New Zealand as professor of music at Auckland University, director of music at Auckland Cathedral, conductor of the Auckland Symphony Orchestra and the Auckland Dorian Choir, conductor of the National Youth Choir, director of music at Wellington Cathedral, conductor of the Wellington Orpheus

Choir, founding conductor of the Kapiti Chamber Choir, conductor of the Kapiti Chorale and founding president of the New Zealand Choral Federation.

Peter has always retained links with Cambridge, visiting his family home in Bluntisham and returning in 1978 to take over the King's College Choir for a spell. His many honours, including FRCO (Fellowship of the Royal College of Organists), Hon FRSCM (Honorary Fellowship of the Royal School of Church Music), and his MBE and CBE are testimony to the regard with which he is held in the world of music.

Over the years I have followed his very successful career with interest and pleasure, and have cherished our long friendship.

Cambridge
January 2009

Opposite: Peter speed skating on the Fens, 1963.

Introduction

Elizabeth Salmon

T HIS BOOK HAS BEEN SEVEN YEARS IN THE MAKING, FAR LONGER THAN I anticipated. Although most of the material was recorded or received in 2008 and 2009, and the book was largely put together then, Peter's circumstances changed. He was suffering from the beginning of suspected Alzheimer's disease, later re-diagnosed as dementia, which made it difficult for him to remember details from the areas of his life we had yet to explore. Also intruding was the trauma of the breakup of his second marriage, leaving his beloved home in Karaka Grove, Waikanae, and saying goodbye to Dottie, the little Jack Russell terrier who had won his heart.

This meant collaboration on the book was not able to continue for a while, and when it was time for me to resume work, Peter's memory was sadly compromised. Fortunately, he had written several autobiographical accounts of parts of his life, which were of immense value in amplifying the recorded material I already had, as was his son-in-law Simon Tipping's generous permission to use material from his books on the Orpheus Choir and the New Zealand Youth Choir. In fact, it would be true to say that the interviews with Peter on those two subjects are as much my construction as Peter himself speaking. Peter understood the modified process, and has read all of the edited interviews with his name on them, accepting them as true to his life and his telling of it. I was delighted to be able to complete a draft of the manuscript to the point where he was presented with a printed version for his ninetieth birthday in 2012. By then he had forgotten so much that a great deal of what he read was a revelation! Peter was very pleased with it.

Only a fraction of the many recordings and written submissions have been used. I have also, with the approval of the other interviewees, edited the transcripts of all the recorded interviews to streamline the huge wealth of material I was offered, as well as to avoid repetition and ensure readability. The written responses I received were lightly edited and, where necessary, condensed, before being returned to the people involved to approve for publication.

Peter lives now in an apartment at Parkwood Retirement Village, Waikanae, and is not enjoying this stage of his life as he has little to keep him occupied, including no garden and no computer. However, until recently he played the organ most Sunday mornings at St Michael's. And he still finds pleasure in singing in the St Michael's Church Choir every Tuesday evening, conducting the Parkwood Singers and going to concerts. Here he is always surrounded by people who want to chat with him, as so many remember the great gift of music that he shared with them over the years. And all is not forgotten. Recently Peter astounded the St Michael's choir by singing a lengthy psalm from memory as they listened to a recording of it by the St Mary's Cathedral Choir.

I am grateful to all of Peter's friends, family and colleagues who agreed to be interviewed, and who sent material, and to those who read the draft book. I felt it was imperative that Peter's huge contribution to choral music in New Zealand was recorded and given a final accolade.

Waikanae,
September 2015

Unless otherwise stated, the interviews recorded here are
Peter Godfrey in conversation with Elizabeth Salmon.

P = Peter Godfrey
E = Elizabeth Salmon

Contributors to RECOLLECTIONS in the book are introduced
with their historical connection to Peter, followed by current
roles in the field of music, if relevant.

Māori words are spelled with macrons, with the exception
of song titles or choir names that do not use them.

I

Bluntisham Boy and King's Chorister, 1922–36

P   I was a Bluntisham boy.

Bluntisham is a small village close to the edge of the fens in Huntingdonshire, England, and this is where I was born. My father farmed the Manor Farm of about 350 acres, which has been in the family since the 18th century. Our home was a large house about a mile away from the farm and was called The Manor – although it didn't look like a manor house. I was next in line of succession to the farm, but, as it turned out, my life was to take a very different direction.

I was born into a close-knit family on my father's side. My grandfather was an alderman earlier on and was very much involved with the parish church. And my great-uncle Cyril lived in a lovely big house, Stapenhill, in the centre of the village with his two sisters. He also had a farm in Bluntisham. My mother's parents, the Hensmans, came from Northampton and settled in the village of Earith, two miles away from Bluntisham, where they ran the local shop.

Before she married, my mother had singing lessons in Cambridge on Saturday afternoons, and wandered around Cambridge afterwards before catching the train home. One afternoon she went into King's College Chapel when Evensong was starting. The beauty of the singing and the building inspired her so much that she vowed then and there, 'If I have a son, he *must* sing in this choir.'

Peter's mother, Evelyn.

My parents, Philip and Evelyn, were married in the Bluntisham Parish Church of St Mary during the First World War. Their first child was my sister Ruth. She was born in 1920 and died some years ago. I was the second child, born in 1922 – the son destined to go to King's – and my brother David was born four years later in 1926. He eventually took over the Manor Farm, which was later run by one of his sons and still belongs to the family. David has lived in Bluntisham all his life.

E   *How would you describe your parents?*

P   My mother had a strong personality. Her life was that of a mother and a farmer's wife. She did rather rule my father and could get moody at times – in fact, she rather ruled us all, but I loved her and got on well with her. Pop was a quiet, thoughtful person who rarely had a row with anyone. He was a great hockey player in his younger days and kept an interest in sports throughout his life. Pop was responsible for my great interest in ice skating as a young boy. He would take me in my pushchair down to some land that he owned on the other side of Bluntisham – just past the church and on the way towards Earith. This was Bury Fen, which used to flood and ice over in winter and the national speed skating races took place there. I started skating at a very young age and by my mid-teens was quite a good speed skater. In fact, I was selected for the junior race – which I didn't win because I fell over!

E   *Did you have special childhood friends in Bluntisham?*

P   I used to play with two cousins, and a boy called Alec Moore was a very good friend. He was a Dr Barnado boy who lived over the road from us with a marvellous woman who cared for four Dr Barnado boys until they were in their early teens.

Alec and I used to play together, digging holes and making huts and all the sorts of things that boys do. He was a very clever boy, much more so than I was, and he won a scholarship to Cambridge. Unfortunately, we saw little of each other once I became a chorister, but we met up again as adults in New Zealand.

E   *Did you show any early signs of being musical?*

P   We had a piano at home which my mother and Ruth played. I suppose I tried it out but I didn't have piano lessons in Bluntisham. My musical experience in Bluntisham was singing hymns at school and Sunday school, and later at church at St Mary's where the whole family sat together – my grandfather, grandmother and so on. When I was seven someone said, 'Well, he's got a bit of a voice. Perhaps he should have some singing lessons.' So my mother arranged these with the organist of St Ives Parish Church who lived in Earith, and on Saturdays my father would take me there, two miles each way, on the crossbar of his bicycle.

Peter as a chorister at King's College in Eton dress.

E   *Do you think your mother had King's in mind for you at this stage?*

P   I'm sure she must have, because the following year, in the summer of 1930, she took me to King's to audition for the choir. But I failed! My mother was devastated, but she wouldn't be defeated. At the end of the year I had to try for the choir at Durham Cathedral … and I failed again! As it turned out, that really was a good thing because Durham was not as good a choir as King's, and it was a long way from home. Bluntisham was only about fifteen miles away from Cambridge.

    The following year, 1931, I auditioned for King's again – one of forty boys trying for a place in the choir. We assembled in the college dining hall where we had to do some academic written work – maths, spelling and writing out the Lord's Prayer – which took up the whole morning. During this time groups of about five or six of us went up to Boris Ord's room for our voice test. He was the director of music.

E   *Was it just Boris Ord who auditioned you?*

P   Oh no – we were made to sing in front of a group of very distinguished people: the dean, the chaplain, the provost, the vice provost and the

Boris Ord, the director of music at King's College, 1929–57.

headmaster, as well as Boris. We were given vocal tests, some ear tests and then we had to read a verse or two of a psalm – just the words, not the music – and do a little bit of music reading. After lunch the dean came in to tell us the names of those who had been selected to sing again in the chapel. And this time my name was read out, amongst about eight others. We all sang hymns, my choice being 'Loving Shepherd of Thy Sheep'. I got in! Only four of us from the forty boys were accepted: Patrick Dobson, Peter King, Tim Bolland and myself, so I was very fortunate. The four of us started as probationers in the choir school at the beginning of the autumn term in September 1931.

E   *Your mother would have been overjoyed. Did being a probationer mean you sang with the chapel choir? And how long was the probationer period?*

P   Occasionally we rehearsed with the chapel choir in the morning, but mostly we had our own treble rehearsals. We would stay as probationers until a vacancy occurred. I had just one term as a probationer and went into the choir in January 1932. I was nine.

E   *The impact of King's College Chapel is quite extraordinary on people, so inspirational. What was it like for you as a small boy to sing in such a place?*

P   Overwhelming, really – it was so vast. And the sound was so wonderful. I don't think we ever really got used to it. In fact the time I appreciated its beauty more fully than at any other time was when I took the Dorian Choir and the National Youth Choir there to sing. The looks on their faces said it all.

E   *What was life like at the choir school?*

P   There were sixteen of us choristers and four probationers, together with about forty boarders and sixty day boys. Our choristers' timetable was different from the other students. After breakfast each morning we had a choir practice from 8.30 to 9.15 which was taken either by Boris

Ord or by the organ scholar. It always started late! Then we went into school with the rest of the boys for ordinary lessons. In the afternoon, there was another rehearsal for about an hour which was followed by games. We played soccer in the autumn term, rugby in the spring term, and then cricket in the summer. I enjoyed these, and actually became captain of the cricket team in my last year. There was a particular match each year which was a highlight for us – the match against the fellows of the college. And there would be matches against other local preparatory schools. But we didn't play outside Cambridge very often because we had rehearsals and Evensong each day.

On Monday, Wednesday and Friday afternoons the rest of the school went back to class after games while we dressed in our Eton suits and marched in a crocodile to the chapel for a full rehearsal with the choral scholars. This was from 4.15pm to 5.15pm – Evensong followed at 5.30pm. There was no electric lighting or heating in the chapel. The only electric light was in the organ loft. The rest of the chapel was lit by candles. On one occasion, during a very cold winter, there were only three people in the congregation. It was like singing in a freezing chamber! On Tuesdays and Thursdays we did our afternoon schoolwork with the rest of the school before going to the chapel at five o'clock for a short rehearsal without the choral scholars. They joined us for Evensong. Then we returned to the choir school for dinner and 'prep'.

On Sundays there was a short treble practice at the school before the morning service, usually Matins but occasionally a sung Communion

King's choristers walking to service.

service. This was followed by another full rehearsal of music for the afternoon service. Then we went back for lunch and a short break, before lining up again to march down to the chapel for Evensong at 3.30. This was always the most important service of the week, and it usually attracted large congregations.

E   *What a full life for young boys!*

P   Yes, it was, but I loved it, especially Evensong. After a year in the choir as junior choristers we were examined again to see if we were good enough to be full choristers. Of the four of us who entered at the same time, one did not make that next level. But Peter King, Tim Bolland and I were accepted as full choristers at the beginning of 1932. As members of the choir we had to be well organised and thinking ahead all the time. And there was a lot of music to learn each week for all those services.

E   *You said that non-choristers also went to the school. Where did they come from?*

P   We had a lot of fee-paying boarders and day boys who were mostly sons of dons and lecturers at the university. Our classes were a mixture of choristers and non-choristers, a good thing, really, as it broadened our outlook. The boys mostly came from more cultured backgrounds than I did, which created a problem for me. I arrived with a dreadful Huntingdonshire accent.

E   *Were you teased because of it?*

P   Oh yes, I was. Terribly! But it gradually went because I was with all those boys who spoke well. Inevitably, I had to copy them.

E   *Did you receive free education and boarding at King's as a chorister?*

P   No, we still had to pay a fee, but not the full fee. My parents were not able to cope with this because of the Depression, which affected my father and our farm. But I had two very generous aunts on the Godfrey side who were able to help, Dorothy and Audrey Wright.

E   *How fortunate you were. What was the impact on you of being a boarder at such a young age even though you were so close to home?*

P   It became rather difficult for me because my life was so different from that of the family. And because the holidays of choristers were shorter than ordinary boarders, I saw even less of my family than I might otherwise have done. For example, we had to stay on until after Evensong on Christmas Day, and we returned in the middle of January, earlier than the other boys. As well, we had to sing for Holy Week and Easter services which would often break that holiday up. Even though my parents used to come into Cambridge quite often and give me lunch or tea on a Saturday, I grew out of touch with them and their influence, and I had little time to be with my brother and sister. It was a great pity and I'm very sad about it.

E *It was probably inevitable under those circumstances. What was it like to be a chorister with Boris Ord?*

P He was a very, very fierce person – strict, demanding perfection. We had to be absolutely on time. And if anyone misbehaved, even slightly, or dared to utter a word in rehearsals, he would shout at us. He never made any jokes, or anything like that. We were scared stiff of him, actually. He took most of the rehearsals, although the organ scholar did take some. Boris was half German and had received some of his education in Germany. There was something about him that we thought of as being German, although he had been to school at Clifton on a music scholarship. Later on I got to like him very much, though.

E *Weren't you very homesick? You were so young to be treated like that, and away from home?*

P We got used to it, although Mr Fiddian, the headmaster, was rather cold and distant as well. But there were some very kind matrons who made life happier for us.

E *What was Boris's conducting style like?*

P It was quite unconventional. In services he would often beat time on the desk with only one finger.

E *Then how did he shape phrases?*

P He trained us very thoroughly in rehearsals and so we just sang as we had been taught. Boris was a very sensitive musician and he always produced very musical singing. There was a definite sound he demanded: no wobbles, always a clear tone. He was extremely strict about intonation and clarity of words.

E   *How were the choristers able to learn such a huge amount of difficult music so quickly? The music would be different for every service!*

P   We had two rehearsals a day plus the full rehearsal with the choral scholars before Evensong, and, of course, the repertoire was repeated over a period of time. I think we just gradually picked it up. It was a case of having to!

E   *Were you expected to read?*

P   Yes, most definitely. Boris wouldn't spoon-feed us by playing parts on the piano. He would help us with intervals and so on but we had to be self-reliant.

E   *Did the choristers have singing lessons at the choir school?*

P   No – again, we just absorbed it all and somehow it worked.

E   *Were there any special occasions that you took part in?*

P   There was one I remember in particular. This was the opening of the university library which was a large building with a great big tower built just behind the choir school. The King's chapel choir was invited to sing the national anthem when the library was opened by King George V. There we were, sitting right in front of him. For young boys like us, it was a very special occasion. A few days after the opening of the library, Boris took us up to the top of the tower. I still have a photograph of a group of us up there with him. I remember feeling most embarrassed because he had his hands on my shoulders!

E   *How were you rated as a chorister?*

P   I wasn't a brilliant chorister, but I did my best and I certainly enjoyed it. I was given the odd solo to sing but I didn't ever sing the very special solo in 'Once in Royal David's City'. My great friend, Peter King, sang that in my day. As far as singing in the choir was concerned, I was competent and I think I sang in tune, but I didn't have an outstandingly beautiful or strong voice.

E   *Perhaps yours was one of those voices that develops more as an adult. You certainly had a very beautiful and powerful baritone voice. What was academic school life like for you? Were you a good student?*

P   I enjoyed the work but I can't say that I was very scholastically minded in those days. Peter King and I always sat together, and I think we were more interested in making drawings of underground shelters, or dugouts, than doing schoolwork! I had a passion for dugouts and we did actually make one on the farm at Bluntisham during a holiday when Peter came to stay with us. We often stayed with each other in the holidays. I can remember one time when we went around together singing very loudly, that awful sort of thing that boys do to show off. Quite disgraceful! Peter and I remained close friends, and I became godfather to his first child.

Interior of King's College Chapel.

E   *Did you get into trouble for not concentrating on your schoolwork?*

P   Not that I remember. However, there was one occasion when I did get into trouble, and it was all my own fault. We used to have a scripture class one morning each week. Our class was taken by the Reverend Roy Bowyer-Yin who was assistant chaplain and became a lifelong friend.

On this occasion, probably in my last year, Roy read us the story of the hypocrites. At the end of the story he asked us, 'Now, tell me, who were the hypocrites?' I jumped up and put my hand in the air and said, 'Mr Fiddian, sir! Mr Fiddian!' Now Mr Fiddian was the headmaster. There was a shocked silence in the classroom until Roy said to me, 'You'd better go and tell him that, Godfrey.' So I left the classroom and went to see Mr Fiddian who made me wait for some time in the dining room before seeing me. He'd actually spoken to Roy about this to find out what had happened. He took me up to his study and said, 'Now, what's all this about? 'Well, sir,' I said, 'we were talking about the hypocrites, and I said that you were one, sir.' 'Right – bend over!'

And he gave me five of the best.

E   *Was there a reason for you to say that he was a hypocrite?*

P   Oh no, it was just a young boy's silliness. I was just trying to be funny, I think. On another occasion I remember coming into the dormitory one day, and I saw a very popular junior matron tidying up our beds. She was leaning over my bed at the time. I couldn't resist coming up behind her and tickling her. She was so surprised that she stood up quickly and banged into my jaw, breaking one of my front teeth which has been a problem ever since!

E   *Apart from singing in the choir what other aspects of musical education did you pursue at King's?*

P   I had piano lessons, which my parents really could not afford, but once again help came from members of the family. I was also very keen on composition and I remember getting a group of choristers together to sing some of my pieces. That would be the first time I ever conducted! Obviously Boris thought I should be given the opportunity to do more academic work with music as he arranged for Douglas Guest, the organ scholar at that time, to become my tutor in harmony and counterpoint. Douglas was another person who became a lifelong friend.

E   *You would have formed strong bonds with some choristers. Apart from Peter King, did you have other close friends amongst them?*

P   Peter was my closest friend – I called him Peterkin! But there were two others in particular. Sandy Forsyth was one year senior to me, and as he came from nearby St Ives there was an immediate connection between us. And there was John Gilbert, a second cousin on my mother's side of the family, and two years behind me. Both are still close friends. It's rather interesting that there were two of us from the same side of the family in the choir at the same time.

E   *You've often spoken of the tour of Europe that the choir made. I think it was towards the end of your time as a chorister wasn't it?*

P   Ah, yes. That was in March 1936 when the British Council had just opened. At that time England had no reputation in Europe whatsoever as far as choirs were concerned and Germany thought we were useless! So it was decided to show the Continent that there were some good choirs in England, and the choir of King's College Chapel was the

The King's College Choir arrives at Hamburg, 1936.

first English choir to tour the Continent. The whole chapel choir went with Boris Ord and Douglas Guest. The dean, Eric Milner-White, the chaplain, Roy Bowyer-Yin, and the headmaster, Mr Fiddian, came with us as well. Quite an entourage!

We left Cambridge on 19 March, catching the 6.30pm train, which linked up with the Harwich Boat Train. It really was a great adventure for us boys, sleeping on the boat train, waking early the next morning and then travelling by train to the Hague. I remember being most impressed by the fact that it was an electric train! That day we rehearsed in the morning and sang Evensong later in the day followed by a short recital. The programme we sang everywhere was a mixture of early composers: Tallis, Byrd, Hilton, Weelkes, Sweelinck, di Lasso, Purcell, and, what were to us then, more contemporary composers: Battishill, Wood, S S Wesley, Howells and Parry.

We left by train the next day for Amsterdam. I remember being most disappointed because there was not even one tulip open, but that was partly compensated for by the fields of crocuses. There was the usual rehearsal and concert there, after which we went back to our hotel to pack for the trip next day to Hamburg.

There were swastikas everywhere in Hamburg – Hitler had been

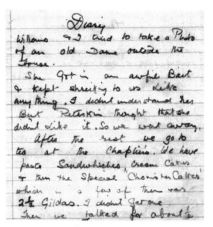

Peter's tour diary.

there only three days before. If we wanted to go walking anywhere we always had to be accompanied by a choral scholar. One boy was arrested for some reason and had to be rescued by a choral scholar. And on another occasion a Brownshirt stopped a group that I was in and demanded to know which youth movement we belonged to. Luckily the choral scholar with us could speak German, and told him that we were English, so we were allowed to go on. It was really quite dangerous.

After Hamburg we set out by train for Copenhagen in Denmark, once again sailing on a train ferry with almost a whole day of travelling. It was very cold when we arrived, with a lot of snow. But a lovely thing happened there. We were entertained by the British legation, and each chorister was presented with a grey woolly hat – they were very warm! Mine was in my possession until 2006, when I attended a concert in Wellington Cathedral given by the Copenhagen Royal Chapel Choir. I presented it to the boy I considered to be the most outstanding chorister in the choir. We sang two well-received programmes in Copenhagen, one in a church and one in a museum, after which we left by train ferry for Sweden. We first went to Lund where a most amusing thing happened. We were met by the Swedish press who thought they were there to meet the King and his choir! When they were told that the leader of the party was the dean, they said to him, 'We understand that you are a King.' Eric Milner-White was most taken aback and stuttered, 'No, er, really – that's not correct. We're *from* King's.' It was very amusing. Unfortunately I became quite ill in Lund, and had to miss the recital in the cathedral. But I was well enough to leave with the choir the next morning for Stockholm, a long drive of some eight hours.

We travelled up to Uppsala for a performance in the cathedral, which was recorded (it was heard back in England); and then we returned to Stockholm en route to Hamburg, where we had our final engagement. We were delighted to sing in St Jacobi Kirche, Hamburg, because J S Bach had once played the organ there. I was privileged to spend some time playing that organ. It was a monumental thrill for me, as you can imagine!

EXCERPTS FROM PETER'S TOUR DIARY

THURSDAY 19TH MARCH 1936 – CAMBRIDGE TO HARWICH

Start from school at 6.00pm. Train starts from Cambridge at 6.37pm

We have tea before we start. Peterkin forgets his case. Mr Corbett has to go and get it.

Quite a good train from Cambridge to Bury St Edmunds. We arrive at 20 to 8. We don't change but keep in the same carriage. I play 'Donkey' with Peterkin and Howe, (25 to 9). The boat trip is very calm. I get to sleep after a long time. It is very hot. I am with Peterkin, Bazie and Tony.

FRIDAY 20TH MARCH – THE HAGUE

After breakfast we got in the bus and went to church and sang. Then we went to the prison and saw all the cells.

We come back and have dinner. We have sausages and fryed potatoes and apple slosh. Just after dinner Peterkins, Williams and I try to take a photo of an old Dame outside the house (where they were staying). She got in awful Bait and kept shrieking to us like anything. I didn't understand her but Peterkin thought she didn't like it. So we went away.

After a rest we had tea at the Chaplain's. We have paste sandwiches, cream cakes and then the special Chorister's Cakes which in a few there was 2 ½ gildas. I didn't get one. The Chaplain (Mr Williams) is a very queer man. He is always laughing. He has a very funny laugh.

We change into Etons and then we have dinner. Tomato soup (I don't have any) and a fried egg and chocolate jelly. Then we go down to the church in the Bus. We start singing at about 8.20. Then we go in and have Evensong and, after that, motets. It finishes about 10 o'clock. It is very hot in the church. We are all tired by the end.

SATURDAY 21ST MARCH – TO AMSTERDAM

We get up at 8.00 and we pack. We only have bread and butter for Breakfast. We then get in the bus. Of course Peterkins forgets his case. But Mr Fiddian finds it just before we leave (for Hamburg). We go in an electric train. None of the tulips were out but there were lots of fields of crocuses.

SUNDAY 22ND MARCH – TO HAMBURG

We go over into German territory. We see lots of Nazis. When we arrived at Hamburg we had our photos taken.

When we were going out a Brown Shirt stops Morgan and asks 'What Boy movement we were.' Mr Seymour says we are English, so we go on.

TUESDAY 24TH MARCH – COPENHAGEN

The church is a very nice one. There is a lot of beautiful carving in it. There are two ships hanging from the ceiling.

TUESDAY 31ST MARCH – IN HAMBURG

We go to the church walking. It is quite a nice church. We sing and then I play on the organ which Bach and Handel played on.

E   *Did the tour achieve the desired result for the British Council, Peter?*

P   From reports I've seen on the tour, both churchmen and musicians on the Continent were most impressed and very moved by the music and the standard of singing. There was, however, a repercussion that really affected Swedish choral music in a most important way. One Danish conductor, a chap called Mogens Wöldike, the founder of the Copenhagen Boys Choir, went up to Boris after our first concert in Copenhagen to ask if he could learn conducting with him.

     'No,' said Boris Ord, 'we don't teach choral conducting in England.'

     Wöldike had been so moved by the singing that he approached Boris again after our second concert. This time Boris relented and said that he could come and sit in on choir rehearsals for a month, which he did. Wöldike was a Jew and had to leave Denmark early in the war. He went to Stockholm in Sweden where he met up with Eric Ericson. Together they developed a course in choral conducting, possibly the first one ever, which they established at the Royal Conservatorium. Many young conductors benefited from this course, and went out into the community, schools and churches to work with choirs. Wöldike returned to Copenhagen after the war, and became the most prominent choral conductor in Denmark.

     The importance of all this for Swedish choral singing was that Sweden developed the highest involvement of people in choral music of any country in the world. Ericson has said that the visit of King's College Choir to Scandinavia in 1936 was fundamental to the great choral development that has taken place in Scandinavia. In turn, Swedish choirs have become a source of inspiration to other countries, including England.

E   *Did the choir find it difficult to settle back into routine after the tour?*

P   Possibly for some, but speaking for myself, I had a new role to adjust to as I became senior chorister immediately after our return, which gave me considerable responsibility.

E   *What did this involve?*

P   I had to assemble the choristers for the daily procession to the chapel, and check them for tidiness – they were dressed in Eton suits, gown and top hat – and I had to control the procession, the boys walking in pairs. Once the procession passed over the bridge of the River Cam, the boys weren't allowed to speak. And it was my responsibility to look after the music of the organist and the director of music, and put it in place on their stands. Those sorts of things. I did sing more solos, not the important ones though – I don't think my voice was strong enough – and I now stood right next to Boris Ord in the choir stalls.

Some years ago Roy reminded me of an event that happened on Whitsunday in my last term in the choir. We always sang S S Wesley's anthem *The Wilderness* on Whitsunday. Boris had already told Peter King that he was to sing the treble solo, 'And Sorrow and Sighing'. But during the final rehearsal on the Sunday morning, Boris said that he was not satisfied with Peter's performance and that I was to sing it. This was dreadful because Peter's mother was coming up specially to hear him sing it. So I said to him, 'Well, you *must* sing it, otherwise there will be dead silence – because I am not going to sing it.'

Peter King did sing the solo – he was far better than I would have been. At the end of Evensong we two waited in fear and trembling, expecting the worst from Boris. But he didn't say a word! My guess is that he may even have been quite pleased, realising that he had been rather unkind. He would never say so, though. Peter and I have stayed with each other several times since I left England, and we keep in touch by letter.

Another thing a senior chorister had to do was to turn pages for the organist's voluntary at the end of every service. So, at the end of each service when the procession passed below the organ screen, I would slip out and climb the stairs to the organ where either Boris or Douglas Guest would be playing.

There was one unforgettable occasion. We had sung a special anthem by Vaughan Williams – which I didn't like very much, none of us did –

and when I arrived at the organ console I saw a big man slouching on the spare seat up there. After the voluntary, Douglas turned round and said, 'Peter, I think you should meet Dr Ralph Vaughan Williams.' He had come to Cambridge that day to receive his honorary doctorate and that, of course, was the reason for the special anthem.

E   *There's a story you tell of your use of time during the sermons. Can you tell it again?*

P   I must admit that I find it difficult to listen to and concentrate on sermons. This has always been the case. I remember when we had sermons at King's (and this was rather rarely), it would not be long before I turned around in my seat, and took down from its shelf my copy of the *English Hymnal*. I would spend the whole sermon looking at tunes I didn't know. I would first look through the soprano part, then the bass, and then I would put them together ... in my head. I would do the same with the alto and tenor parts, and finally I would put all four parts together. It stood me in such good stead for my work with choirs.

E   *You say that Dr Milner-White was an important influence on your life.*

P   Oh yes, very much so. He prepared me for confirmation on my own and had a strong impact on me then. Talking about religion has never been part of my intellect. It is just something which I feel, and it has played an important part in my life. There's no doubt that Eric Milner-White and the atmosphere at King's were the foundation of this.

  Milner-White started a summer camp, Batcombe camp, for boys who had been confirmed. This was on a farm in Somerset belonging to an ex-chorister's father and they were great occasions. We played a lot of games – cricket in particular – and we visited various places. I remember going to Wells Cathedral on one occasion.

E   *Was the purpose of the camp partly to develop the boys' faith?*

P   Yes, I think so. I went to several camps, the last one being memorable because I cycled all the way from East Anglia to Somerset – two days each way! I was only fourteen. I stayed overnight with an aunt who lived just north of Oxford. And also memorable during this camp: my voice broke.

E   *Did that mean that you had to leave the choir school?*

P   I went back to King's in September, after the camp, but Boris said, 'I'm afraid your treble voice has gone now, and we can't have you in the choir any more.' So it was decided that I should have my last term at King's as a fee-paying boarder, before leaving for my secondary school after Christmas.

E   *That would have been devastating for you!*

P   Yes, it was a bit. But it was just one of those things that had to be accepted.

E   *And difficult to find another school? There was some mention that parents thought the academic education of choristers had been neglected because of all the time spent at rehearsals and services.*

P   Actually, that was so, because we had so many choral rehearsals in school time. We started schoolwork late in the morning, and three afternoons a week, when the other students went on with lessons, we had to go off to the chapel. But we choristers found that we could catch up quickly because of the high level of concentration and self-discipline we had developed in the choir.

E   *So now, you were at the end of your primary school days and you had to find a new school. How did you make this choice? It must have been difficult for you.*

P   Well, as it turned out, no. My life has been full of coincidences and amazing opportunities. And this was one of them.

    RECOLLECTIONS

Pat Moore (formerly Alec), Peter's earliest childhood and remaining friend from Bluntisham. *Letter, 17 February 2009.*

Eighty years ago, the neighbouring East Anglian villages of Bluntisham-cum-Earith each housed about 300 inhabitants. In Bluntisham there were fewer than sixty children at the three-roomed Church of England school; a uniformed district nurse travelled on a bicycle to render first aid and midwifery; and two doctors, who shared a much wider area, made house calls in response to requests left at one of the shops, ran their surgeries and dispensed their own physic. Milk was delivered from a pony and trap and measured from churn to jug; meat was sold from two little shops whose owners also delivered weekly; and groceries came from two other small shops with competition from salesmen in well-stocked vans invading from nearby small towns.

There was a sole village policeman mounted on a heavy-duty bike – the most common means of transport. The village blacksmith operated a forge, shod horses and manufactured basic farm implements, and farming was a fairly intensive mix of arable and livestock with other large acreages devoted to orchards of plums, apples and berry fruits. These were the Depression years when markets yielded poor returns, but kitchen gardens and free-range hens helped maintain a higher standard of living for working families than for many in the towns and cities. There were few cars, still no electricity or gas or mains water supply.

It was to Bluntisham that I arrived at the age of three to an adoptive home, where I became an early playmate of Peter Godfrey, his younger brother, David, and his older sister, Ruth. They were part of an old, established and quite widespread farming family, and our houses were on either side of the road leading out of the village. We attended the village school together until Peter won his place in the King's College Choir; we played a lot of cricket and built makeshift trollies. Influenced, no doubt, by stories of the Great War, we built trenches and dugouts. During the hardest of winters, many acres of flooded fenland would turn into a huge area for skating, at which Peter was quite talented. In summer we swam in the River Ouse. We shared birthday parties and played 'parlour games', with Ruth as the great organiser. On Sundays we went to St Mary's Church, where we grew up in the Anglican tradition of Sunday school and Matins and Evensong. There was an old organ dependent on manual pumping, which prompted a lead weight to rise or fall indicating the amount of air in the bellows.

Then came the time for Peter to go to King's, and I went to Huntingdon Grammar School on a scholarship. Our lives were separated apart from holidays in Bluntisham. But there were to be coincidences which persistently brought Peter and me back in contact throughout our lives, and which have enriched our childhood friendship. For instance, I just happened to meet Peter on the platform at Cambridge Station. He was returning from East Africa and I was about to go there. He was very recently married, and I lunched with him and Sheila in London. We exchanged a few letters during the next year, and I discovered I was again following in his footsteps in both Kenya and Somaliland, where we both served as captain and adjutant of the battalion. Very shortly after I left the army, I spent some years in India, involved in commerce and shipping. After a further seven years in Ceylon, I decided to give my family a better upbringing in New Zealand. At a farewell party shortly before my departure from Ceylon in 1964, I overheard a guest mention someone who had been at King's College, had later taught music at Marlborough College, and was now in Auckland directing the Cathedral Choir. She was a little surprised when I suggested she might be talking of Peter Godfrey! I wrote to him the next day and dined with him and his family a week later.

Peter's extremely busy musical life, and the demands of business and travel, meant that we had little contact for some years. But Heather and I became admirers and supporters of the Dorian Choir. I had several business friends whose wives sang in the choir, and it was one of them who contacted me to suggest we might be able to do some fundraising to help cover the costs of a planned overseas tour. I heard that funds at that stage were being raised by choir members undertaking such tasks as clearing rubbish at Eden Park after rugby matches. I suggested they needed some commercial sponsorship and as a result my company became their sponsor in the name of our main product, Choysa Tea. It was a new type of sponsorship for us, and obviously the choir supporters found it strange especially when Peter insisted on thanking Choysa Tea at the end of concerts in several of Auckland's churches – the response was invariably a ripple of subdued laughter. An extra concert in the town hall was held, which helped to swell the coffers. Then we had a farewell dinner. That morning I asked the choir treasurer how much we needed to complete our funding, and in the evening presented the choir with a cheque that covered the remaining amount. The Dorians were able to leave debt free and happily for an overseas tour, which was to prove very demanding but an enormous success.

I marvel at what Peter has achieved, and wish his contribution to the country we both adopted and grew to love had been more widely recognised. Fifty years ago the general standard of singing in New Zealand – and the degree of interest in it – was low; there were few choirs to command respect, and school performance levels were indifferent. Now we have so many choirs with singers of all ages, and so many conductors and musicians who draw inspiration from Peter. It is no exaggeration to say that his immigration led to a musical revolution, which has seen New Zealand evolve as a country in which fine singing has become a passion. What a wonderful mark for one man to leave on his adopted home!

Professor Peter King, chorister at King's College and lifelong friend.
Email, 4 December 2008.

Peter and I arrived at King's together and continued to shadow one another during our years there. I don't think either of us was particularly bright at schoolwork at King's, and I fancy that Peter's talents developed along practical rather than scholarly lines. We always sat next to one another in class, and I remember us drawing endless dugouts, one of which we actually built on the farm when I stayed with him at Bluntisham during a holiday.

At one stage he was dead-set on building an organ. He did actually make a pipe, but just one – a diapason pipe.

Peter had a very open and honest nature that could be fully trusted. I felt that I could confide in him unconditionally. We both enjoyed the same things, and we have remained good friends all our lives in spite of the thousands of miles that separate us. He is godfather to my oldest child and, I was godfather to his.*

Sandy Forsyth, chorister and choral scholar, King's College.
Letter, 23 December 2008.

Peter and I have been friends for eighty years. It was through his sister, Ruth, that our contact was first made. She was a boarder at Slepe Hall School at which I was a day pupil. When my scholarship to King's College Choir was announced at morning assembly, Ruth told her mother, as she knew of her ambition in that direction for Peter. In due course, after I had been a chorister for a term, I was invited over to Bluntisham – a short bus ride from St Ives, where I lived – to meet Ruth's brother and tell them all about life as a chorister. He joined me a year later and was to succeed me as senior chorister four years after that. Peter started composing at a very early age – chants at first. Before choir practice, one morning, he had the temerity to ask Boris Ord if he would play his first chant for him. The result was disastrous, much to our amusement, but all credit to Peter!

In 1940 he joined me once again in the choir at King's, this time as a bass. Then war service came, meaning that we did not meet again until 1947, when I spent a week at Manor Farm picking plums for that year's crop. I stayed with my sister at Ely, travelling over in Peter's 'old banger', which he lent me for the week. It was called 'Vain Glory', so-named by Rev Eric Milner-White, Dean of York, on account of its number plate, VG9147.

We seldom met after that week, each going his own way. But I remember attending performances given by two of his New Zealand choirs, one at King's and one at St Paul's Cathedral, London, after which we were able to have a brief chat. Peter is distinguished by being the only person since its founding in the 15th century to have been chorister, choral scholar and director of music at King's.

* Peter's eldest daughter, Belinda, was killed in a car accident in 1973.

.

2

Denstone College and Sheila, 1937–40

E   *So now you had to find a new school, Peter. How did you go about that?*

P   My parents were considering Huntingdon Grammar School for me, but as I had moved into the public school scene at the choir school – and with all my friends going on to public schools – I really didn't want to go to Huntingdon. The problem was that my parents couldn't afford to send me to a public school, and there was no chance of my achieving an academic scholarship after the minimal education I had received as a chorister.

     However, a most remarkable thing happened. About a year earlier, a distant relation turned up in Bluntisham: Uncle Ronald Godfrey. We had never met him before. Uncle Ronald came from Lincoln, but was wanting to make contact with members of the Godfrey family. He was a maths teacher and housemaster at Denstone College in Staffordshire. He visited us several times, and naturally my parents discussed my secondary school education with him. Uncle Ronald returned to Denstone and persuaded the headmaster to award me a music scholarship! This was incredible luck as it was the first music scholarship to be awarded at the school and it paid for most of the fees. I doubt that I would have been a musician if that hadn't happened, as there were very few schools offering music scholarships at that time –

Clifton, Harrow, Rugby and Eton were the only ones, if I remember correctly.

My younger brother, David, also came with me to Denstone, but he went to the prep school, some miles away. My mother had wanted him to go to King's as a chorister, but in spite of two attempts and singing lessons from Douglas Guest, he didn't get in. Just as well, I think, as he eventually took over the Manor Farm and was very successful at farming. Far more so than I ever would have been.

I hadn't been in the college long before I was asked – actually, I was told – to conduct the house choir in the house music competitions. The whole house had two rehearsals a week. They had to sing a unison song and one in four parts. Here I was, just a new junior boy, being expected to tell my seniors what to do when I hadn't done any conducting. Amazingly, we won. There were seven other houses.

E *Was there a choir at Denstone?*

P I sang in the chapel choir. I don't remember how good it was, but we sang two services a week. And I learned to sing bass. The music master when I first went there was Hugh Denton, but his successor was John Alston who was to be a very important influence on me. He had been at school with Benjamin Britten and was a great friend of his. John taught me piano and organ. In my last year I won the Senior Piano Prize – I played Beethoven's 'Pathétique' Sonata – and was awarded a lovely volume of Beethoven Piano Sonatas. I also had singing lessons and won that competition as well. On one occasion the adjudicator was Heddle Nash, the famous tenor!

And so I became very closely involved with the music of the school. I spent practically every afternoon of the week with a great friend, Richard Blakeway Phillips, who was a year older than I was and a very good pianist. We listened to music on a gramophone and sometimes on the wireless in the music school. That was when I first heard a symphony and a concerto, and started buying miniature scores. The first one was the Brahms First Symphony, I remember. Every Thursday afternoon we would listen to the Bournemouth Symphony Orchestra, which, incidentally, was to play an important part in my life later on.

John took us in his car to concerts of visiting artists who came up to Derby. One of the very first was a concert given by Rachmaninoff. Imagine me sitting on the stage only an arm's length away from the grand piano! My memory is of a gloomy looking man who came on to the stage and improvised before each piece. I could see his hands and the expressions on his face – it really was an amazing experience. And I remember hearing Beecham, Toscanini and Gigli. Heddle Nash came to school to give a recital on one occasion and I sang to him while he was there. John fed me with such a lot of music – I was so very fortunate.

Peter at the Denstone chapel organ.

These experiences introduced me to orchestral music, which was wonderful because I had been so focussed on sacred choral music until then. I began to have viola lessons and, although I didn't ever get very far with them, I gained valuable experience with a stringed instrument. My viola was given to me by John – it just happened to have belonged to Benjamin Britten! I passed it on to my eldest daughter, Belinda – and after she died, we gave it to a great friend of hers who was also a very good viola player. She has it still.

E   *You developed a deep faith at King's. Did that continue to develop?*

P   Oh, yes, it did indeed. For a long time there I would go to the early Communion service every day, and was often a server. Another boy used to attend the services as well, John Goodman (he was eventually ordained as a priest), who became a very good friend. He was senior to me in my house and was keen on shooting. After he left Denstone, I lost contact with him until I went to Marlborough College. He had just been appointed assistant chaplain to the parish of Marlborough. It was one of those strange coincidences. He had arrived in Marlborough for an interview, and was driving in his car trying to find the place – when he happened to notice me, and pulled up to speak.

E   *You were steeped in music at Denstone. Did you continue your interest in sport?*

P   Partly. I did continue with rugby, but soccer wasn't played at Denstone. Instead of playing cricket, I was persuaded to take up rifle shooting by my uncle Ron who was a very fine shot. He coached shooting in the college. During the winter terms we shot .22 (rifles) on the short range, and in the summer .303 (rifles) at 200 and 500 yards. In my second year I shot in the college VIII, with John Goodman as captain. We shot at various school competitions and went to Bisley each year where teams from most public schools shot. In my last year I was appointed captain.

E *Would you tell me more about Bisley?*

P Bisley was the national centre of outdoor rifle shooting. There was a lot of indoor rifle shooting at twenty yards going on in special places. But Bisley was the place where they had school, national and international competitions. I was introduced to the Duke of Edinburgh there on two occasions.

E *A very important person came into your life during your secondary school days, didn't she?*

Sheila McNeile.

P Ah yes, that was Sheila! Our first meeting took place in rather unusual circumstances. It was quite a common practice for boys of my age – I must have been about fifteen – to follow fox hunts by foot. During the winter holidays of January 1938, the hunt was on some of my father's land in Bluntisham. There was only one other person there, and that was a girl, Sheila McNeile, the daughter of the Rector of Bluntisham. So we ran together and that was the beginning of our romance. Sheila and I wrote letters to each other all through our schooldays. We met up in the holidays in Bluntisham, and we went up to Cambridge at the same time.

E *What place did music have in your life at this point? Did you have an inborn compulsion to be a musician?*

P No, not really. I was involved with a lot of music – I learnt the organ, the piano and the viola, sang in the chapel choir and took music for School Certificate. But I had no real ambition at that stage of becoming a professional musician.

Even when I left college I didn't know what I wanted to take up as a career. Although I was very focussed on music at Denstone, history was the academic subject that I enjoyed most, and I remember becoming very interested in trees at one point!

I had continued my connection with King's during my Denstone days by cycling into Cambridge in the holidays and going up into the organ loft for Evensong. Douglas Guest was still there (to be followed by David Willcocks). It gradually became clear to me that I wanted to go back to King's to sing in the choir as a choral scholar, but that I would read history. So in 1940 I auditioned for a choral scholarship as a bass and was very fortunate to be awarded one.

This really was one of the most important events in my life.

RECOLLECTIONS

Rev John Goodman, Denstone College student and lifelong friend.
Letter, 8 December 2008.

I first met Peter Godfrey when he arrived at Denstone College in January 1937 and joined us in Woodard House. The house music competition took place in the Lent Term and, as it was clear from the start that he was very musical, we asked him to take charge of the house choir. We numbered, I suppose, about a dozen boys. Peter taught us how to sing better than we had ever sung before, and so we emphatically won the competition. The trophy took its place on our shelf, and remained there not only for 1937, but at least as long as Peter was at Denstone. Not long after he came to Denstone, we realised that he was very much in love with 'his' Sheila.

A prefect on duty would come round at mealtime delivering our mail. When certain envelopes were handed to Peter we would see a gentle blush on his cheek. We knew that another letter had come from Sheila. It was so genuine and serious and natural that there was little, if any, teasing. They were truly in love.

Our housemaster was Peter's distant cousin, Ronald Godfrey, a keen rifle shot who was in charge of the school's shooting. Peter joined me in the sport in the summer of 1937. He was a member of the school VIII in 1939. This brought us close together, exercising, practising, going regularly to the firing range at Burton-on-Trent and competing for the Public Schools' Ashburton Trophy at Bisley. Peter was awarded his shooting colours that year and was Captain of Shooting the following year.

Rev Richard Blakeley Phillips, Denstone College student and lifelong friend. *Letter, 11 November 2008.*

Peter and I went to Denstone College, Staffordshire. I went in 1936, and Peter followed two terms later. I went to Denstone on a minor scholarship and Peter on the first music scholarship ever awarded at Denstone.

Although the school had only about 260 students, it was astonishingly rich in musical talent. There were three boys who between them played the *Rhapsodies* of Brahms, the *Fantasie Impromptu* of Chopin, and his finale from the Sonata in B Minor. Two of them each played Grieg's Piano Concerto and Mozart's Piano Concerto in A, K448, at the college with a county orchestra. Standards were fostered by an annual inter-house music competition judged by a well-known musician. Only Peter and another old Denstonian, Lucy Crowe, became professional musicians. Lucy is now one of our leading operatic sopranos.

We benefited from organised visits to hear Fritz Kreisler, Beniamino Gigli, Rachmaninoff and Jelly D'Arányi. There were recitals in college where we heard the great tenor, Heddle Nash, the violinist Antonio Brosa and Arthur Rubinstein. Amongst choral items, the school produced *The Mikado* with me as pianist and Peter singing Pish-Tush. Several boys tried their hand at composition, including Peter who composed a piano quintet. We were most fortunate in having such a rich musical life as schoolboys.

When I was Rector of a Cambridgeshire parish, I was reading a notice board outside the Porter's Lodge at King's advertising a visit of one of Peter's choirs from New Zealand when, just behind me, Peter himself appeared. Unknown to me his choir was to sing Evensong during the King's College Choir's holiday. They also came to sing at the Three Choirs Festival at Hereford, where I was ordained.

Peter would have made a very fine parish priest, but he chose to serve the church through his outstanding gifts as choral conductor and organist. He was one of the very few who rose early to go frequently to the weekday Holy Communion service in the Denstone College Chapel. He was offered the job as director of music at Eton College some time after leaving Marlborough, but when he visited them he noted that the boys did not sing much in Chapel. He told us that he was not going to a school where the boys did not sing. For ever thereafter he elected to give his unstinted life's work to the southern hemisphere. It was our loss, but I am sure he made the right decision and a happy one for both Peter and his family.

3

King's College Choir and the Army, 1941–45

P I should have gone up to Cambridge in September 1940, as I had been awarded my scholarship in June or July. However, the war was causing great stress in England and so it was decided that the university would be shut down. I spoke to the headmaster at Denstone about this and was offered a temporary position at the prep school to teach there for a term. This part of the school was about fifteen miles away from the senior school. So I accepted that, only to find that Cambridge had reopened in the middle of the summer, and I was told I could go up to King's. However, I thought, 'No, I've accepted this job for a term and I mustn't let them down.' So I didn't go up to the university until January 1941 when I began to sing again in the King's chapel choir as a choral scholar. It was wonderful to be back.

After only three weeks of reading history, I realised that I had made a wrong decision and that I should read music. I was allowed to change to the music department and began reading for my BMus. I had to complete the first year's syllabus, Part I, in only two terms! And in the following year I had to pass the whole of Part II. So I did my full degree in two years minus one term. It was supposed to be a three-year degree, but I think the authorities were somewhat lenient at that time because of the war situation. I was also awarded the John Stewart of Rannoch Scholarship Award in Sacred Music, which was worth £60. I was fortunate to have my degree completed before being called up in the summer of 1943.

E   *Were the numbers of choral scholars at King's affected by the war at all?*

P   Yes, they were. There were fewer men than usual because so many were being called up to fight in the war. Two of them had been choristers with me – Sandy Forsyth and Cecil Paget. I still keep in touch with Sandy.

E   *You said that as a chorister you were nervous of Boris Ord because he was so demanding and critical. Was it different for you as a choral scholar?*

P   Definitely. Most definitely. He was also my organ teacher and so I developed a personal relationship with him. I always had a very great respect for Boris, but my attitude towards him changed at this time. I learned such a lot from singing with him – his conducting, the way he ran choir practices and the music he chose. I built up quite a music library at that time – full scores, miniature scores and copies of the music we were singing in the chapel.

E   *It seems as though you were starting to shape yourself for a career in music.*

P   Yes, I suppose I was.

E   *Were there any aspects of Boris Ord's choir management you decided not to emulate?*

Peter Godfrey, BMus.

P   There was this business of beating (time) with one finger. It was quite amazing how much he achieved with the choir from that technique, but it was not one that I was comfortable with. I have always felt strongly that a conductor's movements should be quite discreet in services, but Boris would stand there in the service, not moving at all, except for that one finger. He was very controlled. His eyes were incredible and they would demand that people look at him all the time. At the same time, I started going to rehearsals of the Cambridge Musical Society Orchestra which Boris conducted and found that his orchestral style of conducting was quite different, even though it was still very ordered and quite restrained. I learnt a lot from him in that area as well.

E   *You also sang with the Cambridge University Musical Society Choir. Who was the conductor then?*

P   Boris was, but he returned to the air force at the end of my first term when Harold Darke took over from him. It was sad that I really had very little time with Boris as a choral scholar until after the war.

E   *Choirs are renowned for being loyal to one conductor. Did the chapel choir accept Harold Darke?*

P   I think we were definitely rather critical. Things seemed to move at a slower pace with him. He was a pleasant and kindly person to get on with, but not as lively and bright as Boris, not as quick. Harold was also teaching organ at the Royal College of Music, and he took over from Boris as my organ teacher. He was a good organ teacher, and I continued with him later on when I went to the Royal College of Music.

E   *What was the rehearsal schedule like for choral scholars?*

P   We actually didn't have a lot of rehearsal time. We had a full chapel rehearsal with the choristers before Evensong on weekdays and Saturdays, plus a rehearsal before the morning service on Sunday, and another one afterwards for Evensong. Some weekday rehearsals were shorter than others, meaning that we had to prepare music for the next day as well.

I was also fortunate in being able to practise on the organ at King's, and there's an interesting story related to this. There was a big heavy door under the organ screen with steps leading up to the top, and this protected us from most visitors. But some people did manage to find their way up. One day a young man appeared beside me, and said that he'd been listening to me practising, and he just wanted to come up to say hello. I asked him if he was an organist but he replied that he was a violinist. After chatting for a while, I discovered that it had been necessary for him to leave France and that he'd been recovering from illness in the Huntingdon hospital. He had visited Cambridge several times to look round the colleges. I said to him, 'If you'd like to play the violin, I could accompany you. Why don't we get together one day?'

He seemed to find the idea quite appealing and agreed to bring his violin with him the next time he was in Cambridge. I suggested that we might play a Beethoven violin sonata, and I offered to get the music from the college library. We set up a time, and a few days later he came up to my room where I had my piano. We had a marvellous time playing together for about two hours. I think he came once more. Obviously I asked him for his name, but it didn't mean a thing to me.

Well, after the war, I told this story to David Willcocks. When I told him who the man was he exclaimed, '*Who?*' He was Stéphane Grappelli, the jazz violinist from Paris! I had no idea who he was until David told me.

E *How extraordinary! Did you ever met up with him again?*

P No, unfortunately, I don't think I did.

E *Were there any other memorable performances that you took part in during that time as a choral scholar?*

P I did have an unusual experience after the war. It was the first time I was invited to be a soloist in a major work. The Huntingdon Choral Society asked me to sing the part of Elijah for two performances of Mendelssohn's *Elijah*. These were bass solos, of course. David Willcocks had been asked to provide the organ accompaniment. I sang the first performance and found it to be a most moving experience. Actually, it was the first time that I had ever heard the work. When it came to the second performance, the tenor soloist, a local singer, was not able to sing as he had fallen ill. You can imagine the panic that it caused! David and I were asked if we could find a replacement, but we couldn't come up with anybody. Eventually we decided that I should sing the tenor solos and John Carol Case, another choral scholar, and later to become a well-known soloist in England, agreed to sing the bass solos. It was quite a challenge to sing both bass and tenor solos within a week but I did enjoy it!

E *Did you ever think of becoming a solo singer?*

P No, that was never a consideration of mine.

E *You have had a beautiful Bösendorfer piano for very many years. How did it come into your possession?*

P　When I went up to Cambridge to read music, it became obvious that I must have a piano. I couldn't afford one at that stage so my parents offered to buy me one and suggested that I should get advice on where to look from a lecturer. I did this and was put in touch with the Wigmore Hall in London, where they had a small Bösendorfer grand piano for sale at the price of £175. It had been in use for only a month before the war and had not been touched since. That's the instrument that my parents bought for me. It was virtually a new piano then, and it has been in my possession ever since. It's a lovely instrument.

E　*Did you continue with composition at this time?*

P　Yes, I did, because I was reading music. But I don't remember anything terribly worthwhile coming out of it. However, I realise now that my work with composition would definitely have been a help for improvisation, which I have always enjoyed. Not that I think I am terribly good at it! But I do a lot of improvisation now before and after services. I don't remember ever being taught the art – I just picked it up.

Engagement photographs of Peter and Sheila.

E　*It must have been a wrench to leave the chapel choir when you were called up.*

P　Strangely enough, I don't remember feeling that. It was what young men were expected to do in those days of war. I just considered it to be my duty.

E　*Now, what of your relationship with Sheila? It continued from that very first meeting at the fox hunt, didn't it?*

P　We wrote to each other while I was at Denstone. And when I was reading music at Cambridge, Sheila was at Newnham College reading medicine. We both sang in the CUMS Madrigal Choir and she also played in the CUMS Orchestra – she was a very good viola player. Our relationship developed, until we became engaged not long before I left for East Africa in the army. Sheila was the only girlfriend that I had ever had.

E   *You were called up at the end of the summer term of 1942. Where did you serve during the war?*

P   First of all I went to officer training for four months on the Isle of Man, and thoroughly enjoyed being there. After my training I was commissioned as second lieutenant, and came back to England to Sheringham on the Norfolk coast to join a battalion. I had to train soldiers in exercises and runs and shooting.

I was very fortunate as my two aunts, Dorothy and Audrey Wright, lived there. And Patrick Hadley, who was professor of music at King's, lived in a house just beyond Huntstanton in Norfolk. He knew Sheila because she played the viola for him at Cambridge, and he used to invite her to stay with him. So I would cycle over to see her during the day, when she was there, and back again at night – halfway over Norfolk! It was wonderful being able to keep in contact like that.

E   *How long was it before you left for South Africa?*

P   I was in Norfolk for three months before my overseas posting came. We left from Liverpool in a convoy of boats with no idea whatsoever where we were going. As it happened, our convoy went to South Africa. We disembarked at Cape Town, and spent two weeks in a camp somewhere out in the country. I remember it being close enough to Cape Town for me to be able to go to rehearsals and performances by the Cape Town Symphony Orchestra.

However, it was not long before we were on-board ship again. We still did not know our final destination. This time we travelled up the east coast and were told that we were heading for Mombassa, the main port for Kenya.

Once we landed we were sent by train to Nairobi for a crash course in learning Swahili. I started writing a diary about that time, which I kept up in some detail until I returned home in 1945. And I got great pleasure from doing drawings, but haven't done any since. After this we went by convoy to Abyssinia, along roads which were little more than dirt tracks. Numerous trucks would break down. The journey took us over a month. I served – first as second lieutenant, and later as lieutenant – in the 66th Battalion of the King's African Rifles, who were acting as protection after the defeat of the Italians. And it was a training period for troops to be sent to Burma. I was promoted to captain in the middle of 1944, and for a while was the only white man among about 120 troops – I was in charge of those men and their training. I got on very well with them, and was given the title of 'Bwana Hevasack' as I always carried a haversack around with me.

Diary writing in East Africa during the war.

E *Did you ever see active service?*

P No. I was extremely fortunate here. Our role was to train troops to fight, particularly against the Japanese.

E *Could you describe how you found your time in the army and your relationships with your fellow officers?*

P I can't say that I enjoyed my time in the army, but I accepted things and just got on with life. I didn't find it difficult to relate to the other officers as people, but I didn't enjoy the huge amount of drinking that went on or the social activities. Small talk was never my strength. I remember nurses coming to the camp from time to time to dance with the officers in the evening. I preferred to put the records on and retire as early as I could!

E *Were you entirely cut off from the things you loved during this time?*

P No, there were broadcasts that I could listen to on the radio. And I went to church every week. Towards the end of my time in the army I was sent east to Somaliland to the base reinforcement's camp up in Jaffna where I was adjutant for a while. I watched African troops passing through on their way to fight the Japanese in Burma. I was able to drive down in my own jeep to Colombo, where I started going to the cathedral. The bishop there was a very nice person who invited me to go and stay with him. But the war ended in Europe shortly after my arrival in Ceylon, and I applied for leave to return to England, the first since joining the army in 1943.

EXCERPTS FROM PETER'S WAR DIARY

Peter's life during the war consisted mainly of training troops in military activities including rifle shooting and office work, and involvement in hearing court tribunals, and general officer's duties. It was not a time that he enjoyed, but the things that were important to him can be seen to have remained so in some of these excerpts from his war diary. Peter kept this journal meticulously for two years while he was in East Africa.

GOOD FRIDAY, APRIL 7TH

Went to Church at 9.30, and a very uninspired service it was, too. I realise that the Padre is under great difficulties but, really, he seems to use no initiative at all in making the services interesting.

SUNDAY, APRIL 18TH

Holy Communion this morning, the first for a long time. Major Ince was Padre and came to breakfast afterwards. Then there was Matins at 11.30, and it would have been good if we had had a good congregation because he preached an exceptionally good sermon to the six people who were present.

This afternoon I wrote letters and then at 4.00 with the doctor we went along to the Armaman's to tea. I haven't played the piano so much for a long, long time. Solos, songs and, to finish up with, duets. Anne and I played most of the 5th and then Isabelle and I went through the 1st, and most of the 3rd*. What a heyday, and very good it was too!

WEDNESDAY, APRIL 26TH

I had my first experience of taking a service, and unhappily this was a funeral! A signaller from Siga Siga had had a brain operation and had died. I arrived on time at the place where I was told to go, but by 5 past 4 no one had turned up, so I wandered to the L of C where I was informed that I was right. I sauntered back again (by which time it was 25 past) when the Major's CO turned up in a lather to tell me that I was at the wrong place, and that the T Major and Staff A were fuming over my lateness. So I had to go up there and fuming they were! I really had not got a great deal of idea what to do, but I think things went OK. Except, as the TM said, I buried him the wrong way round.

* Beethoven symphonies.

SUNDAY, MAY 14TH

I played the organ for the African Service which was altogether quite impressive. I did arrive late for the first hymn but joined in during the third verse. The two pitches did not altogether coincide and we were out for the rest of the time!

MONDAY, MAY 22ND

We suffered really seriously for the first time from locusts. They have been on the way for the last three weeks and bait parties have been out most mornings and evenings. On Saturday at the shoot they were crawling and hopping past us by the millions ... by Sunday evening they were everywhere. The Church was absolutely covered with them ... in the offices, mess, and barracks. A frightful mess. Bait has been thrown everywhere but this generally takes two days to take effect. Orderly officer today.

FRIDAY, JUNE 2ND

Orderly officer again today. For about the umpteenth time another rocket from the C O re the L of C guard. It's just absurd, because as soon as one gets something right something else is wrong – today, for instance, the equipment was ragged – BAH, how can one be expected to do training and keep everything in perfect order for guards! So I've been 'browned off' today again.

THURSDAY, JUNE 15TH

One year ago today since I said 'Goodbye' to my She in that miserable hotel in Shaftesbury Ave. One is inclined to wonder if ... there will be another whole year away from home ...

TUESDAY, JUNE 20TH

... Listened to another Prom concert this evening – Liszt Piano Concerto and 1st Movement of New World ...

MONDAY, JULY 3RD

... I was called to the Adjutant's office and told to wait outside. I saw the C O and Adj discussing something inside in low tones. I didn't know what it was that I had done wrong. In I went and was told that I would be going on a Fieldworks course and that I was, in fact, a Captain and was to put up my third Pip that afternoon! What a shock when all the other officers are older than I am!

FRIDAY, SEPT 8TH

… On the range today and the results again were not good. These people do not aim properly, that's all it is. Phoned up HQ and they seem most uncommunicative. They seem to have forgotten about us altogether …

SUNDAY, SEPT 17TH

… I heard the 'Missa Solemnis' this afternoon on the wireless!! It sounded as if it was coming from America. How wonderful. Bags of office work to be coped with …

SUNDAY, DEC 24TH

… I tried for all I was worth to get the Carols from King's on the wireless this evening but was unhappily unsuccessful. But, however, I was lucky in hearing two services later on from York Minster and the other from Westminster. How wonderful to hear dear old Milner's voice all the way from England. Their choir was good and better than Westminster.

WEDNESDAY, JAN 3RD

A few days ago I got the Denstonian which gave news of a lot of deaths of Old Denstonians. Many of them were at school with me, a lot of them in Burma. And here I am, still sitting in Africa doing absolutely nothing. I feel like putting in for a transfer right away.

THURSDAY, JAN 4TH

… Got the wireless going today. Started teaching the Askaris* to play Rounders this evening, and they quite enjoyed it.

FRIDAY, JAN 5TH

… Played Rounders this evening with the Askaris again and the results were a lot more successful – bags of exercise anyway, which is the most important thing.

SATURDAY, JAN 7TH

Tonight we all dined with the Governor, his wife and two daughters. It really was most pleasant, with helpful moon and all the lights on in the garden, and we sang with the piano later. Oh, if only my She were with me – this is just all right, when the tropics are worth having.

---

* A local soldier or policeman serving in a colonial administration.

THURSDAY, JAN 11TH

This is not my life, just to sit here doing office work, and it's getting me down completely.

MONDAY, JAN 29TH

Went round the Magaha with Dennis who bought a watch. I bought gramophone needles. They wanted 9/– a box. I got them for 5/–.

MONDAY, FEB 5TH

Spent the most shocking night. Goodness knows what was the matter – hardly slept a wink. Even got out and put Brahms No 1 on at 2.00 this morning.

SUNDAY, FEB 11TH

It is always difficult to realise that it's a Sunday when one is on a safari.

SUNDAY, FEB 24TH

Two years ago today since my She and I were officially engaged. God bless her.

4

King's and the Royal College of Music, 1945–49

P My request for leave from the army was confirmed in 1945, at the end of the war as it turned out. When I knew of this, I sent a telegram to Sheila asking if we could get married on my return. She and her father, the rector, were marvellous and planned the whole thing. And my sister, Ruth, arranged for Eric Milner-White to come and marry us. I flew home, the first time I had ever been in an aeroplane, and because of delays, I arrived almost too late for the wedding!

I have been blessed throughout my life, but on the day of our wedding an incredible stroke of good fortune occurred. Sheila's father had been chaplain, head of maths and a housemaster at Uppingham School. In fact, Sheila was born there. Her parents had invited some of their old friends from Uppingham to the wedding and among them was the newly retired director of music, Robert Sterndale Bennett. He was followed by Douglas Guest, who happened to be staying with the Sterndale Bennetts when our wedding invitation arrived. When Douglas saw it on their mantelpiece he exclaimed, 'There can be only one Peter Godfrey. If he was a chorister at King's, please will you pass on my invitation for him to come to Uppingham as my first assistant?'

I was duly given that invitation on my wedding day. Here I was, still officially in the army but with a wonderful career move just popping out of the blue, as it were. I had decided to do an MA, but because I

Married at last.

was still not demobilised and therefore not in a position to return to Cambridge, I accepted Douglas's invitation. This, however, turned out to be very short-lived as three weeks later I was demobilised and able to move back to King's. But it was to lead to important things in my life later on.

E   *You already had a BMus, why did you go back to university for more study?*

P   I needed to have an MA for the teaching career that I had planned. At Cambridge one would take a BA, and then wait for five years for it to be made an MA. We had to pay a certain amount for this.

E   *A strange way of obtaining a higher qualification!*

P   Well, that was the way of it. I was accepted back into King's, and because Sheila was working as a doctor in a London hospital (she was very much involved in women's medicine at the time, but specialised later on in anaesthesia), I applied for a room in King's. And here follows another amazing coincidence. Who should I be sharing a room with? None other than David Willcocks, who became a lifelong friend and who helped me in my career in many different ways! David was a little older than I was, but we were both musicians and hit it off straight away. We had met once before when I was a choral scholar at King's. David had also recently come out of the army, and was later to become director of music at King's College, Cambridge.

E   *Were you taking different subjects?*

P   No. We chose the same subjects because we found that the easiest way to get our BA was to do a mixture of history and economics. I was very happy to take history, but economics was another story altogether. The period we had to study was modern history, particularly the last hundred years of the British Empire. We went to about two or three lectures a week, and had the same supervisor, John Saltmarsh. Each week we would read out our weekly essay to him in his study. David and I would take it in turns to read first. On one particular occasion we were given an essay to write on Cecil Rhodes. David always left his essay to the last moment, but as usual I went up to the college library earlier in the week and found a book on Rhodesia, which helped me to write my essay. On the day of our supervision, I just happened to be passing the library and met David trotting down the steps.

    I said, 'Oh, you've been reading the book on Rhodesia, have you?'
'Yes,' he said.

    Well, anyway, we met together outside John's room and discovered that we both had exactly the same opening words: 'Cecil Rhodes came of yeoman stock.' Of course, that had come straight out of the book! Well, we went into the room in absolute giggles.

    John said, 'Godfrey, it's your turn to read first.'

'No,' I replied hastily, 'it's David's.'

And David said quickly, 'No, it's Peter's.'

I don't remember who read first, but whoever it was managed to get only as far as 'Cecil Rhodes came of yeoman stock' before we both giggled like mad. John was not at all impressed with the situation and sent us both away. But David and I still laugh over it when we meet. Well, we sat our exam and passed it – David got a much higher mark than I did. I have to say that I didn't ever understand economics, and coped only by buying a very easy book two weeks before the exam called *Teach Yourself Economics*. We both got our BAs – David did very little work and got a first. I worked hard and got a second. And five years later we had our MAs.

E *Did you continue as a choral scholar at this time?*

P Oh yes. We were still needed in the choir. And I was asked to conduct the King's College Choral Society. I remember one frightful rumpus during that time. It was the practice for the college to bill all students a subscription of ten shillings to belong to this society, hoping that most students would join. They were asked to write to the society's secretary if they didn't wish to join, otherwise 'willingness to join would be assumed'. This upset one student so much that I received the following letter with an illegible signature:

> Nothing is further from my intention than to join the KCMS, and nothing could annoy me more than to be forced, whether I like it or not, to write and tell you so.
>
> It seems to me little short of blackmail to recruit your members without consulting them, and to throw upon them the onus which is rightly yours, of entering into correspondence on the matter; or else of going to some trouble of having their college bills corrected later.
>
> While I do not anticipate that this protest will have the slightest effect on you, I should like to add that I am not alone in resenting your high-handed, bureaucratic and idle methods.

E *Oh dear – how unfortunate. Did you continue shooting in that year at Cambridge?*

P Yes, I did. I was invited to join a *pro tem* English team in the Channel Islands in the Easter vacation – Uncle Ronald was also in the team – and later to join the Cambridge team to shoot against Oxford. The latter was at Bisley. So all this got me started again.

Peter's first car, a Morris Minor.

E *At the end of your time at King's, when you had your BA, had you decided on being a professional musician as your career?*

P Teaching music seemed the right path for me to follow. I had already spent three enjoyable weeks at Uppingham, teaching mostly practical music – piano and organ. So I decided that I must have an ARCO* and, if I could manage it, an FRCO*. For anyone going into schools, universities or cathedrals it was a necessary qualification. The most sensible way to achieve this was to spend a year at the Royal College of Music. This is what I chose to do, studying organ, singing and piano. The college authorities told me that it was quite possible to accomplish a lot in just one day a week, so I accepted an invitation to teach piano part-time at Felsted School in Essex for two terms, as well as taking the studies at the Royal College of Music.

Taking a class at Felsted.

E *Who were your teachers at the college?*

P Harold Darke taught me organ and I got to know Herbert Howells very well. But I'm sorry to say that I don't remember the names of my singing and piano teachers.

E *Did you study composition with Howells?*

P I may have done, but I'm not certain about that. I got to know him when I was at King's as a chorister, because he took a part-time job

* Associate and Fellow of the Royal College of Organists.

at St John's when the director of music there was called up. Herbert used to come up every weekend, and – as a great friend of Harold Darke's – he would come to Harold's afternoon tea parties after Evensong at King's on Sundays. We became good friends at the Royal College and he became very fond of Sheila.

My move to Felsted made it necessary for me to buy our first car, a little Morris Minor. Sheila was now working as an anaesthetist in London. I would drive up to London for my college work and would spend whatever time I could with her, sometimes staying overnight in the hospital in her room. There was one occasion when a nurse came into the room to say that Sheila was wanted in the operating theatre. So Sheila got out of bed and off to the theatre, where she found the nurse in tears – she was so shocked to find a man in Dr Godfrey's bed!

E   *Attitudes were very different in those days!*

P   I was still at Felsted in January 1947, when we had a really terrible winter with a lot of snow. The roads were very dangerous and quite nerve-wracking, as driving was new to me and I hadn't driven in such conditions before. Then a dreadful thing happened: the headmaster of Felsted was killed in a car accident because of icy conditions. The realisation hit me that it would be like this every year. I found myself dwelling on the warm climate of East Africa and considering the possibility of a move away from England. Where to go, though? I thought about the different nationalities of officers I had been with from the colonies during my time in the army. The people I liked best were the New Zealanders. So I started looking in the papers for jobs in New Zealand, but found nothing at that stage.

E   *How did Sheila react to your desire to leave England?*

P   Amazingly well. She was always a terrific supporter of anything I wanted to do. Her parents didn't like the idea at all, and I don't know if Sheila was keen at first, but she didn't ever discourage me.

After a term at Felsted I received another invitation from Douglas Guest. There was a vacancy at Uppingham again and he wanted me to go back. I couldn't refuse his offer as I had enjoyed my previous three weeks at the school so much. Sheila came with me to Uppingham where we lived in a lovely old house, our first home together. She had strong associations with the school as she was born there. Once again I was involved with playing for church services when Douglas was conducting, and teaching piano and organ. And I became very much involved with shooting, and coached the school teams. They did very well in national competitions although they didn't actually win. I continued with my own shooting.

It wasn't until I got back to Uppingham that I did actually find two music positions in New Zealand that interested me – one was music master at Hereworth School in Hawkes Bay, with the job of organist at St Matthew's Anglican church in Hastings, the other being a music lectureship at the University of Auckland in New Zealand. I wrote to the head of department, Professor Roger Hollinrake, expressing my interest in the position, but said that, because church music was a very important feature of my life, I would like a church job as well. The position at St Matthew's in the City was vacant at the time, but he replied that it would not be acceptable to do any work other than the university work. So I thought, 'Blow you', and left it at that. I continued to look for positions overseas but without any success at that time.

Uppingham was a full-time job, but I continued going up to London to the college until the end of that academic year. It was then that I passed my ARCO in the summer of 1947. And now, here's an extraordinary story.

There were several people who had been at Cambridge with me who were doing the same thing at that time. We'd all agreed to get together for lunch in the middle of the exams – there was a paper in the morning and another in the afternoon. There were about fifty or sixty people there for the morning exam. I had a desk right on the aisle. I completed the paper and when we were told to take our papers up I walked along the aisle and just happened to look down at a paper two rows in front of me. It looked quite different from mine. So I looked back at my paper which gave the *afternoon* times – 2.30 to 5.30. I wondered what on earth to do, realising that the paper would be discussed over lunch and that I could tell my friends what questions the afternoon paper would have.

E   *And you would have been sitting the afternoon paper for a second time!*

P   Exactly. So I told the invigilator what had happened who got into a frightful spin and called other college authorities. In the end I was taken off to a room on my own and locked in! They did bring me food.

And I had to sit the morning paper in a room with blind students. If I hadn't noticed the problem in the morning they would have had to cancel the whole exam! I passed my ARCO and, some time later, FRCO. And so I felt equipped to start my teaching career in earnest.

5

Marlborough College, 1949–58

E   *Peter, you were appointed assistant director of music at Marlborough College in September 1949. How did that come about?*

P   Boris Ord called me to talk over the possibility of a position at Marlborough. The headmaster, or 'master' as he was called, knew Boris Ord, and apparently had discussed the matter with him. I had enjoyed working with Douglas Guest very much – he was so good with choirs – and was reluctant to leave Uppingham, but Boris said, 'Marlborough is a much bigger school than Uppingham and is considered to be one of the top five public schools in England. It is an excellent promotion, which I think you should accept.'

So that's what I did.

We had only about a year and a half at Uppingham before we moved to Marlborough. Our first two children were born while we were at Uppingham: Belinda in August 1947, and our second daughter, Rachel, in August 1949, just before we moved to Marlborough. As a young mother, Sheila couldn't continue to work full-time, but she used to do some part-time work there, as she did later at Marlborough. They were happy days and I was sorry to leave them. We had two more daughters who were born in Marlborough. Diana was born on 28 December 1951, and our last child, Patricia, was born in March 1954.

Apart from the college position, there were two other strokes of good fortune resulting from that move. One was that the main parish church of St Mary in Marlborough was vacant and I was offered that position. It all fell into place so easily! I had a choir of about thirty singers consisting of sixteen boys, women altos and men. And it gave me the opportunity to develop my organ playing – I gave several organ recitals in St Mary's and the other Anglican Church, St Peter's. I was thrilled to meet up with an old Denstonian in the High Street one morning: John Goodman (a member of my house – Woodard, but one year senior to me, and a member of the shooting VIII a year before me). John was coming to Marlborough to act as assistant priest to the vicar. Both of us will always remember a sermon he preached on St John 1 verse 8: 'If we say we have no sin, we deceive ourselves, and the truth is not in us.' John said that we all had dandelions in our gardens. I checked with my garden and could not find a single one, and told him so!

The other stroke of good fortune was the invitation to take a Women's Institute choir of about twenty women in a village called Pewsey, some five miles south of Marlborough. I used to go there every Monday evening by bus. This was a very important part of my training as it was an all-comers choir with very limited skills. I have to say that I was surprised by the patience and tolerance I had, considering my King's experiences! This was the first time I had my own choirs and did any serious choir training. I realise now that these two choirs provided me with preparation for the challenges that I was to meet in my work with choirs throughout my life – singers of all types and abilities, and all kinds of age levels. It was very good of the headmaster to allow me to take on so many extra-curricular activities. We used to take part in competitions and festivals and they performed quite well. I enjoyed working with the choirs enormously.

Another very rewarding thing was the choir I started at Marlborough College: the Marlborough Madrigal Society. This was for members of staff and their wives, though it also included some members of the community. Just digressing a little, one person joined the choir who still sings with me on occasions – and that was Shirley Carson, as I knew her then, now Shirley Burrows. Shirley has family in New Zealand and visits them regularly. She and her husband, Frank, have sung twice with the Nostalgia Choir, which has performed in Auckland each January for the last six or so years. This choir consists of former members of the cathedral and Dorian choirs that I conducted many years ago. We rehearse and sing services in Holy Trinity Cathedral, Auckland, over the period of five days and have a wonderful time together. They sing amazingly well even though the average combined age is probably in the seventies now. Two singers are in their nineties!

Now, going back to Marlborough. By this time David was organist at Worcester Cathedral and he said to me, 'Why don't you come to the Three Choirs Festival. I could put you and Sheila up in the same house as the other two conductors and the soloists.' So I started going each year and just loved it all. The Finzi family attended regularly as well, and this is how Gerald Finzi and I first met. He happened to live quite close to Marlborough and became a close friend. Gerald's lovely wife, Joy, used to come and play viola in the college orchestra. Gerald came over with her but would go up to my study and work on his compositions there. It so happened that the Marlborough Madrigal Society was given the honour of being the first choir to perform his lovely work, *In Terra Pax*.

At one point there came an opportunity when I could very easily have gone to Australia. Marlborough College had quite an attachment with Melbourne Grammar School, with regular exchanges of staff taking place for a year or so. One of those who came to us from Melbourne was their assistant principal. Fairly soon after he returned home, and about two or three years after I had been at Marlborough, I received an invitation to go to Melbourne Grammar School as director of music. This was a permanent position. I went to see Tommy Garlick, the master at Marlborough, to talk this over with him. His reply to me was, 'Well, look, if you are still here in a year and a half's time and I offer you the position of director of music, will you stay here?' I decided to stay.

E   *That must have been a difficult decision for you seeing that you were longing to emigrate to a warmer climate.*

P   Not really. It was to be such a very good promotion for me as director of music at Marlborough that I felt I would have been silly to have turned it down. And we were enjoying wonderful friends in Marlborough, such as the Kempsons and the Byrnes. Girsha Byrne was a fine artist and actually painted a portrait of me which I have still. She had sung in the Pewsey Women's Institute Choir. Sheila and I used to visit the Byrnes often, where we enjoyed evening musical soirées, and I would play four-hand duets with another friend.

I eventually became director of music at Marlborough. This meant a move to the director of music's house, Hamelin, a lovely home on the Bath Road with a large garden. There was a garden at Uppingham, which I realised I had to keep tidy, but it was the garden at Hamelin that first got me really interested. I bought quite a few books to help, which I have in my bedroom still!

Several boys from the college helped me over the years. I remember in particular, Richard Podger, who had been a senior chorister at King's and was one of Boris's favourites; David Garnett, who was my organ student; and Nicholas Hinton, who had been a chorister at Salisbury Cathedral and who later became head of the Save the Children organisation. We were to meet again many years later when he turned up at Evensong at Wellington Cathedral when I was director of music.

I was paid a huge compliment once by the local postman. My raspberries were by far the best in Marlborough, he declared. I often wondered how he knew! The garden developed so well that I actually dug up the tennis court to increase its size. I did feel rather guilty about that – I made it into a vegetable garden!

E   *This new position must have added a lot more work to your already busy life.*

P   The director's job was very demanding and a considerable challenge, but I received tremendous support from Sheila and managed to cope with it all. Sadly, I had to give up both the parish church job and the Women's Institute choir. I valued enormously the chance I had with both choirs – learning to conduct and work with people – and I was very sad about leaving them. But it would have been just too much.

The main part of my job was conducting: the chapel choir, the large choral society and the college orchestra. One of the most memorable large-scale choral events was our performance of the *St Matthew Passion*. And we put on a full-scale opera in the Memorial Hall which was written for us by Anthony Smith Masters, my first assistant.

One of the things I enjoyed most at Marlborough was taking the congregational practice – or 'congregaggers', as it was known – on Friday mornings in preparation for the Sunday service. The school had a lovely big chapel with unusual seating arrangements for the congregation – they faced inwards. I used to walk up and down the aisle and really loved getting these boys to sing. As well, I still taught piano and organ and, occasionally, singing.

E *Choral and orchestral conducting are very different techniques. Did you feel adequately equipped for the latter?*

P I was helped later on by a week of training offered by the Bournemouth Symphony Orchestra, who came to play for us at the college several times. In 1957 I heard that they were to have a week of workshops for training young conductors. This was the brainchild of Sir Charles Groves who gave us the training. So I applied for it and went. And here is another strange coincidence. As I went to the orchestra's office at the beginning of the course there was another man going up the steps at the same time. It turned out that he came from New Zealand. He was Peter Zwartz and I was to get to know him again when I emigrated there. I invited him to conduct the Auckland String Players on one occasion.

There was a final concert that three of the participants were invited to conduct. I was fortunate to be one of them. However, there was an article in the *Times* about the week and the concert, which stated that Peter Godfrey appeared to be rather tense! I think the writer's opinion was that I shouldn't have been one of the three chosen.

E *Interesting. Another reviewer in an unnamed newspaper wrote this …*

YOUNG CONDUCTORS SHOW THEIR SKILLS AT BOURNEMOUTH SYMPHONY ORCHESTRA'S WINTER GARDENS CONCERT

Mr Godfrey took over to conduct the orchestral accompaniment of Schubert's *Konzertstucke* in D with Derek Collie as solo violinist. A stylish conductor, Mr Godfrey commendably resisted the temptation to thrust himself forward and played an intelligent second fiddle to the brilliance of his soloist. The orchestral introduction seemed if anything too leisurely, but thereafter all was plain sailing …

E *… now, can you tell me about shooting while you were at Marlborough?*

P I continued to shoot and coach rifle shooting, as I had done at Uppingham. I found it to be a great form of relaxation and a change from the stresses and strains of teaching.

In 1951 I took a team of national cadets to shoot in Canada. I shot in the competition in Ottawa, coming second in the Silver Cross Trophy. I also shot for England in the international match against Wales,

Scotland and Ireland and took part in the national competitions at Bisley each year. I enjoyed the shooting there tremendously and I got to know a lot of people.

The college team did very well – we didn't ever win but we got very close to it. However, I became aware of a slight lack of hearing in my right ear and was told very firmly by Gerald Finzi that I should not be shooting and to stop it right away. So I did! This was in 1952. I still think my hearing problem was caused by firing an anti-tank rifle during the war as we didn't ever wear any protection for our ears. Even with rifle shooting, we used only two small pieces of four by two pushed into our ears (their real purpose was to clean out our rifle!), and they were always falling out.

E   *All this sounds a very fulfilling way of life. And yet you did eventually make the move to New Zealand. How did that come about?*

Peter at Bisley, 1953.

P   My restlessness never really went away. Strangely enough, it was through the Three Choirs Festival that my opportunity came.

I continued going to the Three Choirs Festival each year and got to know quite a few distinguished musicians. Herbert Howells always attended. In 1957 when it was held at Gloucester, we had a particularly marvellous house party there. David Willcocks, Howard Ferguson, Meredith Davies and all the Finzis came. And also Ralph Vaughan Williams and his wife, Ursula. Ralph conducted his own orchestral and choral works at the festival.

I got to know Vaughan Williams quite well over the years. He was a most kind and amiable man, although people could find him rather gruff – as he appeared to me when I met him for the first time as a chorister. But life can't have been terribly easy for him, as he was quite deaf and had poor eyesight when I got to know him as an adult. He had one intriguing characteristic: at mealtimes he always organised things so that he had an attractive young woman sitting on each side of him. I'm not saying that he was a womaniser, but he did enjoy talking to good-looking ladies! As we became his friends we were invited to call him Uncle Ralph. I remember asking if he would make a piano accompaniment of *Hodie*, his large-scale Christmas work, as I wanted to perform it at Marlborough. He surprised me when he was more than willing to do it.

Coaching a shooting team at Bisley.

David had arranged for us to stay in the headmaster's house of the choir school. It was such a stimulating time, and, as it turned out, a crucial time for my future. I heard of a New Zealander attending the festival who was head of the country's broadcasting service, so I arranged a meeting with him.

He was Malcolm Rickard, the founder and conductor of a large choral society in Wellington, the Orpheus Choir as it became known, and which I later conducted. I told him of my interest in emigrating and had long talks with him about possible employment. Malcolm said that there was a new professor of music at Auckland University and he would find out what his attitude was about outside employment for his staff members. When we parted he promised to tell me of any suitable music positions that became vacant.

Quite soon after this, Malcolm phoned to say that the new professor, Charles Nalden, was very supportive of lecturers taking on extra musical activities in the community. It wasn't long before Malcolm wrote to me saying that not only was there a lecturer's position available at the university, but also the cathedral was looking for a new director of music. I contacted Charles Nalden who told me that I would need to have an interview, which duly took place in London.

There was a panel of very distinguished people to interview me – Sir Thomas Armstrong, Herbert Howells and Ernest Bullock. I knew Herbert Howells well.

P   In mid-December I received a telegram offering me the position at the university, and within twenty-four hours I received another telegram offering me the position of director of music at the cathedral. This was

from
HERBERT HOWELLS
3 BEVERLEY CLOSE
BARNES. S.W. 13
PROSPECT 5119

I have known Mr Peter Godfrey for the past fifteen years. What I most willingly state here is, therefore, based upon direct knowledge of his musicianship.

At Cambridge he was himself the product of the Tutorial system in preparation for Musical and Arts Degrees in that University — an unsurpassed system —

His 'University sense' of things — if I may use that expression — is keen and highly-geared, and would add greatly to his own effective directorship of any University Degree Course in Music. Academically he is finely-grounded. It would be a powerful influence in his lecturing.

One knows his musicianship to be well-balanced: a fine blend of theoretic and executive ability. In his case, moreover, one stresses his marked gifts as Conductor — orchestral and choral.

With these aptitudes there goes a firm, attractive personality. He 'mixes' well. His colleagues respect him immensely. They know — and his pupils know — that he is a fine 'energiser' in all his musical undertakings.

I regard him, therefore, as a man and musician fit for the responsibility of a major post.

He has my warm, confident support.

Herbert Howells:

(27 Aug: 1957)

A reference for Peter written by
Herbert Howells.

the first and only time that I have ever applied for jobs. It was the major turning point in my career. Auckland let it be known that they wanted me to assume duties there as soon as possible. However, because the academic year at Marlborough had already started, I insisted on seeing out the full year. We left England towards the end of September 1958. David Willcocks was quite dubious about this appointment, and told me that I would be back in England in two years!

E   *How did the family feel about this momentous change in their lives?*

P   Our parents were very sad, particularly Sheila's parents. They really didn't want to see us go. The children were excited about the adventure, but Sheila found it difficult to leave her family and England. It had to be, though. So we packed up. I made boxes for everything, even the Bösendorfer piano! Some students at the college helped us to pack everything, including the antique furniture which my mother had bought for us earlier and which I still have. It was a big job.

Last glimpse of England.

E   *Then you were faced with the long voyage out to New Zealand. How long did it take you?*

P   We were at sea for five weeks, sailing on the *Southern Cross*.

E   *You are not known to enjoy holidays. Didn't you find that an impossibly long time to be doing nothing?*

P   Well … what I did was start a choir! But I had to wait until we arrived at Cape Town where I found a music shop and bought some scores. The choir proved to be quite popular and we decided that we should meet every day. So preparation for rehearsals, and taking them, filled in quite a bit of time very pleasantly for me. We sang in the ship's concert.

There were two people on-board the ship who were to become very well known to me in the future. One of these was a New Zealander named Maurice Faulknor who was returning home with his wife, and she sang in the ship choir. Maurie now sings in the St Michael's Parish Choir with me in Waikanae, and composes for us. Also singing in the ship choir was Malcolm Gray who later married Coreen, a fine soprano who sang in the Dorian Choir for many years. As well, there were two other people on-board who were old Marlburians!

After Cape Town we berthed at Durban, Fremantle and then Melbourne where we met up with an old Marlburian, Frank Woods. He had recently been appointed Archbishop of Melbourne. Frank had two sons at Marlborough while I was there, Theodore and David.

I've continued to keep in touch with David who became a teacher at Melbourne Grammar School. I met up with Frank again when I was director of music at Trinity College, Melbourne, as he was a trustee to the college.

Finally, we crossed the Tasman on the final leg of the voyage to Wellington, New Zealand.

RECOLLECTIONS

(née Maurice)

Caroline Gowers, organ student, Marlborough College.
Email, 2014.

I first came under Peter's spell when I was ten years old, and he was coaching my younger brother who was about to audition for the Winchester Cathedral Choir. I begged my parents to allow me to have singing lessons too. Almost immediately I was singing such things as, 'Where the Bee Sucks' and 'Where E'er You Walk'. I loved it, and I also loved his, then, small children. I would spend a great deal of time at Hamelin, where the family lived, playing with the children and being musically educated in about equal quantities. I have a strong memory of Peter playing me old 78s of Beethoven's *Pastoral Symphony* and telling me all about it in such a way that it has always remained a favourite with me. He had a way of bringing music to life because of his own love of it.

When I was eleven, I went to boarding school, but continued my contact with the Godfrey family in the holidays. At some point this extended to my having organ lessons with Peter in the college chapel. I don't really know how he managed to teach me to become a good organist. I have no recollection of his ever mentioning the word technique, and we just seemed to progress from one piece to the next via volumes of Bach preludes and fugues and not much else. All the same, by the time I was seventeen I remember playing Bach's great G Minor Prelude and Fugue after Evensong in the chapel. Peter persuaded my parents that I should try for the Royal College of Music with the result that I was a student there from 1958 to 1961, learning for the first year with Peter's old teacher Harold Darke.

Though I loved my organ lessons with Peter, I certainly felt that his real gift was as a choral conductor. I sang in the Marlborough Madrigal Society and it was a most exhilarating experience. Everyone came under his spell. Though I have sung in many choirs since, I have never experienced the same degree of sheer musical pleasure that he managed to communicate.

In 1961 I married Patrick Gowers, a composer, and we saw Peter, and sometimes Sheila too, on their intermittent returns to the UK. After Belinda's tragic death, Peter asked Patrick to write an anthem which was to be sung at her memorial service in Auckland Cathedral. Some years later, when Peter took over from David Willcocks at King's for a term, he performed this anthem – *Holy, Holy, Holy* – and Patrick recorded it illegally with a small recorder hidden under the pew.

Marlborough College Chapel.

Looking back now, I realise how lucky I was to have known someone like Peter when I was a child. He was a sort of musical mentor and a huge inspiration. He wanted to share his love of music with anyone who showed an interest, and then nothing seemed too much trouble. I remember he took me to my first prom in the Albert Hall and we heard the Brahms *St Anthony Variations*. By the time we went he had played them to me so many times that I was completely familiar with the music. It was a very different approach from the sort of academic analysis that went on later at the RCM, and had a far more lasting effect. It is no exaggeration to say that without Peter's influence and teaching I would not have become a musician, and I owe him a huge debt of gratitude.

Trevor Gartside, assistant music teacher, Marlborough College.
Letter, 2009.

In 1954 I was appointed as assistant music teacher at Marlborough College when Peter became director of music. I was no stranger to the school as I had been a war-time evacuee in Marlborough, coming from the City of London School in 1939. My appointment included the post of organist of the two town churches. I began work there before the school term started, and Peter was keen that I was of use before college pupils began the new school year. I inherited the parish choir from Peter, which was very good of its genre, and during my time sang Evensong in Salisbury Cathedral. There was only one choir between the two churches in Marlborough, both within sight of each other at either end of the High Street. Traipsing cassocks and surplices back and forth for the Sunday services was a real bore. St Peter's at the college end hosted a said Communion and sung Matins, and was where Cardinal Wolsey was priested and where the majority of Charles II's ministers have their tombs.

For my pre-appointment interviews Peter collected me in a grey Dormobile at Savernake Station, a nearby junction. Even now I recall its registration number – JMW371! Peter set me the task of making a card index of orchestral parts in the library, and this is still in use from over fifty years ago. This taught me many things that I still remember e.g. that Mozart's 38th Symphony, *The Prague*, has no clarinets in the score and the 39th has no oboes!

I also took over the Pewsey choir from him – a village choir bursting with ladies who adored him, but nevertheless they continued to be regular winners at the local County Music Festival in Devizes.

Small-bore shooting was another of Peter's hobbies he was keen to pass on, so he involved me in that too. This eventually led me to command the College Cadet Force, before becoming a housemaster and deputy head.

I remember especially the care he took in making sure that I was capable and confident before playing morning service for the whole school (800 plus), and before I first took the weekly congregational practice – an alarming experience for anyone, let alone a novice! I owe all this to Peter, and I shall always be grateful to him for giving me a very good start as a schoolmaster.

John Hunt, student, Marlborough College.
Letter, 2009.

Having been accepted for the choral society on arrival at Marlborough College in the Lent Term of 1955, I was one of the trebles in that year's performance – Mozart's Requiem Mass, if my memory serves me correctly. During an early rehearsal all sections were lustily singing some pianissimo passage when Peter tapped his baton.

'Something wrong there. We'll do it again.'

More lusty singing and another tap of the baton.

'Something wrong. I think it's with the trebles. We'll try your part again.'

Another repeat of the lusty section, or as much as we trebles could muster, anyway.

'Yes, something wrong there, trebles. We'll do your bit again.'
Yet more lusty singing, but this time without my contribution.
'Perfect, trebles.'
As a new boy, fearful at the thought of my absence being noted, I continued to attend rehearsals and the actual performance, but felt obliged to mime my way throughout.

Charles Waterfield, student, Marlborough College.
Letter, 13 February 2009.

I went up to Marlborough in 1954 with little idea that music would play a very significant part in my education. Academically I did well (on the science side) and eventually left with a place at Oxford. However my time at Marlborough College was hugely enriched by many musical discoveries, nearly all of which had behind them Peter Godfrey's guiding hand.

Of course there were piano lessons with Trevor Gartside, and a start made on the oboe – initially with the bandmaster! But I also discovered that there was a chapel choir to join where the high musical standard was a revelation. Peter had been the moving spirit behind the renovation of a magnificent five-manual organ, and I made sure (as a bass in the choir) to have a seat near enough to watch his nimble footwork in the voluntaries.

Chapel was also the setting for Choral Society, where we were introduced to several great works under Peter's baton – Bach, Mozart and Brahms amongst them. Later on I got to play in the orchestra for this, alongside visiting professionals.

My progress with the oboe was helped by a good peripatetic teacher, and by getting involved in the orchestra. I remember that on at least one occasion where there wasn't an oboe part (Mozart's 23rd Piano Concerto), Peter wrote one to keep me happy! He was also more than supportive when the chance to audition for the National Youth Orchestra came up. Successfully, as it turned out.

Then there were of course the annual music competitions. We were encouraged to enter a variety of classes – instrumental solos, piano duets, small ensembles – on whatever instrument(s) came to hand. One year Peter had managed to get the eminent Herbert Howells as adjudicator – all I remember Howells saying, after yet another of my many appearances, was that Waterfield seemed to be 'ubiquitous' (not entirely a term of approval).

Many others fortunate to have been at Marlborough College during Peter's time as music director, will agree that he created a remarkable musical tradition, which has continued to this day. He is remembered across the years with affection and gratitude.

Michael Boxford, student, Marlborough College.
Letter, 25 May 2009.

At the age of thirteen, as a new boy at Marlborough College in 1955, I was overawed by this huge institution where all 800 other boys seemed to be bigger and tougher than me. So I was apprehensive when asked to audition for the chapel choir, and very surprised when Mr Godfrey, the director of music, accepted me as a treble. I was even more astonished when I later played my latest piano piece to him, *Water-Wagtail* by Cyril Scott, for he assessed me as Grade VII standard and said he would teach me himself! That was a good start to my first year at the college. Although I was lucky enough to have a modicum of academic and sporting success, it is my musical memories that are the most vivid.

Chapel was at the centre of school life. There were compulsory services attended by the whole school every weekday morning and on every Sunday morning. There was also a voluntary service on Thursday evening and a Sunday Evensong. The choir had to prepare a different psalm to be chanted in four-part harmony every day, at least two new anthems every week, and of course there were the different settings of the responses, Te Deum, Magnificat and the other canticles to be learned. Peter directed all this with huge authority and skill, and I loved every moment. Our musical education continued at the end of each service with an organ voluntary played on the newly renovated Norman and Beard instrument, alternately by Peter and his two assistants, Tony Smith Masters and Trevor Gartside. This was no doubt of little interest to the majority of the boys, but to some of us, these voluntaries were a great introduction to the organ repertoire. One of Peter's party pieces was the Bach Prelude and Fugue, the 'St Anne'.

A weekly chapel highlight of more general relevance was congregational practice – or 'congregaggers', as it was affectionately called. One would think that this would be the ultimate in boredom for most public school boys, whose main enthusiasm tended to be sports, not music. But Peter managed to coax a sound out of them – always impressive and sometimes thrilling. On one particularly memorable occasion, he chose a unison chant in triple time for the words of the Benedicite, sung as a two-part canon. There were 800 boys, arranged in two halves facing each other, Decani and Cantoris, vying at each swell of the melody to drown each other out, and nearly blowing the roof off in the process.

The chapel also hosted one of the main events of the college musical year in the form of a grand concert, which I think formed part of the annual subscription concert series. The musical forces consisted of a large choir of boys (with representation well beyond the eighty-strong chapel choir), 'beaks' (masters) and/or their wives and other grown-ups from the town of Marlborough, together with an orchestra made up of the college's best instrumental musicians, reinforced by college staff (Reginald Jennings on his bassoon, Margaret Kempson on her violin) and other outsiders, with Peter of course conducting. It was here that he introduced me to *Zadok the Priest* when I could still sing a treble top A and, in subsequent years, to Bach's *St Matthew Passion* and Brahms' *German Requiem*. Performed in two halves with a longish interval for tea, these concerts were real adventures. The subscription concerts were otherwise given by exclusively professional musicians. One I particularly remember was given by Benjamin Britten and Peter Pears; and there was the annual visit of the Bournemouth Symphony Orchestra conducted by Walter Susskind.

Not all musical excitements during Peter's tenure as director of music happened in the chapel. Other highlights of the musical year included the music competitions that took place in the Winter and Easter terms in the Memorial Hall. In my first term, Peter accompanied me in the junior singing competition where I came third with the aria 'Voi Che Sapete' from his beloved *Marriage of Figaro*. This competition was won by Nicholas Hinton, who came to Marlborough as a Salisbury Cathedral chorister. After Marlborough, Nicholas went on to be director first of NACRO (National Association for the Care and Resettlement of Offenders) and then of Save the Children Fund, whilst still finding time to direct the Edington Music Festival – at which the leading cathedral choirs get together to 'let their hair down'.

Peter also teamed me up with Nicholas Hare in the piano duet competition, which we didn't win. Hare however went on to become an organ scholar at Oxford and a distinguished music publisher. In my second term, and to my complete surprise, I won the junior piano solo competition, playing the first movement of Beethoven's Sonata in E Flat that Peter had taught me, and which I had to repeat in front of the whole school at the end-of-term concert in the Memorial Hall. I took this as a great honour. To the school at large, the events of most interest in the music competitions were the 'House Shout,' an inter-house challenge featuring a unison song sung by a 20-strong group from each house, and in Easter Term, the 'House Glee' in which a smaller group from each house performed a part-song. These were highly competitive affairs with strong partisan support from the audience.

My first year ended with what must rank as a unique happening at a British public school: a series of six performances of a full-length opera, *Circe*, composed by Tony Smith Masters, with a libretto by Michael Davis, head of the English department, and performed entirely by a cast of boys and the school orchestra. Two of the three main roles of *Circe* were played by Richard Podger, later to become a King's College, Cambridge, choral scholar, and Nicholas Hinton. I played a minor role as a priestess. The opera received national press attention, and I still have a clipping of a photo which appeared in the *Illustrated London News*.

There were many other activities in Peter's crowded musical calendar. The school orchestra met once a week to rehearse, and performed at least once a term in the end-of-term concert, and twice in the Summer Term at the Prize Day concert. There were some good instrumentalists at that time including Charles Waterfield, oboist, who also played in the National Youth Orchestra, and Crispian Steele Perkins who remains one of the best known trumpet soloists worldwide; also David Woods, a fine violinist, who emigrated to Australia in 1958, where his father had been appointed Archbishop of Melbourne at the same time as Peter left for New Zealand. I started in the orchestra on the triangle and cymbals, graduating to the tympani on the departure of Tim Lowden whose finest hour had been *Finlandia*. I can't say that the quality of the orchestral playing was always good. It wasn't; and there were many hilarious moments, which only musical mishaps can produce. Other groups meeting regularly included the Madrigal Society conducted by Tony Smith Masters, and of which I was an enthusiastic member, and Brasser, a military band consisting of brass, woodwind and percussion, which had associations with the college's cadet corp run by an ex-army bandmaster. So there was always a lot going on.

A big favourite of mine was the music club that met occasionally in the housemasters' quarters of the individual houses, or at the appropriately named Hamelin, the residence of the director of music. The evenings consisted of a short concert given by both boys and staff, followed by glasses of sherry and something different to eat from the usual fare in the dining hall. Enthusiastic housemasters and their wives included Derek Seymour of B2 House, whose wife Betty was a good soprano and of whom I was very fond, the Kembers of Cotton House and Arnold Wright of Littlefield. As a traditional boys school, we were somewhat short of feminine company and these evenings, enlivened by the ladies and no doubt by the sherry, were enjoyable occasions. Particularly memorable were those hosted by Sheila Godfrey, Peter's lovely wife. Before Peter left, he appointed me secretary of the music club, and I organised their meetings for my final two years at the college.

This habit of making music informally became part of our lives. Later on, whilst still at Marlborough and then at university, a group of us gathered in the Christmas or spring holidays to give a short series of concerts in aid of charity. Nicholas Hinton was the prime mover and conductor and I think most of the concerts benefited a school run by Franciscan Friars in Hook, Dorset. In addition to us boys, we co-opted Caroline Maurice, daughter of Dr Tim Maurice, Marlborough town's GP, and Nicola Ferry, the daughter of Peter's successor as director of music, Robert Ferry. Peter had prepared Caroline for entrance to the Royal College of Music and she became a fine organist. She later married the distinguished composer Patrick Gowers, and continues her music as a leading exponent of piano teaching using the Suzuki method. Nicola studied the violin at Guildhall with Yfrah Neaman and still teaches at Bryanston School. Other members of our group included Nicholas Maurice, Caroline's brother, and George Howarth, formerly chorister at St George's, Windsor, who became director of music at Malvern College.

What was so special about Peter that he was able to instill such a love of music that it has continued to enrich the lives of all of us, whether we became professional musicians or simply enthusiastic amateurs? Although I had no experience of King's College, Cambridge, at the time, I later came to think that the way Peter approaches music – the way he sings and conducts, the way he phrases psalms and responses – owes much to his training as a choral scholar there. I subsequently went up to Trinity Cambridge where I sang in the Cambridge University Musical Society Choir under David Willcocks. There is a remarkable similarity of style, approach and conducting technique. David is a better organist than Peter, but then Peter is a much better singer. (One of my favourite recordings is of Peter singing the Vaughan Williams *Five Mystical Songs* in Chapel, during his last term at Marlborough.) And of course, one of the highlights of Peter's subsequent career has been the year he exchanged with Philip Ledger, bringing him back to King's College, Cambridge.

If Peter is a wonderful singer and musician, I can't say that he was the best piano teacher I've ever had. Yet I felt his piano lessons at the time were the best thing that had happened to me. When he announced he was moving to New Zealand in 1958, I felt the end of the world had come. Why?

I was once asked to say what single event or saying had had the most impact on my life. After much thought, I decided that it was something Peter had said to me during my first year at Marlborough: 'One day you'll be a prefect.' Not very deep, perhaps, but at the time I was feeling insecure as a very junior SOB (small out-boarder). Peter seemed to be able to give me the confidence to tackle any task however difficult, however remote. I did indeed become a prefect and head of C1 House during my last year. So Peter's greatest power is the power to inspire. I know that there are many who remember his inspiration over fifty years ago here in England, and who are still grateful for his influence. I am sure that we have been joined by many others in New Zealand and Australia since.

I last saw Peter during his trip to the UK three years ago (2006). I was delighted to be able to play to him a piece that I was shortly to perform with London's Orchestra of St John's in Chichester Cathedral in Sussex. It was a piece that I had loved all my life, even before meeting Peter, and I certainly never dreamed that I would ever get to the point of being able to play it, let alone in public. It was Rachmaninoff's Second Piano Concerto. I was so pleased to be able to thank him for what he had done for me all those years before.

Rev John Goodman, chorister and friend at King's College.
Letter, 8 December 2008.

Peter and I were in Cambridge together from 1940 to 1942, I in Selwyn and Peter in King's, so we met from time to time. Several such occasions were at Evensong in King's College Chapel followed by tea in his rooms. But, inevitably, the war separated us. It was not until 1953 that I learned of Peter's teaching positions as assistant director of music, first at Uppingham and then Marlborough. So when we met again it was a complete surprise to us both.

After the war I resumed my long-intended preparation for ordination and was ordained priest in 1950. In 1953 I applied for the position of curate at St Mary's, Marlborough, and went down to Marlborough for an interview with the rector. In order to find my way to the rectory I stopped my car, wound down the window to ask someone the way only to hear a very familiar voice – Peter's – say, 'John! Whatever are you doing here? Did you know that there's a job going?' What a wonderful surprise that was. We had met again.

I got the job, met Sheila and the girls for the first time, and our families became great friends. What's more, Peter became the organist at St Mary's, so we worshipped together. When it was my lot to sing the Versicles he would hum the note and off I would go, just like the old times at school. I listened to his organ voluntaries and he (maybe) listened to my sermons. They were exceedingly happy days and, to our delight, Peter accepted my invitation to be godfather to my daughter, Philippa. They have always enjoyed a very close relationship.

Maurice Faulknor, St Michael's Church Choir.
Letter, 14 November 2008.

New Zealand, until recent times, has historically been populated by people arriving by sea. Peter Godfrey with his wife and three daughters were no exception. Their 'waka' was the Shaw Savill and Albion liner *Southern Cross*, which departed from Southampton and arrived in Wellington in October 1958, just before Labour weekend and on a perfect day. My wife Lucy and I happened to arrive home on the same ship, having toured England and Scotland with the City of Wellington Pipe Band.

I became acquainted with Peter in three ways during the journey.

One afternoon three of us listened to Sibelius's *Finlandia* with him in the lounge during siesta time. I learned then the reason for Peter's move to New Zealand, and I remember telling him that Christchurch Cathedral had the best choir in New Zealand. What he thought of that I do not know, but it was true at that time!

We played deck tennis in the shipboard competition, Peter cutting a fine athletic figure, resplendent in his 'Bombay Bloomers'. I was not pleased when he beat me.

Someone was quoted once as saying, 'Peter cannot bear being without a choir to conduct.' Five weeks was a long time without involvement in music for Peter and the long sea voyage bored him. One day a notice appeared on the noticeboard which told of a meeting for anyone interested in singing in a choir to be formed. When the ship arrived in Cape Town, Peter visited a music shop to purchase choral music for the choir to sing in the ship's concert. To my dying day I regret that I did not join the choir, but it was not my scene at that time. However the choir's performance in the concert made a great impression on me.

The programme opened with a Peter Godfrey composition based on the chimes played every night over the loudspeaker system to announce the first sitting for dinner. Other pieces included 'An Eriskay Love Lilt', a negro spiritual 'De Gospel Train', a setting of a John Masefield poem 'Cargoes', 'I Got a Robe', 'Old Mother Hubbard', 'What is Life to Me', and 'Little Polly Flinders'. Copies of these pieces cost a singer the princely sum of 5/10 (five shillings and ten pence).

Many years later, I had the tremendous joy of singing in several massed choirs conducted by Peter in Wellington. That huge pleasure was heightened when I shifted to the Kāpiti Coast and started to sing in the Kapiti Chorale and later in the church choir of St Michael's, Waikanae. Peter was amazed when I told him we had met before, and that Lucy had sung in his shipboard choir. Little did I envisage that, fifty years after first meeting him, I would be privileged to be singing choral masterpieces under his direction. Someone once said that the best thing that ever happened to the Kāpiti Coast was Peter Godfrey settling here.

6

New Zealand and
St Mary's Cathedral, 1958–61

E   *Peter, New Zealand was a rather raw and young country in 1958 when you arrived. Did you, as English people, still consider it as one of the colonies?*

P   I suppose so. Yes, I do think that was so. But it was all such an exciting challenge, and I don't think any of us was against the idea of coming out at all. We were excited by the prospect of somewhere new.

E   *What were your first impressions of New Zealand?*

P   Our immediate reaction was that we had come to a lovely country. We were welcomed with a card from Margery Charlton and her husband. She was secretary to the dean of Auckland Cathedral and Albert was on the vestry. Margery was to become a most important person in my life. And we were met at the ship by Stanley and Ruth Jackson and another couple. Stanley was the director of music at Wellington Cathedral. We spent our first day with them before we travelled overnight to Auckland by train. We had wonderful views of the country before it grew too dark to see. And then in Auckland, we were met by, dare I say it, two quite short men.

E   *They could only be …*

Peter and Sheila's house
at 448 Parnell Road.

P   Yes! One of them was Dean Monteith, and the other, Professor Nalden from the university. They were so kind and welcoming. The dean took us up to Parnell where we saw first the magnificent old wooden building of St Mary's Cathedral, and then our house, which was down a long drive just opposite the cathedral.

E   *Wasn't the house a shock to you both? It was an old house and not at all what you would have been used to.*

P   The house was done up pretty well – I didn't mind it, but I think Sheila was rather disconcerted. The ladies of the parish had stocked the cupboards with every kind of food you could imagine, though, and Sheila was very moved by their great thoughtfulness and kindness. It wasn't an easy house for her to care for, but it had character. It was quite large with plenty of bedrooms for us all, a good-sized room for my study, and a nice drawing room. It was well-positioned for my work, being opposite the cathedral and close enough to the university for me to walk there. There was a garden of sorts around the house and spare land adjacent to the house, which I soon dug up and made into a vegetable garden. It, too, had once been a tennis court! Soon after our arrival I found myself busy making beds and bedroom furniture for the children who were sleeping on camp beds. And I had to make several bookshelves for the study.

E   *What was your first impression of St Mary's Cathedral?*

P   It was a beautiful wooden building, but completely different, of course, from the stone churches of England. It had a very dry and difficult acoustic. It certainly wasn't easy for singers. They couldn't get away with any imperfection as anything less than perfect was so obvious.

E   *The music department building at the university must have been even more of a shock.*

P   Well – yes. It was quite dreadful! It was an old tin shed that had been sentenced to demolition in the 1930s, but which somehow had survived. It wasn't until the 1970s that the music department moved into decent accommodation. Strangely, none of these things upset me at the time. I just got on with the job.

St Mary's Cathedral, Auckland.

E   *Your previous teaching had been more practical – piano, organ and conducting. Was it a big change to become a lecturer and work in the purely academic area?*

P   I had taught individuals harmony and counterpoint so I did have a certain amount of experience. My lecturing duties were quite light at first – history and harmony for first-year students, keyboard (score reading and reading from a figured bass) and aural training. I continued as a lecturer for the next ten years and as I wasn't really stretched by this, I was able to take up the various conducting opportunities which presented themselves over the next few years.

My work at the university had an additional benefit: there was a succession of very good students, and I was able to invite them to sing in the Cathedral Choir. The younger voices were able to give me the pure, straight sound I was looking for. And they were musically literate as well, which was so important for us to cope with the large amount of music for the two services we sang each week. The sound that the Cathedral Choir achieved was quite amazing. I suppose I was trying to establish a choir like King's. I must say that the sopranos did sound very much like boys in those days. It was only three years after I took it over that a recording we made was received in England as being 'better than many English cathedral choirs'. Quite honestly, my work in the church was more important to me than that at the university.

There were two difficult things that I had to do when I took over the Cathedral Choir: one was to hold auditions – I'm afraid there were quite a few older people who weren't accepted – and the other was to ask the headmistress of a nearby school for Māori girls, Queen Victoria School, that her girls not sing in the choir in the future. I hated doing this as they were lovely girls, but their voices were very strong and they didn't blend. As well, I imposed an age limit of thirty-five for the women and forty for the men. I know the singers found it very hard to accept retirement from the choir when their time came but it did allow for consistency of tone.

The choir very quickly established a great reputation for fine singing, and gave me such joy over the years I was with them. We sang not only weekly services, but also gave recitals, and made a number of LP records. The choir became a very valuable musical asset in the city and we developed a strong bond as a group.

E   *What were your most memorable services?*

P   It's difficult to remember now, but the ordination of Bishop Gowing was one – we first sang that difficult anthem *Faire is the Heaven* by William Harris. Choirs sail through it these days, but for the choir then it was a real challenge. And the Advent carol services were great occasions. Quite early on we gave broadcast services from time to time, and there were one or two televised services as well. But all services were equally as important to me.

E   *What assistance did you have with the choir?*

P   I was very fortunate in having a most able and lovable person as my assistant, and that was Bill Power, a dentist. He was always full of enthusiasm for whatever I asked him to do. I did most of the conducting while he played, so he had a lot of new accompaniments to learn. But he always had them ready. He was also keen on recording music and built up an enormous collection of recordings of the choir. After Bill died in December 2007, a memorial service was held in Auckland and the Nostalgia Choir sang. This was a combination of singers from both the Cathedral Choir and the Dorians. I must tell you of a very amusing thing. I don't think it could have been on purpose, but the psalm chosen for the occasion couldn't have been more relevant. One verse was: 'Open thy mouth wide and I shall fill it.' We needed huge self-control to sing that verse with a straight face! I'm sure Bill would have been chuckling as well.

Speaking of psalms, I think they were the things I loved to work with most. Getting the speech rhythms right, changing the pointing so that the stress of the words made clearest sense, singing in tune, clarity of words. And I think they provided a basis for the choir's good singing in other areas.

E *You built up a considerable library of sacred choral music at the cathedral.*

P There was hardly any music for the choir to draw on, so I began the task of ordering music from overseas. I was very fortunate to have the support of the dean who gave me carte blanche to order what I needed. That music is still being used today because we organised each piece to be covered in coloured card and housed in strong cardboard boxes. The librarians did a great job. Incidentally, the dean and I would meet once a week to discuss services for the week and to choose appropriate hymns.

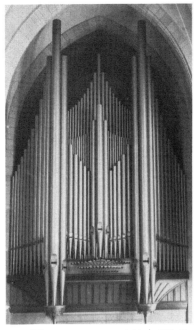

The new organ at Holy Trinity Cathedral, designed by Peter.

Later on we were very fortunate to have a new building to sing in, although it was only a chancel with no nave – Holy Trinity Cathedral – where the acoustics were far more sympathetic and the choir enjoyed singing there.

I had the challenge of designing a pipe organ for the new cathedral which was built by Harrison & Harrison of England. It was installed while I was in England on a sabbatical. Incidentally, while I was away I was invited to become director of music at Gloucester Cathedral. That was a difficult decision to make, but in the end I was enjoying the enthusiasm and excellent work in Auckland so much that I really couldn't walk away from that. And the family was enjoying Auckland. Getting back to the organ, it did receive some criticism at the time as yet another romantic organ in Auckland! That was at the time when Baroque style was becoming fashionable. Since that organ was installed, a large nave has been added to the building, which meant that the existing organ was inadequate, so a new organ is being planned. The position of the console was always a problem – it was shifted several times, but it was never very satisfactory.

Of course, the other thing that shifted was lovely old St Mary's Cathedral itself. It was moved on railway lines over the road to become attached to Holy Trinity Cathedral as the Lady Chapel. Sheila was severely critical about the move.

E   *Before we leave your cathedral days, we shouldn't forget your work for the Royal School of Church Music.*

P   Yes, of course. I hadn't had much to do with the RSCM either in England or in my early days in New Zealand. But in the early sixties I was invited to act as assistant to Roy Massey, organist of Hereford Cathedral who came out to run a summer school in New Zealand. Not long after this, Gerald Knight, the director of the RSCM, paid us a visit in 1962, and from that there came a number of invitations for me to direct summer music schools for the RSCM in Australia (Sydney and Canberra), the USA, and in England. I also directed a number of the English Summer Schools at the RSCM headquarters at Addington Palace, and in 1968 I ran the summer school in America. Once I became a professor, I gradually dropped my involvement with the RSCM, but over a period of ten years, I enjoyed these courses greatly and was awarded the Fellowship of the Royal School of Church Music in 1974.

E   *And we mustn't forget the summer school courses at St Peter's, Cambridge. How did that come about?*

P   They were very enjoyable times. These had been held for a number of years before I became involved, and were financed by the university. The main organiser was Ronald Dellow, musician, and on the staff of the Department for Adult Education. The venue was a boys prep school in Cambridge – New Zealand! – called St Peter's. It had excellent facilities for the various musical activities, concerts, living in and camping out in the grounds. I was invited in January 1959, shortly after my arrival, to visit this school. And the next year I was invited to be the choral director of these courses. I continued this for a good ten years. They were immensely popular courses, and the source of wonderful fun as well as good music-making – both choral and instrumental.

The time came when my workload became so great that some things had to be sacrificed. That was when I became professor of music at the university in 1974. The day that I had to announce my resignation to the Cathedral Choir was one of the saddest in my life.

RECOLLECTIONS

Mary Ann Hetherington, St Mary's Cathedral Choir.
Interviewed, 29 January 2009.

My choir mistress at Auckland Diocesan School for Girls was asked to provide some sopranos to build up numbers in the Cathedral Choir for the Queen's visit in 1953. I was head chorister at the time so I was one of the girls selected. There were a lot of old ladies and some girls from Queen Victoria School for Māori girls in the choir at that stage, and I didn't think the singing was very good. I went nursing the next year, but, as I had enjoyed singing in the choir so much, I stayed on.

Then Mr Godfrey arrived! We were told that everyone would be auditioned. There were two delightful older ladies, Mrs McMillan and Miss Waterworth. They were just horrified. They had never, ever been auditioned! I remember them saying, 'I don't know why this man is doing all this auditioning. We are perfectly happy as we are.' We had to sing something – scales, I think; do some ear tests and sing something at sight. As a result there was quite a clean-out of members of the choir. And Mrs McMillan and Miss Waterworth didn't get back in. They were the kingpins of the cathedral and were devastated by it. There was a great anti-feeling about Mr Godfrey for a while. But a lot of new singers came, I got in, and it was all just marvellous.

Rehearsals were totally different from anything we had ever encountered before. Peter was very strict: we had to sing in tune; we had to raise our hands if we made a mistake; we had to have a 2B pencil at all rehearsals; and we weren't allowed to sit down. But the more we became used to Peter, the more we realised the worth of it all, and those auditions were more than justified. I think that even dear Miss Waterworth, who really had sounded like a fog horn, and Mrs McMillan, who was far too nice to hold a grudge, settled down eventually. A major issue Peter had with us was our speech – our vowels. The New Zealand habit of saying 'uh' instead of 'i' was particular anathema to this very English-sounding gentleman, who complained constantly about our agricultural vowels. I was rather

St Mary's Cathedral Choir, 1963.

naughty and teased him by saying words from hymns in the best New Zealand accent: 'Ut uz a pulgrum', and more daringly, 'Ut uz an unvuzuble pulgrum'. And even, 'Ut uz an ummortal, unvuzuble pulgrum'. But that was pushing things a bit!

We would listen to Peter's recordings of King's after rehearsals quite often, over at 448 Parnell Road, where Sheila would provide us with generous suppers of tea and flapjack. And that sound became a model for us, a sound to emulate. It seemed to work as it was only three years later that our recording of psalms and hymns was described as better than most English cathedral choirs!

Our choir parties were great fun. We played various games based on the psalms, one where a team would be given a verse which had to be acted out for the other teams to identify – like 'Neither delighteth he in any man's legs'. And we had wonderful picnics at the various Auckland beaches. Peter had the ability to bind us into a choir family.

I also went to the summer school at St Peter's in Cambridge (New Zealand), which was wonderfully stimulating but absolutely exhausting.

We didn't sleep much as it was all such fun. There was a large communal, tiled bathroom where Cathedral Choir women would arrange to bathe at the same time so that we could sing in parts in this wonderful echoing acoustic – we thought we sounded rather like King's choristers! What we didn't realise was that Peter's bedroom was immediately below. On one occasion, when Peter was trying to have a nap, there came a loud repeated noise from below – Peter banging on the ceiling to let us know that our singing was not appreciated!

They were such happy days.

Allan Thomas, St Mary's Cathedral Choir; ethnomusicologist.
Interviewed, 2010.

A   Peter came to New Zealand at a most fortuitous time for us. New Zealand was still regarded as a colony by many English people, and we accepted that attitude – many New Zealanders still referring to England as 'home'. And so we absorbed Peter's insistence on English vowels and inflexion of speech without any bother. I think that if Peter had come, say, twenty years later, he may have had considerable difficulty with this Englishness.

For me, his style of psalm singing was very important. One of the great European composers once described psalm chanting as 'monotonous repetition of a bad melody'. And certainly, before Peter's arrival, congregations would sing the psalms to chants in a most unmusical kind of metrical form. With Peter, however, psalm chanting took wings. The short psalm chants were the perfect vehicle for Peter to develop the intonation that was his passion. Also, we learned to listen to each voice part so that we were unanimous in our singing – absolutely together.

Peter liberated the psalms with his insistence on speech rhythm, and with his sensitive pointing of the words. Before we rehearsed a psalm there would be a pencil session where he would give us any revised pointing, where dynamics were determined and where words of special emphasis were marked. We had to concentrate as he would say it only once. Then the chant would be learned, which had to be sung perfectly in tune. He demanded sharpened leading notes and major thirds and would hold on to a chord until the errant part was in tune.

We sang the psalms unaccompanied for many years. I think Peter's reason for this was to make it easier for the congregation to hear the words. But later, he added the colour and heightened expression that a

St Mary's choir singing in the unfinished
Holy Trinity Cathedral.

good organ accompaniment was able to give. I can't help but wonder
if his choice of unaccompanied psalm singing was a deliberate ploy
to train the congregation to listen to the choir instead of joining in.
Anglican chanting really is too difficult for congregations, even if they
do want to sing it. But at that time there was tremendous resistance to
choirs 'taking over' what the congregation considered was theirs by right.

E   *I asked Peter about this. His response was that the choir was a cathedral
choir and that, apart from the hymns, everything would be sung only by the
choir – psalm, responses, and settings of the canticles and the Communion
service. And that is how it was, right from the beginning of his time at the
cathedral.*

A   Peter's training in psalm singing was the kernel of what we were doing
then, and its influence flowed on into our polyphonic singing. You
can hear choirs today that, because they are based so much on hymn
singing and metrical music, do not sing polyphony as well. They
don't know how to let the music flow through the bar lines. Peter's
intuitive musicianship allowed the words to be liberated from metrical
boundaries.

Peter enjoyed psalms so much that he wrote an amusing one of his own to farewell the assistant curate, Richard Buttle. Over the years, others wrote 'psalms' also, and this became a tradition for special occasions – parties, anniversaries, people leaving the choir, and so on. They were very funny!

As our repertoire expanded, so did the degree of difficulty. We were given such things as Harris's utterly beautiful *Faire is the Heaven* for example, and Parry's *I was Glad* which seemed almost beyond our reach when we rehearsed them for the first time. And then there were those big 16th century anthems, such as Gibbons' *O Clap Your Hands Together* and Byrd's *Haec Dies*. Wonderful music and so new to us. As a result of all this, the ability of the choir improved with amazing rapidity! I didn't ever hear Peter admonish the choir. He simply showed them how something must be sung and then underpinned it with thorough practise.

E   *Peter had a very simple technique: if we hadn't learned the set anthem well enough, we would have to sing the hymn, 'There is a Green Hill Far Away'. How ignominious!*

A   Did that ever happen?

E   *Only once, as I remember. It was mortifying.*

A   I must comment on the enormous library of music that quickly came into being at the cathedral. When I joined the Cathedral Choir there were three or four new choral items quite regularly – anthems, services, responses – and these were separate pieces of sheet music, not from collections such as the *Red Anthem* book, which I think was scarcely ever used.

I remember Herbert Howells's settings of the canticles, Ireland, the Stanford services, through to the verse anthems and the great Byrd, Gibbons and Tallis motets. He must have spent a fortune, and planning must have been so difficult because everything took about two months to come by sea from England in those days before airmail.

Over the years quite a few choir members of the Cathedral Choir have gone on to take church or school choirs, and to play the organ. Through them Peter's influence has spread far and wide throughout the country – from the thorough grounding in 'Godfrey technique' that he unwittingly gave us in training and conducting a choir, choice of repertoire, conduct in services and basic disciplines like being on time. We would rather die than be late and suffer the 'sniff', the silence and those eyes following us as we went to our seat, found the music and the right place!

I found that I was constantly referring back to my experiences with Peter. They were the foundation of my many years of working with church music in parish choirs and in church schools. I have great admiration, fondness and respect for Peter Godfrey.

Gillian Lander, St Mary's Cathedral Choir; organist, church musician. *Interviewed, 26 January 2009.*

E   *Gillian, you had considerable experience with Peter as your university lecturer, and as a singer in St Mary's Cathedral Choir. What impact did that have on your life?*

G   Although he was too busy to give me lessons after my organ teacher died, Peter gave me permission to practice on the cathedral organ and eventually surprised me by asking me to play for some of the 9.30 services in the morning. This was a great thrill!

Eventually I joined the Cathedral Choir. One thing that impressed me hugely about Peter was his sense of spiritual devotion. Before each service Peter would come up to the nave after rehearsal with the choir and spend some time in private prayer at the back of the cathedral. That is something I fully understand now, because I realise that when you are involved in the creation of a service as a conductor of a choir, you cannot worship fully as well. You're really in a work space, not a worship space.

Peter didn't conduct a choir at the university until the early 1970s, when he had the University Festival Choir and an all-comers choir. Singers would come for the lunchtime practices – staff members joined, and students as well. We sang some demanding music, including Tallis's *Spem in Alium* on one occasion. As there were over 200 singers in the choir it wasn't difficult to manage the forty parts! And one year we sang some early music – Dufay, Ockeghem and others – that Peter had edited, and which was photocopied from his own immaculate manuscript.

I saw Peter in a very different light in the all-comers choir from his work with the Cathedral Choir. Here he had an easier, more tolerant manner, which demonstrated just what could be achieved with average singers. One extraordinary thing was his acceptance of a young man who stayed in the choir for two or three years, and sang on one note! I couldn't believe that Peter would allow him to stay, but his attitude was, 'He wants to sing, so sing he must.' He did, however, tell him on occasions, 'This bit's unaccompanied, so don't sing here.'

My time in the Cathedral Choir with Peter gave me a foundation of a huge amount of wonderful repertoire, and the necessary knowledge to work with my own choirs. I am deeply indebted to Peter.

Anita Banbury, St Mary's Cathedral Choir, Dorian Choir; conductor of the Orlando Singers. *Interviewed, 20 January 2009.*

E   *Anita, you have conducted the well-known Orlando Singers for many years. Have you studied choral conducting, or are you like a lot of us, just picking it up from singing with Peter?*

A   During my holidays in Auckland I asked Peter if I could observe his rehearsals with the Cathedral Choir. Instead I found myself invited to sing with them! Later, when I moved to Auckland, I joined the Dorian Choir. I have never had much choral conducting training, so I am sure I have absorbed a lot from my experiences with Peter. Choral conducting tends to be like that.

E   *What stands out in your mind from your time in his choirs?*

A   With Peter, precision and tuning always comes with equal importance to the musical considerations. I have always been impressed with Peter's acute, innate musicianship. There is an absolute affinity with a style for each piece. But typical of Peter's choral sound is his love of a pure top line. I remember asking him one day what he listened for in a choir. He hesitated, and then said, 'I suppose it would be the sopranos,' which is what I really expected him to say.

There's an example of Peter's caring nature that I must comment on. When I decided to leave teaching at St Mary's, Stratford, and move to Auckland, Peter invited me to coffee one Saturday morning and handed me an advertisement for the position of organist and choirmaster at St David's. 'I would accept that,' he said. He also introduced me to Jane Barnett (later to become his second wife) because both she and her mother were teaching piano in Auckland. And that introduction helped me to get started as a private music teacher. He also found me a relieving job at Queen Victoria School for the best part of a term as well, and told me which suburbs I should consider living in. He really got me sorted in a morning, and I simply did as I was told.

Noni Kenny and Hilary Monteith, St Mary's Cathedral Choir, Auckland Dorian Singers and Dorian Choir. *Interviewed, 21 January 2009.*

E *Hilary, how did you come to join the St Mary's Cathedral Choir?*

H I had been going to Evensong for some time before 1958, when Peter came. I soon noticed that the Cathedral Choir under Peter was going to be something very good. So early in 1959 I asked Mr Godfrey if I could join. I was told that I had to have an audition, which, for someone who had never learnt music, was very daunting! Peter, at that time, was in need of people with reasonable voices that would blend, and so my complete lack of reading skills didn't stop me from being accepted. He offered me lessons, but he was very scary and I waited for him to say something more about them – which he never did. So I just had to do my best.

I got quick at following the music from instinct. Peter insisted that we took our music home to learn it. But I had no piano at home, and couldn't play anyway. So the only way I could learn the music was at choir practice. There were one or two others in that situation. One of the tenors was also a non-reader but with a wonderful voice. He used to meet with another tenor at lunchtimes during the week who would teach him the music! And another singer worked with some unconventional method of her own, and insisted on her copy being given to her each time we sang the work because of her markings. It was amazing how we coped.

We sang a huge amount of early music. Later on with other conductors, I realised that there was a great deal of later music that we hadn't ever sung with Peter – such as Howells. When I commented on this to Peter later, he said that he thought it was too hard for us! I guess he had a point. Of course we did sing some Romantic and 20th century composers. But in the early days, a lot of this music was quite formidable for us to learn.

E *Noni, how did you come to join the Cathedral Choir?*

N I was a member of the Dorian Singers, conducted by Harry Luscombe at that time. Peter came to one of our concerts in which I had a solo to sing. After the performance he asked me if I would like to join the

Cathedral Choir, and so I did. That was in 1960. It was all marvellous. I don't think I had been inside the cathedral before and was in awe of the long aisle and the lovely red carpet, and the robes and the candles. It was so beautiful compared with the little parish church I had attended. I'll never forget the Advent carol service for Christmas – the cathedral was just packed and it was all magical. The cathedral was in darkness for most of the service, the choir being lit by candles carried by servers. We had to know the entire music very well as it was not the easiest light to read by! I'd never seen anything like it before – it was wonderful.

H We became fairly well known throughout New Zealand quite quickly because of the broadcast services we used to sing. In those days there was a broadcast church service every Sunday morning, and we would be asked to sing quite frequently during the year. And we sang at least two televised services. Of course, we had to make sure we really were perfect because we were being heard nationwide. Peter was a bit of a tyrant in those early days! But it certainly raised the standard of the choir very quickly.

I must share a story about the time I was late for the rehearsal before a service. It was well known in the choir that my car was not the most reliable of vehicles and on this occasion it let me down once again. I arrived just at the time Peter was rehearsing the psalm for the service. And what were the words of the psalm? None other than 'Some put their trust in chariots and some in horses'! Needless to say, the singing was interrupted by much mirth for a minute or two.

N The thing I found really difficult was Peter's insistence on having an age limit for his singers in the Cathedral Choir. Here I am, still singing in the Cathedral Choir and I'm in my seventies, but I had to leave the choir in Peter's time when I turned thirty-five. My birthday was in August, and I remember saying to Peter at the end of the year, 'By the way, I turned thirty-five earlier in the year.' He was quite shocked. 'You didn't!' he said. But that was it – out I went! The men could stay on until they were forty. I think he thought better about this in later years. I was fortunate in that I sang with the Dorians as well where there was no such age restriction, but it affected a few people quite badly.

E *How did Peter achieve that high standard of singing?*

H He got us to do a lot of chording and we were always working on intonation. He got us to listen. He got us to blend. Other conductors don't seem to do this. People in other choirs think that all they need to do is to sing out – and then that special blend of sound is lost. Choral conductors don't want people to sound like little boys any more, but they seem to go to the other extreme. Peter did achieve a beautiful, pure sound with his sopranos.

John Hume, St Mary's Cathedral Choir and Dorian Singers.
Note, 2009.

On occasion, during the sermon in a service at St Mary's Cathedral, the organists would disappear from the organ console for a short time. The reason was never clear to us lesser mortals in the choir. One particular Sunday, Peter disappeared, this time for much longer than usual. The first lesson that day had been about the Queen of Sheba visiting Solomon. We became worried that he wouldn't be back in time for the next hymn, but he was.

All was explained when, at the end of the service, he launched into Handel's *The Arrival of the Queen of Sheba*. It turned out that he had dashed across the road to his house, found the music and had a quick practice on the piano, to give the service an appropriate ending.

Janet Wilson and Judith Goodall, St Mary's Cathedral Choir.
Note, 2009.

After one Sunday Evensong in St Mary's Cathedral, the choir processed out to a heavily disguised version of 'Happy Birthday'. This was recognised by 'Monty', as the choir affectionately called the dean, who was keen to discover who was celebrating a birthday*.

Another improvisation on a well-known song took place after a heavy defeat of the English cricket team. 'There'll Always be an England' was detected. The choir processed out with broad smiles on their faces.

Peter made it known to the choir that a tipple of sherry prior to singing was very helpful for the vocal chords. On one occasion, when the Cathedral Choir gave a recital in the Auckland Museum, he had the bottle of sherry in his briefcase. It seemed inappropriate to swig from it in the museum corridor, so Peter and the tenors and basses repaired to the men's washroom. After their return, the sopranos and altos followed suit, much to the confusion of the solitary museum attendant! Where there's a will, there's a way …

At a Wednesday evening choir practice, two section leaders of the choir had problems with their throats. Peter recommended sherry as a panacea. The two singers heartily agreed with this and, much to Peter's astonishment, went down to the choir vestry. There, unknown even to the choir, they had a private supply of sherry!

During one of the choir's recording sessions, it had great difficulty in maintaining pitch throughout a certain hymn. After several failures, and with Peter becoming more and more stressed and upsetting the choir, he turned to the recording engineers and announced with great venom, '"When I Survey the Wondrous Cross" – for the last time, I hope.'

Following Peter's decree that there was to be a retirement age – thirty-five for the women and forty for the men – it was considered appropriate that he, too, should undergo an audition when he reached his two-score years. Three members of the choir went over to Peter's home a little before choir practice, and they tested him with stringent ear tests and some demanding pieces of sight-reading. Finally, and fortunately, Peter was deemed to have passed, thus retaining his position as organist and choirmaster.

* It was the author's birthday!

7

Auckland University Tours, 1972 & 1974

E   *Peter, you had been lecturing at Auckland University since 1959 without being involved with any choir work there, and yet you formed a university choir to tour overseas in 1972. How did that come about?*

P   Well, it was quite extraordinary. I think it is worth going into in some detail, as it was the first major tour I was involved with. At that time, Auckland University had two choirs – a large all-comers choir and a small madrigal choir that was conducted by a fourth-year student, Brian Webb.

However, in the middle of 1970 the four largest New Zealand universities were invited to send a representative choir to the Third International University Choral Festival to be held in New York, in April 1972. The director of the festival, Mr James Bjorge, was to visit New Zealand towards the end of 1970 to hear choirs, and to discuss whether or not New Zealand would be able to accept the invitation.

Auckland University felt strongly that we should accept the invitation, and so I was asked to start auditioning and interviewing prospective members in August. By September we were rehearsing! We also formed a committee of staff and choir members in order to show the festival director that we could organise finance for the journey to New York.

Mr Bjorge duly came to Auckland in November 1970, and

auditioned our two-month-old choir. We had only enough material to sing for half an hour. Afterwards he met with both university officials and the committee where he answered questions about the festival and gave us background information.

The origin of the festival was quite remarkable. A young American man, Marshall Bartholomew, was studying music in Germany – and about to sign a contract as assistant conductor to the Mannheim Opera – when the First World War broke out. He volunteered for War Prison Relief Service and was sent to serve among the 400 thousand war prisoners in Central Siberia. I'll quote him:

> Throughout that bleak, frigid winter of 1915–16 there was misery and despair which I shall not attempt to describe. I had the privilege of bringing music, particularly singing, to the prisoners of war. As soon as musical activities became well organised there appeared a noticeable improvement of morale, and it was then I witnessed the miracle of the power of music to reawaken the wish to live and the courage to carry on in spite of homesickness, enforced idleness, and the deep despair which made suicide a frequent occurrence in the Siberian prison camps.

This wonderful man decided to use music as a means of bringing together the peoples of the world. He became involved with university music after the war, making two attempts at creating an international festival; but these were prevented first by the Depression, and secondly the Second World War.

When Mr Bartholomew retired from choral conducting in the 1950s, he passed on his idea of an international festival to one of his enthusiastic singers – James Bjorge. James shared the potential of the idea with William Schumann, composer and president of the Lincoln Centre, and suddenly the festival had a base. The first international universities choral festival took place in 1965, a second festival in 1969, with a third planned for April 1972. As well as choirs from sixteen different countries singing together, each choir was to undertake a ten-day recital tour before the festival, all organised for them, and all expenses paid for by America, apart from travel to and from their own country.

Mr Bjorge then went on to visit Wellington and Dunedin. However, it was our Auckland choir that was selected, his only comment being that we should look as though we were enjoying ourselves more! The official invitation came early in 1971, which left us with just fourteen months to prepare ourselves musically, and to organise and finance the tour.

We discovered that it would cost us only an additional thirty-five dollars per head to travel right round the world. So it seemed sensible to include England and Europe in the tour, especially as it would happen in the university vacation. Very soon we received invitations from King's College, Cambridge, and Westminster Abbey, which were a great help in arousing public interest in the tour and the fundraising. The Ministry of Foreign Affairs showed considerable interest in our plans, and eventually the New Zealand ambassadors to the Hague and Bonn made arrangements for the choir to sing in Maastricht in the Netherlands, and in Düsseldorf in West Germany. In Maastricht we were offered free accommodation in return for our concert presentation, and in Düsseldorf the embassy arranged for very inexpensive accommodation at a youth guest house.

E   *With no previous experience in fundraising and organisation of this stature, it must have been an enormous task to undertake.*

P   Yes, it really was. I don't think we realised just what we were taking on at the beginning. However, we had excellent people to help us. I don't want to single out anyone, but Margery Charlton was a first-class executive officer with a great deal of experience, and Carolyn Jackson was a most efficient secretary. The committee of sixteen people held regular meetings, usually once a week. Nineteen subcommittees were formed to deal with all aspects of organisation: travel, fundraising, uniform, brochures, publicity, concerts in New Zealand, acknowledgement of donations and so on. We worked out that the total time spent in meetings equalled about 600 man-hours of work in committee time alone!

Sir Arthur Porritt, the governor general, was invited to be our patron, and we were very pleased when he accepted. The chancellors of other New Zealand universities agreed to be vice patrons, which gave us their blessing as representing all universities. And a number of prominent Auckland people agreed to be trustees.

We needed expert advice about fundraising, and were most fortunate to have the services of a chartered accountant and experienced fundraiser, Mr Rolf Porter. Our first telephone conversation was most amusing as he mistook me for a namesake who had once sold him dogs! He became very enthusiastic about the choir's venture, especially when he heard that members were prepared to help themselves to the extent of paying half their airfares, as well as providing their spending money. The university had no funds for such a project, so we found the remaining funds by appealing to official bodies, trusts and private individuals.

Rolf met with considerable resistance amongst business associates, however. They were quite strongly prejudiced against university students because of the time they wasted on protests and marches, together with a perceived lack of cleanliness! But the Auckland businessmen did actually contribute about $11,000 of the total of $40,000 needed. The singers' share was $16,000. We hoped that the government would be able to make a sizeable contribution, but they could give us only a few thousand dollars. However, by various means we did achieve the total amount by the time we left, with a farewell benefit concert raising $2,700 at the last minute. It was a wonderful feeling to know that we wouldn't return in debt, and we were very grateful to all organisations, choirs and individuals who helped us.

E   *Uniforms are a tricky business. It's almost impossible to please everyone. Was this difficult for the committee?*

P   It was no easy task! We chose to promote New Zealand wool, and were very grateful when we were told that the materials would be donated by the Wool Board and three other firms. This left us to pay for the manufacture of the garments. Colin Cole, a fashion designer, produced designs which co-ordinated the fabrics into the garments that we needed. There was a last minute panic when one firm pulled out from making the evening blouses and shirts only three weeks before we left! Fortunately Colin was able to get the material, and made them for us in that short remaining time. I must say that the uniform was particularly striking and received many compliments while we were overseas.

We took small souvenir gifts with us to promote New Zealand. Our choir members showed their sense of 'public relations' and friendliness by approaching all kinds of people – bus and lorry drivers as well as other travellers – with kiwi lapel pins and brochures. This made many unexpected friends for our country. One of the singers even pinned a kiwi pin on to the lapel of Mr Kurt Waldheim, the secretary general of the United Nations. Jim Bjorge was the first to receive the kiwi

lapel pin, and he was never seen without it for the rest of the festival –
although he did not always wear the pins of the other participating
choirs. When asked later why we were accorded this honour, he replied
that of all the countries he visited in preparation for this festival, he had
found New Zealand to be the most hospitable and friendly.

E *How did you prepare a new choir for such a large and prestigious tour in
   such a short time?*

P It was very intensive work. We rehearsed twice a week, with additional
   rehearsals where necessary. Our first concert was in May 1971, and
   we undertook an extensive concert tour of the North Island in August
   1971, to develop concert experience and polish repertoire. We also had
   an intensive training weekend six weeks before we left. So by the time
   of the farewell benefit concert, the choir was singing very well.

E *A newspaper review of that first concert gave the choir considerable praise.
   'It is a measure of Peter Godfrey's skill and authority as a choral conductor
   that within a few weeks of the formation of this choir that it was possible
   to include a recital in the Auckland festival. Already the choir bears Mr
   Godfrey's fingerprint: clarity of diction, refinement of tone, and rhythmic
   certainty – to a marked degree.' How did you go about selecting repertoire
   for the choir's various engagements?*

P We needed more secular music than sacred for the American university
   campuses. But for places in England and Europe – such as King's
   College, Cambridge, and Westminster Abbey – we needed quite a large
   amount of sacred music. I felt that it was most important to promote
   New Zealand music, but this posed considerable difficulties. Practically
   every country taking part in the festival had a considerable heritage of
   great choral music of their own culture. But we had practically none.
       We had some excellent contemporary composers but nothing of
   Māori music. Māori chant used micro-tonal intervals – extremely
   difficult to learn – and was in unison, monotonous to Western ears,
   and not appropriate for us to perform. The festival director requested
   some Māori music, but I was reluctant to include any 'typically Māori
   music' as it was quite recent and strongly influenced by the melody and
   harmony of missionary hymns.
       However, it was obvious that something of the kind had to be
   included, so eventually I asked Dr Douglas Mews to find three 'typical

Māori songs' and to harmonise them for the choir. Actually, they gave me the opportunity to talk about Māori music to audiences and to spread awareness in that way.

Douglas Mews also wrote a piece for us that was enormously effective and popular – *Ghosts, Fire, Water.* This was a setting of a poem by the English poet James Kirkup based on *The Hiroshima Panels,* a series of paintings by the Japanese painters Iri and Toshi Maruki. These depicted the horrors of the atomic bomb dropped on Hiroshima. It dealt with the psychological and philosophical implications of the bombing, ending with the words, 'Forgive us that we had to see your Passion to remember what we must never again deny: Love One Another.'

At the end of the setting, Dr Mews introduced the Latin plainsong hymn 'Ubi Caritas et Amor Deus ibi est'. While this is sung, the words 'love one another' were spoken in each of the languages of the choirs participating in the festival (the Māori language representing New Zealand). We sang this work in our main thirty-minute programme in the Philharmonic Hall at Lincoln Centre, as well as on every campus, and in Europe. It always produced a profound reaction from the audience. Its most startling effect was in the southern Dutch city of Maastricht, in a recital in the ancient Church of St Servaas. The audience, which was predominantly non-English speaking, had sat quietly up to this point in the recital, but after *Ghosts, Fire, Water* they started clapping spontaneously, culminating in a standing ovation. It was incredibly moving.

There were other excellent pieces from our contemporary New Zealand composers, and eventually I selected sixteen fine pieces for our repertoire. Three of these composers have become internationally successful – Gillian Whitehead, Jack Body and David Griffiths. I had to select the rest of our repertoire rather haphazardly from what was available in other choir libraries in Auckland.

And then it was time to go. *April?*

We were given a very moving farewell at Auckland International Airport, and arrived in New York on 8 August where freezing temperatures and snow awaited us. Jim Bjorge was a very welcome sight, and the only person to meet us. We started our campus tour immediately, travelling many miles down the Eastern seaboard and back again. We couldn't believe our ears when our bus driver told us that his surname was Van Winkle and he was known as Rip!

Festival Choir at Auckland airport, 1972.

Our first performance was at Suffolk Community College, Selden, Long Island. Considering the obvious fatigue after twenty-five hours of travel prior to this, the first concert went off amazingly well and we were very well received. Before we set off the next morning, we were given the opportunity to attend choral classes in the college. I still do some of their choral warm-up exercises of slapping and pummelling the back of the person standing in front. Then followed seven more campuses, both secondary and tertiary where we saw a good cross-section of American education. Our tour took us from Long Island to New Jersey, Pennsylvania, Philadelphia, Maryland, Virginia and North

Carolina – where the temperature was up to 29 degrees and spring was well advanced, with the lovely dogwood trees in flower.

I must say that the numbers attending our concerts were very disappointing. We discovered later that the English and West German choirs had enjoyed large audiences wherever they went, so it was obvious the name of New Zealand carried no cultural weight in America, in spite of the extremely complimentary reviews that were written about us and the standing ovations we received after almost all our concerts – not a common occurrence, we were told. Regardless of this, our young people carried off all the concerts in a thoroughly professional manner. I was very proud of them.

There were two rather frightening moments during this tour. Some of our group were woken one night by a bomb scare that kept them up for two hours. It turned out to be a hoax but was not at all a pleasant experience for them. And during one concert a fire started in the library. We were halfway through the first half of the programme when the stage lights began to flicker, and then went out. There was just enough light reflected from the 'Exit' lights in the hall for us to continue the programme by singing three madrigals which we knew from memory – including *Fire, Fire*.

I was just about to walk on to announce a further bracket of songs, when the school's choral director walked on to the stage from the opposite side and asked us all to leave at once as the library was on fire! Considerable damage was done, but the fire was soon under control. It was thought to have been arson. We gave an impromptu performance outside, which, of course, had to include *Fire, Fire* again, much to the amusement of the fire fighters! (Once back in New Zealand, the choir decided to send a number of books on New Zealand to the school library.)

And so we returned to Washington for the festival.

E *How had the choir stood up to this intensive tour with all its travelling?*

P Towards the end of the tour about a third of the choir had succumbed to throat infections and colds, and we were all very tired. But they still managed to carry off the concerts very professionally. It was rather worrying, but by the time we got to Washington they were on the mend.

We had been told by the festival organisation that all sixteen choirs were to arrive at the Kennedy Centre's Hall of Nations on 20 April, arriving at ten-minute intervals with ten minutes on stage to rehearse their individual four-minute items. After this all choirs were to join in the first massed rehearsal. This was daunting organisation to say the least, and we were quite apprehensive about arriving precisely at the time given us! However, there had been some delay by the time we got there, and we were able to hear some of the other choirs rehearsing. This turned out to be very useful, as it was the only time we were able to compare other choirs and ourselves (we had to remain backstage during the Washington and New York gala concerts). It was interesting to observe our singers – it didn't take them long to start making friends amongst the other choirs, and I found myself soon chatting in Swahili to the Ugandans.

The conductor of the massed choirs was Robert Shaw, although we didn't see him for the first three days as he was ill. Dr Willi Gohl was associate musical director of the festival who had come from Switzerland. He conducted the first massed rehearsal and quickly won the hearts of all the singers – a most precise, musical and stylistically sensitive musician. And so began a period of intense rehearsing and education with many workshops to attend.

One of the highlights of this time was a visit to the White House to meet the first lady, Mrs Nixon. The following day, again at pre-arranged times, all sixteen choirs in their buses converged on the White House. It was a most moving occasion. Of course there was much spontaneous singing as we lined up to shake hands with Mrs Nixon – who was given a kiwi pin by one of our singers. And, as well, Willi Gohl conducted them in some of their massed items in front of the White House. I've never seen anyone move so fast as the plain-clothes security men did when the German choir, who were to sing an echo part, were gestured by the conductor to sing on the steps leading up to the first floor of the White House. Even when it was obvious that there was no danger, they still hid behind the large white columns, watching carefully. After the singing was over, we were invited to walk through the various state-rooms. What a privilege it was for us to experience all this.

Saturday was the day of the first concert in the Kennedy Centre. Each choir appeared in alphabetical order to sing two works in the first half, and then the massed items in the second half. Our madrigal and Jack Body's carol 'People Look East' received reassuring compliments. And then we were off to New York, a long, five-hour drive without consideration for comfort stops by our driver, following which we

Festival Choir performing at the Kennedy Centre, 1972.

gave our first concert in the evening. A highlight was to receive an invitation from the organist, Dr Alec Wyton, to sing some motets at the Cathedral of St John the Divine.

The daily rehearsal routine was two hours on our own and three and a half hours under Robert Shaw – exhausting! And as well there were seminars for conductors, which I attended. In the evening there was always a concert at which four of the choirs provided thirty minutes of music. We had to sing in the final concert, so the problem was to maintain fitness during the week. We reminded the singers constantly of Friday night. That evening was the final gala performance of the festival. Each choir sang one piece, no longer than three minutes. Again, the second half consisted of the massed items. But the concert concluded with a most emotional performance of 'Gaudeamus igitur' conducted by Mr Marshall Bartholomew himself, now ninety years old. A perfect way to end this momentous time in America.

E   *What was the overall impression of the New Zealand choir?*

P   I think it can be summed up by this quotation from a letter written to me by the festival director:

At last I have an opportunity to thank you, and the University of Auckland Choir, for the extraordinary contribution which you made to our festival. I really can think of no way in which you could have been better. You and your choir won the hearts of everyone during the festival. You sang absolutely magnificently and, on top of that, were the most splendid representatives of New Zealand. If a vote had been taken among the choruses, I'm sure that you Kiwis would have been selected the most friendly and popular group. And, in saying that, I do not mean to detract in any way from your stunning concert performances.

E *How would you sum up the overall benefit of this experience?*

P Without a doubt it was the enthusiastic willingness to exchange ideas and music that was one of the festival's greatest assets. I was often asked by New Zealanders, 'Who won the competition?' It wasn't a competition. If that had been the case, there would have been no such exchange of ideas and music because everything would have been too closely guarded.

And so it was on to the next stage of the tour – England, Europe and Singapore. The first highlight was our visit to Peter Pears and Benjamin Britten at The Maltings, Snape, on our way to Cambridge. We didn't give a concert there but we received an invitation to meet them as one of our singers, Christopher Lackner, was the first holder of the Pears/Britten Scholarship that they had set up when in Auckland. The singer and the composer had given an unscheduled recital during an informal visit to New Zealand, and had donated the proceeds to set up this scholarship. They gave us a sumptuous lunch in the concert hall restaurant. It was a moving experience and so kind of them – typical of these good people.

On our way to Cambridge we passed within a couple of miles of Hengrave Hall just outside Bury St Edmonds, where John Wilbye, one of the great 16th century madrigalists, had worked as a musician in residence. The hall was now a Roman Catholic girls convent school, but, according to the guidebook, could be visited by appointment. Although we didn't have an appointment, we just had to visit. It took several minutes to manoeuvre the bus through the very narrow gateway, from a narrow English lane – hair raising! We were welcomed by the reverend mother and the school was hastily assembled to meet us. Incidentally, I remember the choir being highly amused when I

Peter (seated) with composer Benjamin Britten (left)
and tenor Peter Pears, at rehearsal in Auckland.

returned from asking if we could visit and said that I had 'tackled the reverend mother'. I was invited to address the students and the choir was invited to sing. It was a very moving half hour, especially when we sang Wilbye's madrigal *Sweet Honey Sucking Bees* in the very room where it had probably received its first performance nearly 400 years before.

On our arrival in Cambridge we rehearsed for our recital in the chapel the next evening. For some this was the climax of our tour, and the choir sang their very best there. Obviously it was quite momentous for me to take my own choir back to the place that had been the beginnings of it all for me.

Then it was off to London where we sang to a packed Westminster Abbey – first a recital, and then the anthem during the service. It was amazing to see many people standing at the back of the nave.

We then went on to Europe where we sang first at Maastricht. The Church of St Servaas, where we were to sing, was consecrated in 1030, but a chapel dedicated to the saint (a local bishop) had been built in the fourth century, and the first St Servatius Church was erected in the sixth century. You can imagine how inspiring this was to our young New Zealanders. The acoustics of the church were absolutely superb.

We also gave a concert in Düsseldorf where we sang in the Orangerie of Schloss Benrath. This was very well received by a capacity audience – in spite of it being Ascension Day and a public holiday – before we flew to the last leg of our tour, Singapore. Our final concert there was a disappointing way to end the tour. The acoustics at the Shangri-La Hotel where we sang were very difficult for choral singing, and we also had to contend with noisy air conditioning. However, this was a concert arranged by the hotel in association with Air New Zealand, as part of our contra-deal with the airline, so it was more a 'bread and butter' kind of arrangement. We also sang an anthem during Evensong and gave a recital afterwards in St Andrew's Cathedral.

And so we boarded our plane for the return journey home to New Zealand, weary, but elated by the ecstatic reception we had received wherever we sang. A fortnight later we gave the final concert of the 1972 Auckland festival, where the difference in expertise of the choir's singing was remarked on by many.

E   *What happened to the choir after the tour?*

P   It was obvious that the choir should continue, so the choir became the Auckland University Singers. It was to consist of forty singers with an age limit of twenty-five, and with annual auditions.

After only two weeks of rehearsal in 1973, this choir was invited by the New Zealand Broadcasting Service to record four works for the BBC choral competition, Let the Peoples Sing. To our astonishment we were placed second! Fairly soon afterwards we were invited to sing at the eleventh conference of ISME, the International Society of Music Education, in Perth in 1974. We were advised that no other similar group should be touring at this time, as funds would be limited both from the government and from the public. This was embarrassing as the Dorians were already fundraising for their 1975 tour. But we decided to go ahead, anyway.

As it turned out, we had only $2,000 to raise after choir contributions and a grant of $2,000 from the government. Once again, Margery Charlton was executive officer and a tower of strength, as was Margo Knightsbridge who, although now too old to sing in the choir, remained on the committee.

The most difficult part of it all was coping with travel in Australia because of strikes. We were a day late getting to Perth as a result, and bus strikes meant we had to walk long distances between the university and the city concert hall. However, we managed, and greatly enjoyed all that was provided for us: seminars, lectures and marvellous concerts. Once again, our choir was praised for its friendliness and readiness to mix with other groups, and our singing was received with praise and enthusiasm. After spending a night on a very hard and cold floor at Perth Airport as we waited for a plane to become available, we left for Adelaide, Melbourne, Canberra and Sydney. There was one delightful incident that I recollect. We sang at a smallish town, Albury, where we were asked by a helpful traffic warden if we were singing any works by Beethoven in our concert. He particularly loved the concertos. I didn't spot him in the audience, so at least he wasn't disappointed.

What grew from these two tours was the understanding that music is invaluable for promoting and encouraging international goodwill, and that we New Zealanders had the musical and social ability to play a vital part in international areas such as these.

One more thing about the choirs at Auckland University. Towards the end of the 1960s I started conducting an all-comers choir there for anyone at the university who wanted to sing – lecturers, general staff and students. There was even one person who loved to sing but sang on only one note! When there was a part where the basses had to sing on their own I would just say to him, 'Don't sing this bit.' There were over 200 singers in the choir. It was obligatory for all first year music students to sing in the choir. When I was appointed head of the music department I made it mandatory for all instrumental students to sing in the choir. I felt that it was crucial for them to sing as well as play, and that singing would develop not only their ear but their sense of musical line.

Peter was appointed professor of music at Auckland University in 1974.

RECOLLECTION

Margo Knightbridge, Auckland University Festival Choir, Dorian Choir. *Interviewed, 21 January 2009.*

M In 1970 I was accepted into the Auckland University Festival Choir which was formed to sing at the 3rd International Festival of University Choirs in America, and to tour England and Europe. We had just one year to rehearse all the music necessary for the festival and other concerts, and to raise the large amount of money necessary. For most of us it was our first trip overseas, and a major event in our lives! The tour was very exciting. Each choir at the festival had its own campus tour for two weeks before we all met up at the festival. Our area was the Eastern seaboard of the States. When the choirs all met together we had several days singing in the Kennedy Centre, which had only just been opened.

E *What was the format of the festival?*

M Each choir gave its own concert with its own conductor, but we also gave combined concerts with the main conductor, who was Robert Shaw, America's leading choral conductor. It was most interesting to hear so many different choirs and observe the different conductors. We learned such a lot.

Then it was on our way to England, where just the thought of singing in places like Westminster Abbey and King's College, Cambridge, was almost inconceivable, and still remains one of the highlights of my life.

I had to leave the Festival Choir after this tour as I was over the age limit by then, so my next step was to join the Dorians, and as luck would have it, I was to have similar rich experiences on tour twice more as a singer. However, I did go on the University Singers' Australian tour in 1974 as a helper to the choir management team.

Over the years, when I've been touring with Peter's choirs, I've had what I call 'transcendent moments' when I simply cannot believe that I'm singing in one of these buildings. It happened on one occasion in 1977 when the Dorians sang in Gloucester Cathedral at the Three Choirs Festival. Just walking out and seeing that packed cathedral giving us a standing ovation, singing a solo in Jack Body's *Carol to St Stephen* made me wonder, 'Am I really here?'

E *What impact has Peter had on your own musical life?*

M Huge! All the experiences of singing in his choirs, his constant search for perfect intonation, blend and balance, have made a great impact on my singing. I learned to listen more carefully. I became confident to hold a part on my own. I was given solos to sing. Later on I sang in smaller ensembles, and in the early 1990s my voice had developed to the point where I began to give solo recitals. Ten years ago I formed a vocal trio that I called The Three Mezzos, which has been very successful. Without the experiences of singing in Peter's choirs, this would not have happened.

8

The Dorians, 1961–82

THE AUCKLAND DORIAN CHOIR WAS FOUNDED IN 1936, RENAMED THE
Auckland Dorian Singers in 1941, and returned to its original name
in November 1975. For the purposes of the world tours in 1975 and 1977,
it was called the New Zealand Dorian Choir. Peter and other interviewees
sometimes use the names interchangeably, or just call them the 'Dorians'.

E   *Peter, by 1961 you already had a punishing schedule of work with lecturing,
    the St Mary's Cathedral Choir and the Auckland String Players. And yet
    you took on another choir, the Auckland Dorian Singers.*

P   Yes, it was another night out, but the opportunity to work with a more
    secular choir seemed too good to turn down. The choir's conductor,
    Harry Luscombe, had just retired and so they invited me to take the
    choir over. I've never regretted taking on the extra work. The Dorians
    became one of the best in the country and gave me great rewards.

E   *What was the choir like when you took it over?*

P   Well, it was more like an all-comers choir of about forty singers, most
    of them older people. But it wasn't long before quite a few of the
    Cathedral Choir singers joined, and the choir began to take on a new
    shape. Of course, I had to hold auditions with the usual results – some

people were very disappointed at not being accepted. It was a pity but it had to happen.

When I began with the choir, they rehearsed in a commercial building in the heart of the city close to the waterfront. I remember people having to sit in rather large armchairs – not the sort of thing that helps with a singer's breathing! Eventually we ended up at the Auckland Teacher's College with good rehearsal facilities there.

E   *Did you do music of a different kind with this choir?*

P   We sang mostly a cappella music, both older and contemporary. I did do a lot of the earlier motets and anthems that the Cathedral Choir sang, as I felt it was important for the Dorian Singers to know these works. And in later years we performed a good deal of New Zealand choral music, some of it written for the choir. The country developed some excellent composers, many of whom had sung in either the Dorian Choir or the National Youth Choir – and therefore had an understanding of choral writing.

I think the first real challenge for us was Penderecki's *Stabat Mater*. But we got to grips with it and performed it several times. I developed the policy of performing difficult contemporary works twice in a programme so that the audience could feel some familiarity the second time. We also sang some unaccompanied music from the 19th century – all the Brahms unaccompanied motets, for example.

Perhaps I should relate an incident that was both amusing and not amusing. On the recommendation of one of our members – Margo Knightbridge – I sought out Mendelssohn's Kyrie and Heilig from his setting of the German Mass. I was able to order a score when I was in Cambridge in 1978, and was lucky to purchase two collections of all his unaccompanied and accompanied anthems and motets. I was charged sixty-five pence for each book. This somewhat surprised me, but the cost is still recorded on each copy. I therefore went ahead, without asking permission, to buy sixty copies of each book for the Dorian Choir.

When I arrived back in Auckland in June that year, the president of the choir, Ian Kendall, was there to meet me at the airport. He was very angry, as the price the choir had to pay for the 120 copies was enormous – at four pounds seventy-five pence per copy. I was in considerable trouble! However, the pieces have been immensely popular and copies have been rented out to numerous choirs since then. So the income

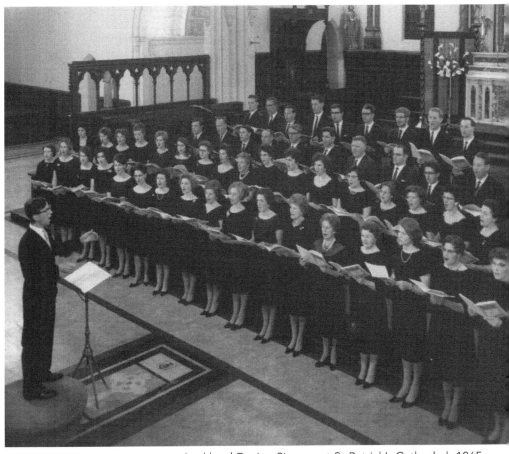

Auckland Dorian Singers at St Patrick's Cathedral, 1965.

from this must have more than paid for the initial cost.

Getting back to the choir in the early days, they became such a talented and enthusiastic group. So much so that I entered them in the European Broadcasting Union's competition Let the Peoples Sing several times – twice, anyway. We received good placings but the Swedish choirs seemed to win each time. However, to our astonishment and great delight, we were judged the best choir in the mixed-voice class in 1972. Malcolm Rickard presented me with the trophy at a public concert, and told the audience that New Zealand should be aware the Auckland Dorian Singers was now a world-class choir.

Rather arrogantly I replied, 'In that case we had better go and show the world.' Of course the Dorians became very excited at such a prospect, especially after the recent success of the Festival Singers overseas.

E   *And so you were involved in organising another tour soon after the University Festival Choir. How did you go about doing that?*

P   I realised that we needed an invitation to a festival of international repute to support fundraising. As I knew Peter Pears quite well, and he was an artistic director of Benjamin Britten's Aldeburgh Festival, I wrote to him to see if they would like us to sing at a festival. We received an invitation by return mail to take part in the Aldeburgh Festival in 1975 – just what we needed.

Our government advised us to check that no other such tours would be taking place at the same time, as that would jeopardise financial support for the Dorians. The way seemed to be clear for us. But ... while I was away in Europe in 1973 on short study leave, I learned that the National Youth Orchestra was also planning a tour in 1975. I also received a letter inviting the University Singers to the 11th International Conference of Music Education in Perth in 1974. So, not only was I faced with preparing two tours simultaneously, but the official finance for the Dorian tour was at risk. We wrote to the government for advice but the letter was not acknowledged. This was very frustrating as we were not sure if we could go ahead with the tour, and I was in Europe at that time, meeting with people who were willing to offer the Dorians concert engagements. However, on my return to Auckland in January 1974, the decision to go ahead with the tour was made.

E   *So once again, you had only eighteen months to raise funds and organise the tour!*

P   Yes, It was a huge undertaking. And all of it was organised outside work hours. By now I had been appointed head of the music department at the university where Margery Charlton was my clerical assistant. Once again she agreed to be tour manager, and was able to work closely with me during the day on tour preparations. Her experience from her similar role in the earlier university choir tours was invaluable. The tour arrangements were carried out entirely by Margery and a committee of choir members, and we planned for a tour of six weeks – two in Europe and four in England. The tour was very expensive as we had fifty-two singers in the choir. We calculated that we needed $110,000 in total. We did receive some government assistance but not nearly as much as had been hoped for. It amounted to a combined total of $16,500 from a government subsidy, the Queen Elizabeth Arts Council and the Ministry of Recreation and Sport. But we still had $93,500 to raise. The financial situation very quickly became a nightmare.

New Zealand Dorian Choir at Tivoli Gardens, Copenhagen, 1975.

The choir members took on a demanding series of fundraising events to raise as much money as possible. They raised $16,000 through such things as sweeping a large football stadium each Sunday morning during the winter; digging and bagging manure at a freezing works, promoting their sales around an Auckland suburb and delivering the bags the following weekend; and cleaning out a bread factory each Friday evening. Together with the $850 personal contribution each singer was asked to make, the choir's contribution to the cost of the tour was $61,000, almost half the total amount of the tour. It was a mammoth undertaking, which put a huge amount of pressure on them. But these physical activities gave opportunities for people to get to know each other better and built a strong team spirit for the tour.

E   *You still needed an enormous amount of money. What sort of public assistance was there for the tour?*

P   We were supported by various private individuals, trusts, companies and clubs, and Air New Zealand and British Airways gave us some advertising contra-deals – we used both airlines for all our major flights. And we organised a 'Friends of the Dorians' list which gave us several thousand dollars. Gradually the money was raised. By the time of our farewell benefit concert the last amount came in. My friend from Bluntisham childhood days, Pat (formerly Alec) Moore was managing director of Choysa Tea, and they decided to sponsor our farewell benefit concert as their main cultural support activity for the year. It was a great relief to know that the tour would take place free of debt. We left in a state of considerable excitement and, dare I say it, some apprehension as well, wondering how we would be received.

Our first performances were at Auckland airport, where we sang rather self-consciously, and on the plane, where we sang 'Oculi' before each meal. As a result, we sold one record to a passenger! Just digressing, the choir got used to singing in all sorts of public places – underground train stations, airports and so on, especially where there were queues of people waiting. They were bored and so were we. I think some of the choir got heartily sick of 'Early One Morning', but the public loved it – especially on a London Underground platform early one morning where we were held up for some time. At Los Angeles on our return journey, we were recognised by an official who asked us to sing again! It was a good public relations exercise, and always received applause.

As for repertoire, I realised how important it was to include works by contemporary New Zealand composers in our programmes and, without exception, they were very well received. Christopher Grier in a BBC broadcast about the choir made the comment, 'I may say that David Griffiths (a singer in the choir) and several other New Zealanders could not have been better ambassadors with their compositions.' Dr Douglas Mews wrote a work based on Māori chant, *The Love Song of Rangipouri*. This was a great success in performance, and once again offered me the opportunity to speak about Māori music.

John Rimmer wrote *Visions I* for us, which was quite different from anything we had ever sung before. It consisted of a tape of electronic music created from the choir's singing, and began with an elaborate high soprano solo, which was sung while processing from the west end of the cathedral up to the choir. The piece ended in reverse. We sang this several times, the most memorable performance being Salisbury Cathedral.

The tour started in Bonn where we were faced with somewhat of a calamity. Some of the choir flew east, picking up 'Delhi belly' on the way. By the time the main party arrived, having flown over the North Pole, these singers were quite ill and unable to sing in the first concert. It put a huge strain on those who were left to sing as one of the works divided into twelve parts! They managed remarkably well.

As the tour went on – we sang in Bonn, Düsseldorf, Paris, Maastricht, Copenhagen, Munster, the Hague, and Paris before the English leg – it became more and more evident that we were making a marked musical impression. Düsseldorf newspapers reported that the standard of the choir's performance was 'unusually high', and that it presented its music with 'overwhelming radiance'. They said the singers achieved a standard of performance rarely heard in Düsseldorf. Other reviews followed on similar lines, a critic in Holland saying that our choral singing reached a standard with which he had seldom been confronted. Audience numbers were disappointing in Europe because of the many visiting choirs from other parts of the world. But the comment invariably made was, 'We wish we had known how good you were, as the hall would have been full.'

Then it was on to England where, amongst many other exciting concerts, the Aldeburgh Festival beckoned us, as well as a broadcast recital to give in St John's Smith Square for the BBC. I think the choir was at its best at a concert in Gloucester Cathedral. I had hoped that we would give a concert in the chapel of King's College, but as the dates clashed with May Week it was suggested that we act as the chapel choir and sing an Evensong instead. It was a great thrill for the choir to sing from the choir stalls where I had sung so often. We sang Dr Ron Tremain's lovely setting of the Magnificat and Nunc Dimittis. Ron was a lecturer in composition at Auckland University at that time, and this work is still being performed and broadcast in New Zealand.

We began the English tour by singing in Marlborough College Chapel where we were told that our singing was magnificent, full of verve and sensitivity, but at times too loud for the building, even though it's a large building! Our soft singing had often received high praise, but never before had we been too loud! As had happened previously with the University Singers, the regular singing had caused individual voices to develop in strength and people were no longer hesitant about singing out.

We sang in other marvellous cathedrals – a lunch-hour recital in St Paul's Cathedral, London; a concert in Chichester Cathedral, which was celebrating its 900th anniversary; concerts in Salisbury and Exeter Cathedrals (where the precentor of the latter wrote, 'Never has such a wonderful choir sung in this cathedral … this visit has added a new dimension to our ideas of that Dominion on the other side of the world'); and then in Gloucester Cathedral, where I think the choir was at its peak. In fact, the organist said after our performance that it was the best choral singing from a large chamber choir that he'd heard in the cathedral. As a result he asked if the choir would sing at the 250th anniversary of the Three Choirs Festival to be held there in 1977, only two years later. The chairman of the festival made the same suggestion the next morning. As far as I know, the only choirs to sing at the Three Choirs Festival had been those of the three cities of Gloucester, Worcester and Hereford, so they were paying a huge compliment to us all. I felt enormously proud of the choir. But I have to admit that the thought of coping with the fundraising and organisation all over again, and in such a short time frame, was almost too daunting!

On our way to Aldeburgh, we called in at Hengrave Hall where John Wilbye had lived and worked as composer in residence, and where the Festival Singers visited in 1972. We enjoyed a most moving experience after an evening meal there when we went out into the garden to sing Wilbye's great madrigal 'Draw on Sweet Night'.

Our concert in the Aldeburgh Festival was to take place in the old church of Blythburgh. Unfortunately conditions there were less than favourable for us. The acoustic was completely dead and we were crammed on to a small raised space very close to the front rows of the audience. We were not altogether satisfied with our performance, but the BBC, who recorded it, expressed great satisfaction with the result.

Our last two performances were the broadcast concert at St John's Smith Square, and at New Zealand House, both of which were very well attended and received. The final event of the tour was a very happy reception at New Zealand House.

E   *How would you sum up that tour?*

P   It was an amazing success and we returned to New Zealand in a spirit of triumph. I must admit that before we left, I was slightly apprehensive that we would not meet the standards of other choirs outside New Zealand. I had heard a number of professional and semi-professional choirs while on leave in 1973, and was very aware of their high standards. But quite early in the tour, after our concert in Düsseldorf, we were given a clear indication of our reception when we received an enthusiastic invitation to return and give another concert under the auspices of the Benrath-Orangerie Council. We had to turn that down, but the invitation boosted our confidence enormously.

Everything went beyond our expectations and we were hailed as one of the great choirs of the world. Much comment was made about the friendly nature of the singers, and how we had presented New Zealand in a different light from sportsmen and farming – or to put it more plainly, rugby and sheep! The great acclaim that our singing received and the many glowing comments on our role as ambassadors made it obvious to us that the tour was an event that should be repeated.

So we accepted the invitation to sing at the Three Choirs Festival in 1977, and the hard work began all over again. We also received an invitation to give a concert for the BBC Proms that year, so the tour had to be organised around those two dates. I must confess to having made a discreet enquiry to the BBC to see if they would be interested in having us.

Touring was no holiday for the choir. They had to make considerable sacrifices in different ways. There was fundraising, extra rehearsals and concerts, and many families had to cope with a parent being away for six weeks. People lost salaries while away during that first tour. A particular bone of contention was the non-payment of school teachers, of whom we had more than twenty in the choir. This brought to a head the question of national status for groups such as ours. The choir was not selected nationally, so government employees were not eligible for special leave like those in representative sports teams. It was quite impossible at that time to train a choir on a national basis, and my opinion is that even though a choir is trained locally, it should be considered as a nationally selected team when it is invited to perform at prestigious overseas events. Unfortunately the same situation prevailed for the next tour in 1977.

Our fundraising for this tour was done differently. I went to Foreign Affairs to see if they could help us but came away feeling quite taken aback. Before our first tour, officers involved in cultural affairs in New Zealand House in London had been keenly interested in our tour, and very willing to act as a co-ordinating agency for the English part of the tour. However, I was handed a report from New Zealand House which was critical of the management of the choir, and claimed that we had expected far too much of their limited resources, and that financial estimates for this help had been considerably underestimated. The Bonn embassy made the same comment.

E *It sounds as though knuckles had been rapped rather too hard!*

P Quite possibly. But it was sad that the warm relations we felt we had with

New Zealand House had been blighted like this. Another staggering comment was that the choir's singing in England had not been of the standard which had been reported in the New Zealand papers. This was unbelievable as the English papers had given us very positive reviews to the point of being ecstatic at times. This was exemplified by such comments as in Colin Ross's criticism in the prestigious *Musical Opinion* which ended: '… this is one of the finest choral bodies one has ever heard'. And the organist of Salisbury Cathedral wrote that our concert 'was something of a landmark in Salisbury's musical history … it was probably the first time that singing of this quality had ever been heard here … certainly their performance can equal if not surpass that of similar English choirs (and I include London choirs too) …'

So you see, I really couldn't accept the adverse report from New Zealand House!

It was obvious that we would have to do this tour on our own. New Zealand House said that we should engage the services of an entrepreneur or agent for another tour. So we organised an agent in England, which did not work out favourably, and then the services of Don Mugridge to visit and organise concert venues in England. This proved to be excellent. Don was a former singer in the choir and treasurer, who had recently retired to Southampton in England. He travelled to the various venues by train as the choir would do, and at the same times, so was able to anticipate any problems that we might experience. He kept in touch with all the authorities who were putting on our concerts, and arranged advertising and hotel bookings where necessary. He was invaluable.

The choir's fundraising was different this time, as we raised money by giving concerts in different parts of Auckland – and throughout the North Island – rather than undertake the exhausting activities of the last tour.

We were a larger choir of sixty singers because of the multi-choral works I had programmed, and as a protection against sickness, although the choir generally remained in good health on this tour. The enthusiastic reception of New Zealand choral music in the first tour made it clear that we should include a good representation of New Zealand composers in this tour. I have to say that one or two of the works were very difficult, both to sing and to listen to, and as a result were not so well-received by some audiences.

We confined this tour to England. While the singers in the 1975 tour had been billeted, and we had travelled by coach, we decided it was easier this time to organise central accommodation in London, and to travel to the various places by train from there. Each choir member was given a BritRail pass, which some people used extensively in their free time. One bass travelled quite a bit of London on foot. That was Charles Naylor, a Presbyterian minister, who loved to keep fit by running. One morning he ran all the way from Victoria to the British Museum, returning via Oxford Street. When he asked a window cleaner for directions back to his hotel, he got the following response: 'Hell, mate, you're bloody miles away!'

We sang first in New Zealand House, with a concert for the Music Club of London, before travelling to Yorkshire for the Harrogate Festival. I made a mistake here by making the programme too long – this was noted in a review. We then travelled to the other end of England to Dartington Hall in Devonshire where we gave a concert for the Summer School to a packed audience. This was followed by a very successful performance at Chichester Cathedral, which earned us a remarkable write up in *Musical Opinion*. Then we were off to Gloucester after a memorable day at Lydney Park, where the choir was hosted by Lord and Lady Bledisloe, as it had been in the 1975 tour. The Bledisloes had commissioned a work from Professor Ronald Tremain – a New Zealand composer then living and working in Ontario. It was in memory of Lord Bledisloe, our former Governor General. The choir sang it in front of his memorial window in Lydney's parish church. It was a memorable day.

Obviously, the concert at the Three Choirs Festival in Gloucester was a highlight for us all. It went extremely well and the audience received us very warmly. One of the works we performed there was Jack Body's dramatic *Carol to St Stephen* for choir and soloists. St Stephen is represented by a solo soprano who 'dies' at the end after a series of piercing top As. The audience loved that. They had been instructed not to applaud during the concert, but they broke out into spontaneous applause at the end of that work.

After a concert in Canterbury Cathedral – unfortunately the choir was very tired after singing at Gloucester the day before and every piece flattened – it was time for the Prom concert, which was held at St Augustine's church in Kilburn and not the vast Albert Hall. It wasn't easy for the choir, as it was a much smaller space compared to the huge cathedrals such as Gloucester and Canterbury that they had been singing in. But once again the audience broke into spontaneous applause in spite of having been asked to desist. I have a letter here which I received from the Controller of BBC Music, Robert Johnson, dated 15 September 1977:

Dear Peter Godfrey,

... will you please tell the choir that their concert provided us with some of the best a cappella singing we have heard at the Proms for some time. The programme was in every way extraordinarily demanding but I have rarely heard such sustained expertise: ensemble, intonation and stamina were all remarkable. And, if I may say so, your interpretative control was very distinguished ...

Yours very sincerely,

Robert Johnson, Controller, Music, BBC

After that came our concert in King's where we gave a lunch hour recital. The choir relished the amazing acoustic – the reverberation period was so long that when an ending tapered to a pianissimo it was hard to tell just when the sound dissolved into an echo. With my background at King's and the choir's excitement over singing there, I had to begin the concert with Bruckner's *Locus Iste*.

We ended the tour with a lunchtime concert in Norwich Cathedral – combined with noisy sightseers – where we were given a civic reception by the Lord Mayor, and a concert at York Minster. We were tired but hugely satisfied and quite jubilant with the outstanding success of the tour. About two thirds of the choir chose to stay in England for a few weeks before returning home. I returned to New Zealand several months later before having one of the most memorable times of my life – becoming acting director of music at King's for four months. More of that later!

I was to have five more years with the Dorians until I made the decision to return to cathedral music by becoming director of music at Wellington Cathedral. That was one of the hardest decisions I've ever had to make, but it had to be done. Our last concert together was in the garden of my new home in Waikanae. It was a poignant farewell concert. During my time with the Dorians we made some fine LP recordings and, later, CDs were made from recordings of concerts that had taken place over the years. It is good to know that the great music we made together has not been lost.

RECOLLECTIONS

Noni Kenny & Hilary Monteith, St Mary's Cathedral Choir, Auckland Dorian Singers and Dorian Choir. *Interviewed, 21 January 2009.*

E *Quite a few Cathedral Choir singers also belonged to the Dorians. You both did. Was there a difference in Peter's style of working with a secular choir?*

H I think Peter showed more of a sense of humour with the Dorians than with the Cathedral Choir, possibly because the Dorian Choir was a secular choir and not rehearsing in a church. He would say things that were very funny with a straight face – which made them even funnier. These were usually accompanied by the rather self-conscious 'Godfrey sniff'. The occasional good laugh was such a tonic. It relieved the hard, concentrated work he demanded.

We had wonderful experiences and developed great friendships. Peter has an amazing ability to create a sense of family in his choirs. This was very helpful when it came to the tours, where we needed to get on well with each other. The tours were, of course, the highlights of my time in the Dorians with the exciting concerts, glorious buildings and acoustics to sing in, and other unforgettable experiences.

We saw Charlemagne's marble throne in Aachen, we enjoyed a mayoral reception on our arrival in Copenhagen, where we were fêted with a breakfast of delicious Cherry Heering liqueur accompanied by wonderful filled pancakes, we visited Hamlet's castle, and we were given a mayoral reception in Munster.

The good thing about touring was that all the extra rehearsals and performances gave us real mastery of the music. I don't think this degree of polish is possible in ordinary circumstances. It was quite overwhelming to experience the reception and high praise that our singing always received.

N We did work very hard but I don't think any of us felt hard done by – it was all such a privilege, and so exciting. And even though our audiences were often on the small to very small side, we always gave of our absolute best. I remember people saying after our concerts, 'If only we had known how wonderfully you sing, there would have been many more people here.' The problem was that we were just one of many visiting choirs – an unknown, unheard of group.

E *What do you think Peter's 'X factor' is?*

H Somehow he always seemed to make rehearsals fun. He's not really a funny person, but he has a good sense of humour. When he first came to Auckland he was young and stern. He's continued to be stern, but there's a sense of humour behind it. Nobody else seems to be able to take rehearsals like him. Most people hated to miss a rehearsal. We always looked forward to them.

N Yes. But there was one thing we sopranos didn't like. Peter had this nasty habit of going along the front row and listening to each individual as he tried to find out who was singing out of tune. On one occasion when he passed me my leg developed an urgent twitch, and I kicked him in the shin! I believe that story has gone right round the world.

Margaret Barriball, St Mary's Cathedral Choir and Dorian Choir.
Interview, January 2009.

The Dorians usually had a rehearsal weekend at the beginning of each year to learn new music. One year, when the choir was at Knock-na-gree, a camp out of Auckland, Peter was quite ill with shingles and so stayed at the camp while seven of the singers went to Karekare beach for a swim. This lonely and wild west coast beach is notorious for rips, and is quite a dangerous beach for swimming. There have been many fatalities there. Nevertheless, the group of seven went into the water, five men and two women. The inevitable happened: they got caught in a rip.

'Keep calm,' one of them advised. 'Just tread water and you'll come into shore eventually, further down the beach.'

The two women, both non-swimmers, panicked and were unable to follow his advice, so one of the men stayed with them to support them. As they saw the other four swimmers being swept out to sea, they despaired that they wouldn't see them alive again.

After some time the women were brought into shore. Imagine their delight when they saw the other group walking towards them along the beach. They had been carried into shore further along and were safe. They decided that they should tell Peter what had happened in case he heard it from someone else. Peter's reaction? 'Oh dear. Were any of them tenors?'

Ian Kendall, chair of the Auckland Dorian Choir.
Interviewed, 20 January 2009.

E *Ian, you had a long association with the Dorian Choir, including many years as the chairman and those busy years touring. How did you come to join the choir in the first place?*

I Friends of mine, Alan and Bryan Cammell, were both in the choir and were very impressed with what Peter was doing. So I went to a concert in St Mary's Cathedral given by the Cathedral Choir, which was really excellent, and I joined the Dorians.

E *How did you find Peter as a conductor in those early days?*

I He was pretty intimidating! One thing you didn't ever do was to come in late. I didn't have a car at the time and so I was given a ride to choir practice by another singer. If we knew we were going to be late, we'd walk around the block a couple of times and go into the rehearsal a good ten minutes late – never just a couple of minutes late! Of course, we were working full days with responsible jobs, and it wasn't always possible to drop what you were doing and get there by a quarter to eight. So we had to play that trick several times, but I think it was wearing a bit thin towards the end. What intimidated us was Peter's technique of dealing with lateness. When the offender arrived, Peter's arms would drop and there would be deathly silence while the chorister found his or her seat, then the music, the page, the line and the bar number. Then there was almost an implied but unspoken 'Thank you for coming – may we start now?', followed by the 'Godfrey sniff' before the rehearsal resumed.

For all that, one could only admire him. He had these standards, and they were the right ones. He never came to a rehearsal without knowing precisely what he was going to do, in what order, and what he was seeking to achieve. It was meticulous planning. And the choir improved immensely and so quickly. We had a bit of fun as well, but we were always ready to work hard. I was apprehensive at the beginning, but the bass I sat next to said to me, 'Don't worry too much, just hold your music up the right way and you'll be okay.' And then he said, 'If you're a tenor, you don't even have to hold your music the right way!'

E *Peter could indeed be very funny which broke up any tension that might have been forming. He was quite skilful the way he used it – 'Sopranos,*

129

you're too long on the loo' (alleluia), or 'Sopranos, you're flat on top'.

I   Yes! And there was, 'Altos – roll your "arrrrrs"'. And 'Gentlemen and the basses'. I remember one occasion when there was a rest, and of course I sang a little personal solo! The comment was: 'Bloody accountants – they can't count'. But he became much more tolerant over the years. A lot depended on how he assessed the person he was dealing with. If he thought they were honest and doing their best, he was prepared to forgive the odd lapse. For the person who just breezed in and breezed out, there was no tolerance whatsoever. His insistence on singers putting their hands up when they made a mistake helped to keep rehearsals moving.

E   *Could you talk about the tours, please?*

I   Yes, most certainly. They were extraordinarily hard work from the beginning to the end, but the choir developed a strong bond as a result. Previously we had turned up at rehearsals and gone home straight after, with only a five minute break in the middle. But the preparation for the tour and the weeks away developed a really good camaraderie, which lasts today.

We did such a lot. I don't know how we achieved it all: rehearsals, concerts, fundraising and our jobs. It was a mammoth effort – cleaning a bakery every Friday night; cleaning the grandstands at Eden Park football stadium on Sunday mornings; digging manure at Southdown freezing works – more than once – then promoting it in a garden area and selling it the following weekend; Peter growing potatoes and selling them; auctions and things like that which are too numerous to name. These fundraising efforts raised relatively little of the total we needed, but they gave us great publicity. We came across as people who were prepared to help ourselves rather than just wait for a handout.

I was approached to be chairman of the tour committee. And when the chairman of the choir, Neil Dow, resigned I took over that role as well. It was such a big exercise that the tour committee met every week. It was important to track things as they were happening, and not to leave anything too late. There was a huge amount of detail to deal with. Margery Charlton was instrumental in organising the tour. She did a tremendous amount of work and gave her heart and soul to it.

E   *Am I right in thinking you had only one year to organise that first tour?*

I   About eighteen months, I think. In 1972 the Dorians won the mixed-voice section of the international competition Let the Peoples Sing, and the trophy was presented to Peter in 1973. This made a considerable impact on the musical scene in New Zealand, so the decision for the choir to tour England and Europe came quite soon after that.

We began the tour in Europe, which was disastrous financially, because of very small audiences. We learned that many choirs visited each year and audiences became blasé about attending concerts. As a virtually unknown country, we were courting disaster as far as audience numbers was concerned. And yet I don't remember being demoralised by the small audiences in Europe – only twenty at the Hague. We sang as well as ever. That's to Peter's credit, I think. We sang for the sake of the music and for our own pleasure. We also knew we were there to represent our country. I remember one man who stood up in the church in Amsterdam after we'd sung and said, 'This is the day when all Amsterdammers should be ashamed. You've brought such great music.' Perhaps our publicity wasn't good enough. But we did have a full chapel for our first concert in Bonn. I'm sure the representative from Foreign Affairs cajoled people into coming! She did a very good job.

At the beginning of the tour, half the choir was ill with 'Delhi belly'. As our repertoire contained works of many parts – as many as twelve, I think – it took courage for a depleted choir to carry on with the concerts. And a virulent strain of 'flu hit some singers. We didn't give concerts with a full choir for two weeks into the tour. And yet we were a huge success as far as audience enthusiasm was concerned. I remember coming off the stage at the university chapel in Bonn after our very first concert of the tour. The person the Ambassador had appointed to look after us said, as she heard the applause, 'They liked you. They liked you!' in a tone of great surprise. And that was typical of the response all the way through Europe.

We were away for six weeks in that first tour with only three or four days off. It was hard work. Copenhagen was the toughest part of the European tour with nine appearances in two days. We'd had a horrific journey to get there – from Munster to Cologne, where we changed trains. We had to cross from one platform to another via an overhead bridge, with only one and a half minutes to get sixty-two people and their luggage on to the train! It had to be organised so carefully.

The women passed the luggage to the men who passed it through the train windows into the carriage. The station staff applauded us when we were all on-board! And the couchettes weren't ready for us, so we had to stand for some time. Then it was a car ferry trip from Puttgart followed by a train journey to Copenhagen. I seem to think that our hotel rooms weren't ready and we had to wait for quite some time. We were exhausted by then! But what a grand welcome we were given by the Lord Mayor, followed by Cherry Heering liqueur and pancakes.

E   *Peter has given a full description of the tours, but what were the highlights of the English part of the first tour for you?*

I   It was all wonderful – St Paul's Cathedral, Canterbury Cathedral, Gloucester Cathedral. The list goes on and on. But singing Evensong at King's, from the choir stalls where Peter had sung as a boy and as a choral scholar, was very poignant. And likewise, singing in Marlborough College Chapel where Peter had been director of music. Our concert at Gloucester Cathedral saw the choir at its peak and was probably the real highlight of the tour.

We were better regarded in the second tour because our reputation seemed to have spread. And although the organisation of the tour in Auckland followed the same pattern, we were fortunate to have someone – Don Mugridge – in England visiting venues and arranging concerts in person. This worked very well. Another difference was in fundraising, which was mainly from concerts, not only in Auckland but all round the North Island. This allowed the choir to develop tour repertoire in performances, and avoided the exhaustion that had come from fundraising activities of the first tour.

We were now known as the New Zealand Dorian Choir because we were representing New Zealand at prestigious events. And we hoped that the government would consider continuing payment of the salaries of teachers and other government employees' salaries while we were away. But that didn't happen in either tour.

A new strategy of Peter's was to have the music critic for the *New Zealand Herald*, Lin Saunders, accompany us overseas and send regular reviews back to New Zealand to show the progress and achievements of the choir. Actually, I don't think that achieved much as far as the general public was concerned. It was very demoralising to arrive back from a triumphantly successful tour as though we were yesterday's news, with very little publicity given the choir. Rather typical of a country focused on sport, I have to say! But we returned with brilliant reviews from our many concerts overseas, which was very reassuring.

It was such a privilege to experience the tours, and only made possible by having Peter as our director of music.

It should be recorded that wives, husbands and families made considerable sacrifices in allowing singers to be away so much from home for rehearsals, fundraising, concerts and tours. At one stage, Ian's daughter, Susan said to her mother, 'Mummy, when I grow up, do I have to be a Dorian?'

9

Return to King's College, 1978

E   *Peter, you hadn't been back in New Zealand for long after the Dorians' second tour before you were back in England. How did this come about?*

P   I was chatting with Philip Ledger while I was at King's with the Dorians. He mentioned that he would like a break from the King's Choir, a sort of sabbatical. He had taken the choir over from David Willcocks, not the easiest thing to do! So the arrangement was made that he would come to New Zealand and take over all my choirs – two at the university and the Auckland Dorian Choir – and feel free to do any other conducting which came his way. He and his wife would live in our house. And I would take over the choir at King's, and Sheila and I would live in their home.

To take over King's College Choir for four months was one of the greatest honours I ever received! Here I was, the first person to be chorister, choral scholar and director of music at King's. It was hard to believe it was happening.

I started with the choir in January 1978. It was certainly a challenge and I enjoyed it immensely, but I found it slightly inhibiting in that I was not in a position to implant too many of my own ideas. I had really looked forward to doing psalms with them, but I found that Philip's style was not the same as mine, so it was generally a matter of

Back at King's College as acting director of music.

just running through them before each service. I got on quite well with the choir and made several friends, but it was not my choir. I always remember stopping in the middle of a rehearsal, and saying, 'Don't you enjoy this?' They certainly never showed it! But then, I've always held that a chapel or cathedral choir should not show their enthusiasm when singing sacred music and the conducting should be discreet with little arm movement showing. My time at King's reinforced my love of the enthusiasm of New Zealanders. Always an important feature! I also conducted the Cambridge University Musical Society Choir (CUMS) and took the opportunity to introduce some New Zealand music to them.

While I was at King's I received an invitation to have lunch with the Queen, which I very much enjoyed, and was able to return to the Palace for the award of my MBE a few weeks afterwards. The Queen actually remembered me!

RECOLLECTIONS

Simon Halsey CBE, choral scholar, King's College Choir; international choral and orchestral conductor including conductor laureate of the Berlin Radio Choir, chorus director of the City of Birmingham Symphony Orchestra Choruses, artistic director of Berlin Philharmonic Youth Choral Programme. *Letter, November 2008.*

I was in my second year at King's when Philip Ledger, our director of music, decided to take sabbatical leave. There was great excitement and curiosity when it was announced that Peter Godfrey was coming to take charge as acting director of music. I'd been a boy chorister at an Oxford College when our organist there went on sabbatical leave, and I had not enjoyed the experience of a different conductor. Choir singers identify very closely with their conductors and a change can be dangerous!

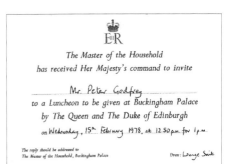

Invitation to lunch with the Queen.

At King's we knew that Peter was an 'insider', in that he had sung in the choir himself. I was particularly interested as I had already decided I would like to be a conductor myself, and I was intrigued to see whether it was possible to win round a young choir quickly – Peter was with us for just one term. Of course Peter had just the right experience and calmly won us round. We were not used to calmness! Philip Ledger – whom we all greatly admired – was extremely demanding of us and put us under a good deal of pressure to excel every day. Peter, unlike Philip, did not have any 'power' over us, in that he was not responsible for having brought us to King's. But with his great professionalism, his evident love of King's, its traditions and the music, we began to sing well. He was particularly well supported by his wife, Sheila, who entered wholeheartedly into the adventure and whom we quickly grew to love.

The repertoire changed a bit – I remember a Flor Peeters Mass that caused us great difficulties! As well as new pieces, Peter gave us pieces that he had loved at King's but which had passed out of the repertoire. Above all we felt secure with Peter because we knew he was making music for the right reasons – for the glory of God, in daily services. I learned a great deal from his integrity. I will not pretend that we did not miss Philip Ledger's great energy and the great excitement of his music-making, but we really grew to appreciate the very skilfully managed, gentler way of making music under Peter. King's, in that year, had a lot of new singers. More than half the choral scholars were new. It cannot always have been easy for Peter. But his time with us was a great success, and it was the beginning of a long friendship between us. I have been three times to New Zealand at his instigation, for which I am unspeakably grateful.

Stephen Cleobury CBE, director of music, King's College, Cambridge.
Letter, 6 January 2014.

I have not had the chance to get to know Peter Godfrey well, and indeed have had the pleasure of meeting him only on a few occasions, but when I arrived in King's in 1982, Peter Godfrey's reputation was palpable. He was clearly regarded as one of the most distinguished of those choral scholar alumni who have gone from King's, and who took what they experienced here, mixed it with their own talent and personal qualities, and created extremely successful choirs in many other parts of the world. In Peter Godfrey's case, it is my perception that he became to New Zealand music what David Willcocks was here in the United Kingdom. Moreover, he is a huge supporter of New Zealand composers, and has a highly imaginative sense of programming. The high regard in which he was held here was exemplified by the invitation to him to direct the choir during the absence of the director of music on sabbatical leave. My only personal regret is that I was never able to observe his work at close hand, since I would have learned much.

Sir Philip Ledger CBE, director of music, King's College, director of the Royal Scottish Academy of Music and Drama.
Email, 24 January 2009.

There are many good choral directors and choirmasters in the musical profession, but really fine choral directors are a rare breed indeed. Peter Godfrey has a most impressive and extensive range of both musical and administrative accomplishments, but his gifts and achievements as a choral director are quite exceptional. We first became acquainted after a Choral Evensong at King's College. As we walked together on the back lawn of King's, by the River Cam, we realised that we had a great deal in common. Peter had been a chorister and choral scholar at King's when the renowned Boris Ord conducted the choir, and I had been taught by Boris when I was first an undergraduate at the college. It was quickly evident to me that the ideals and traditions of the King's College Choir had guided and inspired Peter's own music-making – and that, with these in mind, he had initiated and nurtured the highest possible standards in choral music in New Zealand. He spoke to me with enormous enthusiasm about his life there, and I knew immediately that I wanted to visit this wonderful country and to hear and see for myself what he had created.

I can't remember which of us suggested exchanging posts, but before we ended our walk on the back lawn of King's, the idea had been born. So it was that, in the English winter and the New Zealand summer of 1978, we did just that. Each of us made suitable arrangements with our institutions. We not only exchanged choirs, we swapped houses, cars and secretaries! Peter and Sheila could not have been kinder. When Mary and I arrived in New Zealand with our two children, we were driven to their house and given the most wonderful welcome by their many friends and colleagues. By this time, Peter and Sheila were settling into our house in Cambridge.

Perhaps the greatest tribute that I can pay Peter is to say that all of the members of his choirs in New Zealand spoke with real affection and not a little awe about 'Prof'. I remember in particular an outstanding performance of Bach's *St John Passion* when I conducted the Dorian Choir. This choir was one of the most disciplined and musically aware that I have ever heard, and it was entirely due to Peter's conscientious and rigorous training. I know, too, that the King's Choir tremendously enjoyed the time that Peter spent with them as the acting director of music.

During our stay in New Zealand, we made numerous friends, and Mary and I have returned there on several occasions. It was perhaps the nature of the exchange that Peter and I did not get to know each other as much as we would have liked, but I have abiding memories of our friendship in subsequent years. I can still hear in my mind a magical performance of Bruckner's motet *Locus Iste*, with Peter conducting it in King's College Chapel. In 2005 I was absolutely delighted when Peter was made an Icon of the Arts Federation of New Zealand. No other musician is as worthy of such a distinction.

Sir Philip's email was read to Peter at the end of the Nostalgia Choir week in Auckland, January 2009. Peter was so moved by this that he was reduced to tears. It is rare for him to express emotion publicly.

10

National Youth Choir, 1979–89

E *Peter, another choir!*

P Well – I really started off in an advisory capacity in 1979. It was to become a most amazing opportunity, the most inspiring I've ever experienced.

It began with Guy Jansen who was the Department of Education's national adviser on music. Guy, as a secondary school teacher, had assisted in holiday choral courses for secondary school students. When he became national adviser he re-established these courses, which became very popular. After some singers had left school they expressed their disappointment at not being able to continue singing in the choir. Various other things led to Guy's passionate idea of starting a national youth choir. Guy came to see me to discuss his plans, and asked if I would be a guest conductor for this choir. He was a man with a lot of drive who had started his own choir in Wellington, the Festival Singers, which had a special character of its own and was making a name for itself.

So I agreed to join his staff and, after auditions had been held throughout the country, a choir of about a hundred began to rehearse in the Wellington area. We had tutors for the four sections who helped with note-learning and voice production. They took a rehearsal each day, and sat in on the full rehearsals to take note of what needed to be worked on. They were also responsible for the note-learning of one work each in the first course. It worked well as far as the choir was concerned, but I think the tutors found it a bit irksome to have to sit around for so many hours each day.

Anyway, the National Youth Choir of New Zealand gave its first concerts in August 1979, and received very encouraging reviews – except it was noted that the balance of male and female voices was less than satisfactory. There were two girls for each boy.

E *What kind of music did you choose for these initial concerts with so little time to train a new choir?*

P Well, we certainly didn't spare them! I remember them singing the three Bruckner motets: *Locus Iste*, *Virga Jesse* and *Ave Maria*; Pachelbel's *Magnificat*; the Schütz *Psalm 100*; three movements of Randall Thompson's *Peaceable Kingdom*; and Chris Norton's *Children's Voices*. So it was quite a substantial programme for them. Of course, Guy and I shared rehearsing them and conducting the concerts. He had sent the music out earlier to each member of the choir, so that was a great help. It also helped Guy to check on individual preparation for the course, as he re-auditioned them during the rehearsal week!

E *How did the young voices stand up to such an intensive week of singing?*

P Quite well on the whole although there were signs of vocal strain. It was obvious that professional voice lessons were of the utmost importance for each singer, and these became mandatory from then on.

The following year, 1980, we gave our first really important concert – Tippett's *A Child of Our Time*, in the Wellington Town Hall with the New Zealand Symphony Orchestra. Sir David Willcocks was the conductor. This was David's first visit to New Zealand. He was so impressed by the National Youth Choir's performance that on his return he suggested the formation of a national youth choir in the UK, which they did.

Guy's imagination and energy lead to the next major event for the National Youth Choir or NYC – an overseas tour in 1982.

E *Goodness, another tour for you! Were you involved in the organisation of this one?*

P   Thankfully, no. An excellent administrator, Colin Brown, was appointed – Colin had recently retired as general manager of a major insurance company – and a very able board and committee of trustees were set up. They took care of all the fundraising and tour arrangements. It was a huge task, as New Zealand was in recession at the time. But, amazingly, not only were the necessary funds raised but there was an excess of $26,000! At the end of the tour it was decided that each singer should receive a refund of $300. Having paid a large subsidy of $2,500 each, they really appreciated that.

   To establish the national identity of the choir, and to help with fundraising on a national level, we gave concerts in various cities throughout the country before the tour. These mini-tours were invaluable as they gave the choir some experience of touring. In July 1982 we left New Zealand to begin a substantial tour of England and Europe. We flew via the United States, and took advantage of that by giving our first concerts at Long Beach in Los Angeles, and Disneyland – much to the joy of the young singers!

   In England, we stayed at the Royal Holloway College for three rest days to get over jet lag, followed by a concert in St Margaret's, Westminster. The tour was very comprehensive: Shrewsbury; Chester, where we sang at the opening of the Chester Music Festival; Bristol, where we sang for the International Conference of the International Society of Music Education; Wells, where they were celebrating the 800th anniversary celebration at the cathedral – we included Professor Ritchie's *Lord, When the Sense of Thy Sweet Grace* in this programme, which was received well, as was Guy's conducting of Lotti's *Crucifixus*; a second performance at the ISME Conference; Plymouth; and Salisbury, where we sang Evensong in the cathedral with a greatly depleted choir owing to brake failure on one of the two buses we were travelling in, followed by a recital in that wonderful building. On 2 August we gave a concert in Marlborough College, which meant a lot to the choir because of my past connection there. The next day we sang Evensong at Gloucester Cathedral, followed by a recital at Coventry Cathedral.

E   *I imagine that Coventry would be a very moving experience for the choir.*

P   Quite so. Two things were of great importance to them. The starkness of the ruins of the original cathedral destroyed by a bomb during the Second World War was an illustration of the reality of war that they had not experienced themselves. And part of the programme was David Hamilton's very telling composition *Lux Aeterna,* which we sang in memory of those who had just died in the Falklands war on the British ship *Coventry.*

Then we moved to York Minster where we gave a lunch hour concert, which laid the foundations for a week's stay there, including an evening concert at Harrogate the next day. Next we drove down to Cambridge where we gave a concert in King's Chapel on the steps underneath the organ loft. I think this was our best performance of the tour. In our programme was the Charles Stanford Magnificat for double choir, which the Dorian Choir had sung in 1975. Other conductors at the concert had never heard the work before, so it provoked a lot of interest. And the choir sang that marvellous double-choir motet by Bach, *Singet dem herrn,* from memory!

E *What a remarkable achievement!*

P Yes – they gave a really great performance. Then we were off to London again, where a rather disastrous problem with accommodation arose. We were to spend four nights in the Chelsea youth hostel, but after a night of the women in the choir being hassled by some fellow guests – and the choir in general hassled by people who tried to peddle drugs – we beat a hasty retreat back to the Royal Holloway College!

On 12 August we gave the long-awaited concert at Wembley with Kiri Te Kanawa, in the presence of the Prince of Wales. There had been some adverse publicity from a gossip columnist prior to this concert, suggesting that after having Kiri sing at his wedding in a rather odd outfit, Prince Charles would suffer attending this concert where she would be singing. Snide remarks indeed! Fortunately we had supportive publicity, which described the columnist's comments as 'pure fabrication', and from New Zealand House 'a load of rubbish', and we sang to a full house with all 2,700 seats sold two weeks before our performance. This really was the most exciting event for the choir.

They were thrilled when Prince Charles spent half an hour chatting with them and Kiri, and presented him with a woolly toy lamb for Prince William, which Prince Charles immediately named 'Cutlets'. The choir sang Schubert's *Ständchen* and Mendelssohn's *Hear My Prayer* with Kiri, as well as three arrangements of Māori songs. The acoustic was uncomfortably dry but the choir responded to the special nature of the occasion and we were warmly received by the critics.

Meeting Prince Charles after the concert at Wembley Stadium,
Peter, centre, with Kiri Te Kanawa on his right.

After a very successful lunch-hour concert in St Paul's Cathedral, our final concert in England, and three free days, we flew to the Continent for the next leg of the tour. It proved to be more relaxing.

Here we sang at Waalsekerk (where we were given a standing ovation), Amsterdam, then Bonn, where we gave an outdoor concert at city hall. Then there were two concerts at Cologne, a concert at Hoechst and finally Eppertshausen, where the choir shared the stage with a local mandolin orchestra of international renown. On our way back to New Zealand, we sang in Singapore, where my friend Roy Bowyer-Yin gave his great support. Finally, we were back in New Zealand after a most successful tour.

E   *Were there any problems with taking a young choir away on such a long tour?*

P   Not really. They stood up to it all very well. There were one or two occasions when their youthful exuberance bubbled over. Someone created a competition to see who could jump out of the back door of the bus at red lights, run round the bus and get back inside before the lights turned green! And on another occasion, young enthusiasm had a less than happy outcome. During the 'free' week in York some singers decided to hire four cars and drive to John o'Groats in the far north of Scotland. Unfortunately they arrived back too late for the rehearsal for the Harrogate concert. Guy and I had to make the tough decision to bar them from singing in the concert that night. We needed to maintain standards, no matter how unpopular a decision might be. But, really, they were a pleasure to travel with.

E *It sounds like another breathtaking tour, in more ways than one! I understand that there was a rather difficult issue arising from the tour that needed to be resolved.*

P Yes. It *was* very difficult and had been growing since the early days of the choir. Problems had arisen through two conductors working with the choir. Guy and I got on well, but there appeared to be some lack of complete support for him from some members of the choir. Unlike orchestras, who are used to working with various conductors regularly, choirs are usually devoted to one conductor. The result of all this was that Guy decided to hand over his appointment as musical director to me at the beginning of 1983. At the same time he decided to go to the USA to do further studies in choral conducting and, in fact, received a doctorate as a result of this. After the tour Guy flew to the States to prepare for his study there. I was now the permanent conductor of the choir. The Department of Education needed someone to take over Guy's role as national adviser and appointed David Wood as a temporary secondment. The NYC Board appointed David as assistant administrator in Guy's absence.

I now needed to work closely with the administrator, Colin Brown, and the committee, which was centred in Wellington. In the early days I would fly down once a month for meetings. But I shifted down to Wellington in late 1982, and so I was able to call in to see the administrator at least once a week. I was so fortunate to have the wonderful help of Paddy Nash, who became the administrator in 1985, as well as an excellent committee. And of course, we had a superb Board of Trustees to help with financial matters and so on.

Over the next six years we scattered rehearsals and concerts as widely as possible throughout the country to make it a truly national choir.

E *Now that the choir was yours, were there changes that you wished to make?*

P Yes. I decided to form a chamber choir of forty voices. This was in 1983 after David and I had held auditions throughout the country. The policy of the choir was to hold national auditions every two years. There were several reasons: I felt that the best young singers needed more challenge; a chamber choir could perform works not suited to the larger choir and give variety in concerts; it would be the required size to enter the Let the Peoples Sing choral competition; and we realised the choir we had taken on tour was too large. In future, a touring choir should consist of forty singers, enough for one bus. They became known as Choir A and Choir B.

I know this wasn't a popular decision with the choir and there was quite an undercurrent of unrest for a while. They felt that we'd created first and second-class singers, which in a way I suppose we had. In a way, it provided incentive for the singers to work hard in order to be in the chamber choir. One good thing that came out of all this was the appointment of two singers, Oliver Drennan and Hamish Morrison, to the recently formed management committee. They were able to pass on the concerns of singers, which provided for better communication. One such issue was the inclusion of some lighter music. I tried to do this, but what they were suggesting wasn't my musical experience, and so things remained much as they had been. I know Colin Brown supported them in this, but it wasn't until Karen Grylls took over that programming changed in this area.

The Board decided in 1984 that I should continue as conductor until 1988, and David Wood was appointed my assistant and concert manager. They also had to accept Colin Brown's resignation who had been administrator for five years. Not only had he been an excellent administrator but he had established an excellent rapport with the choir, rather like an elderly grandfather. I was so fortunate when Paddy Nash was appointed as the new administrator in 1985. It was the beginning of a very long and successful working relationship – right through to the end of my conducting life. She has also been a greatly valued friend.

E *How did you manage rehearsals for the two levels of the choir?*

P We got over that problem by rehearsing the chamber choir for three days or so before the big choir met. That worked well as far as I was concerned, but I realise now that it must have been difficult for singers to arrive for a course that had been going for a few days already. It just couldn't be helped.

The chamber choir recorded a contribution for the youth section of Let the Peoples Sing in 1984. We sent it in, although I wasn't happy with the recording. We were placed fourth. We entered again in 1986 and were absolutely delighted when we learned that we had been placed first in the youth section. We were now recognised as being one of the world's top young ensembles. I'll always treasure one comment made by the international jury: that choral singing in New Zealand is not an end in itself, but a spiritual achievement. This was borne out by the conductor, Nicholas Braithwaite who conducted them when they sang Andrew Lloyd Webber's Requiem with the New Zealand Symphony Orchestra. He described the chamber choir as '... Without question the most outstanding choir with which I have ever worked.'

There's such a lot to say about my time as conductor of NYC – the concerts, the recordings, the successes in Let the Peoples Sing, but too much for this book, I feel. I suggest that readers who are interested in more detail read Simon Tipping's excellent *Choir of the World*. The choir experienced some ups and downs, but it grew from strength to strength and some world-class professional singers, not all in my time, have come from its ranks – Paul Whelan, Martin Snell, Teddy Tahu Rhodes, Sarah Castle, Simon O'Neill, Jonathan Lemalu, Anna Leese, Anna Pierard and Madeleine Pierard and probably others. The conductor Tecwyn Evans was also a member of the choir as were the composers David Hamilton and Anthony Ritchie, and quite a few other professional musicians once sang with NYC.

I felt so often that this was the most outstanding choir I had ever conducted. Sadly, this was to come to an end in 1988, but not before another tour.

E *I have spoken at length with Paddy Nash about her years in association with you and NYC. Rather than duplicate things, would you like to let her take over at this point?*

P I think that would be an excellent idea! But I must make mention of Karen Grylls. Karen was the obvious person to take over NYC. She had studied choral conducting and vocal production in America and had achieved a doctorate there. She was young, very able and highly enthusiastic. And with her the choir was to rise to new heights.

RECOLLECTIONS

Paddy Nash QSM, administrator of the
National Youth Choir 1985–89.
Interviewed, January 2009.

Peter and Paddy Nash at their
investiture, Government House.

E *Paddy, you became administrator of the
National Youth Choir in 1985 after Colin
Brown retired from the position. Had you
met Peter before?*

PN Yes, briefly, in my time as manager of
the Wellington Youth Orchestra. The
Orpheus Choir was to sing with the
orchestra in a concert at Mana near
Porirua. It was quite amusing, actually,
as Peter and the conductor of the orchestra Bill Southgate (now Sir
William) were worried about how many people could be seated on the
stage. They solved the problem in an unusual way by lying down on
the floor one after the other. They were able to calculate the width of
the stage by multiplying the sum of their individual heights and the
numbers of moves they had to make from one side to the other. Quite
ingenious, really!

E *Were you full-time as administrator of National Youth Choir?*

PN No, it was four days a week only, with no assistant for the first year.
The choir office was in the Department of Education building in
Wellington, which – being close to the cathedral – was handy for
Peter to call in regularly for meetings. My job was to make all the
arrangements for the various courses, to be at the courses and to
arrange the overseas tours. I also had to liaise with choir contacts in
the centres we were to visit, in order to arrange billeting, venues and
publicity. I was given an assistant in 1986, however.

E *What a mammoth task.*

PN Yes. It would have been impossible without Peter's administrative
experience. We quickly established a sound, collegial working
partnership.

E *I understand that there were some problems with the choir when you took over.*

PN The tour to take part in the Australian Youth Festival, held in Melbourne, was on my plate when I arrived, but fairly quickly it became apparent that the organisation on the Australian side was having difficulties, and eventually the tour was cancelled.

Some singers who had been on the 1982 tour may have felt that things were now less stimulating. There had been some criticism earlier in the year of the repertoire that Peter was choosing for the choir. It was likened to 'Auckland University choral programming'. As a result of this, Peter offered to resign from the conductorship of the choir. Now, I had been at the very first concert that NYC gave, and had been amazed at the standard he achieved in only a week with a new choir. Having been so closely involved in 1985, for whatever my opinion was worth, I was acutely aware that Peter should continue with the choir.

The difficult issue of biculturalism was rising at that time – the lack of Māori and Polynesian singers in the choir, and the need to introduce more Māori and Polynesian music to the repertoire. Peter did try to achieve this by commissioning a work from David Farquhar, *Waiata Maori*, but this work was not really successful and this area really was not Peter's forte. It had also been suggested that some more light-hearted repertoire should be introduced. Peter had actually already ordered some songs by Rutter, so he was doing his best.

Fortunately, his letter of resignation was not accepted by the trustees.

E *Bearing in mind that this was a choir of students and young adults, were there any problems with discipline that Peter had to contend with? I imagine that could have been quite a tricky age combination to manage.*

PN I found the singers to be very well-behaved and self-regulating – they had fun, but they obeyed the rules. However, just before the second tour in 1988, Peter wrote a long list of rules for attendance and behaviour on the tour which each singer was expected to sign. We felt this was heavy-handed and would create ill feeling so it was decided to handle things differently. Peter's reason for this was to avoid some problems that had arisen on the first tour. A few singers took off on a sightseeing trip in free time. Others missed a pre-concert rehearsal so were forbidden to sing in the concert. And someone missed a plane to Cologne, arriving a day late.

The National Youth Choir of New Zealand in Peter's garden, Waikanae, 1988.
Courtesy of Choirs Aotearoa New Zealand Trust.

It was easier for us to manage the choir this time as it was smaller than in 1982. We had only one coach and one management team. There had been two coaches and two lots of choir management for the previous tour, which must have been rather unwieldy.

To achieve the smaller choir for the tour it had been decided to have two choirs in New Zealand – Choir A (the touring choir) and Choir B, which would rehearse as usual and give concerts in New Zealand.

E   *Did this produce any sense of elitism?*

PN There were mixed feelings, but we tried to give Choir B something appealing. For example, Choir A rehearsed in January one year and sang the Lloyd Webber Requiem in the Wellington Festival of the Arts. Choir B sang *Messiah* in Nelson in May.

E   *It must have been difficult for you to manage two courses held to rehearse each of the choirs.*

PN It wasn't always easy, I must admit. I remember a situation in 1987 when the course for Choir A was in Dunedin. The weather was frightful and we had a problem getting there. Peter and I were late getting to the course because of it. Added to that, Peter was jet-lagged having just come back from a trip to England, and a group of singers arrived late because of the weather. We were meant to be recorded for TV but that fell through at the last minute, meaning that we lost some high-profile publicity.

There was another very difficult issue for Peter to deal with. Just prior to this some singers had been in the Mobil Song Quest and one of them, Paul Whelan, won it. As part of his prize he was offered a recital in Salt Lake City, which coincided with part of the tour in England. Paul wanted to join the choir halfway through the tour, but Peter decided that it wasn't fair to the others and he had to leave the course straight away. A tough decision to have to make, but Peter had very strong principles and felt that it wasn't right for one person to be dealt with on a different basis from others in the choir. This did cause unhappiness in the choir, but it just had to be accepted.

Following straight on from that was the course in New Plymouth for Choir B. We all bent over backwards to make that course a success. Peter told that choir that he would be happy to take them on the tour if necessary. That was excellent psychology for those singers, but it also put singers in Choir A on their mettle – they could be replaced if necessary.

E   *You went on the 1988 tour, didn't you?*

PN   Yes – it was a fantastic experience, but exhausting. We had a marvellous farewell concert in Auckland, where people had to be turned away because of a full auditorium. We were to have gone first to Germany for a few days of recovery from the trip, but earlier in the year the High Commissioner in London had given a strong recommendation that we should take part in the very important Llangollen Eisteddfod. So we went first to Royal Holloway College in London where, jet lag or no jet lag, rehearsals quickly took place for the Eisteddfod. Of the five pieces we were to sing there, only one had been rehearsed before we left. Even after these few days Peter was concerned that the choir was still under-rehearsed for this.

The choir sang in two classes: the Youth Class and the Mixed Class. The first category posed a huge problem – because of the late inclusion of this festival in the lineup, a quarter of our singers were over the age limit set by the festival and were not able to sing. The choir was left with only two basses! A few tenors had to learn the bass parts and help out. Amazingly enough our depleted choir was placed second in the Youth Class, and the full choir came second in the Mixed Class! It was a good start to the tour.

After that we left for Germany to give a series of concerts in Freising (near Munich), Salzburg and Vienna, where we sang at the eighteenth international Youth and Music Festival. Almost 2,500 young musicians from all parts of the world gathered in Vienna for this. Our choir was competing with twelve other choirs, all invited, from Europe, Canada, the USA and Great Britain. The festival took place over three days, and the choir gave several concerts and sang Mass on Sunday in two different churches. Prior to the final gathering we had been warned that we had won a prize, and that we would be expected to sing at the final ceremony. But we didn't expect the news that was announced that evening: we had been awarded first place! The joy that we all felt was immense. However, it should be noted that our choir was a little more mature, age-wise, than the others. This meant that the organisers did tend to treat them as teenagers!

Following that emotional time, we left for Budapest for a few days rest, and then on to Pecs, a Hungarian city, for the big Europa Cantat Choral Festival – a non-competitive festival which brought choirs together from all over Europe. Only five non-European choirs were allowed to attend. Choirs sang their own repertoire in concerts in the evening as massed items. They took part in choral workshops for different large-scale works with different conductors. The New Zealand music that our choir sang produced a great deal of interest. Most of that music was unpublished, and Peter noted that New Zealand composers needed to act quickly on getting their works published, if they were to take advantage of such worldwide interest.

The European part of the tour concluded with concerts in Venice and Paris. Then we flew back to England to spend two days at Ely Cathedral, and a week at York replacing the Minster choirs. Peter thought that it would be interesting for the choir to sing some of the sacred music from their concert repertoire in the actual church environment. This wasn't the most popular part of the tour, and Peter later thought it had been a mistake on his part. A very successful concert was given in York as well, followed by a concert in Hereford at the Three Choirs Festival – following in the Dorian Choir's footsteps – then Wells Cathedral, St Paul's Cathedral in London, and finally a recital in King's College, Cambridge.

This was an emotional end to two months of travelling and singing together, not only because of Peter's strong association with King's, but because Sir John Marshall, the choir's founding patron who was to have attended, had died that very day. This was the longest tour that Peter had ever undertaken, but the length was judged to be good sense considering the overall expense of getting there. That the tour was debt-free was thanks to the major sponsors, the financial contributions of the singers, and the enthusiastic work of local committees. The National Youth Choir demonstrated to Europe, England and Europa Cantat that its standards and qualities were at least equal to theirs.

RECOLLECTIONS

Teddy Tahu Rhodes, National Youth Choir; professional opera singer. *Letter, 2010.*

As a former member of the New Zealand National Youth Choir, as it was called in the days when Peter was music director, I had the pleasure of getting to know and admire a man who had an enormous influence on the lives of so many talented young New Zealanders. A bond of not just respect but friendship was forever established with 'Prof' – as he was, and still is, affectionately known by all those who have had the privilege of being part of his choir.

Many of the members of the choir during that time have gone on to have professional careers in music in many different areas, from teaching to performing. Without doubt, my passion for music and singing was established through my days with the choir, and the joy imparted to me by Peter. I now have the privilege of performing internationally as an opera singer. It is quite amazing that all my New Zealand colleagues and friends who have international careers were all in the National Youth Choir. Two of us are currently performing at the Metropolitan Opera House in New York.

I was recently in New Zealand touring with the New Zealand Symphony Orchestra, and the opening concert was in Wellington. Sitting a few rows back from the stage was Peter Godfrey. Twenty years after leaving the choir he was still there to support me. Prof seems to remember each one of us individually – quite incredible as the number of young musicians he has influenced must be endless. It is his caring about each of us that influences us more than anything.

Oliver Drennan, National Youth Choir. *Email, 2009.*

You could always tell those in the National Youth Choir who knew Peter

Godfrey from Auckland University experience: they called him 'Prof'. I have always called him Peter, or used the initials PDHG. I guess this was due to the fact that Peter and my mother had been friends in the UK before they both – for quite different reasons – moved to New Zealand in the late 1950s. Indeed, on arriving first, my mother searched for the 'director of music's house' near St Mary's Cathedral, and having found and assessed it from the outside, told the dean that she felt Mr and Mrs Godfrey's residence would need some serious smartening up before their arrival!

It wasn't until I joined the National Youth Choir in 1980 that I got to know Peter myself. At the beginning of my first audition, he announced that he and David Wood 'will have Oliver with a cup of tea'. Thereafter, I had the immense privilege of singing under Peter in the most wonderful cathedrals and concert halls (not to mention pubs, restaurants, bars, buses and airports), in both New Zealand and in Europe, during the choir's first overseas tour in 1982.

We all know that Peter's standards were high: my continued aversion to poor tuning comes from him. He was also a lot of fun in rehearsal. I recall one occasion when he lambasted us for a lack of attention to detail in a piece with, 'you seem to think backwards'. Immediately he called for us to go to the end of the piece and start to sing it backwards – with his eyes and ears not missing one of the many errors. We sang that page over and over till we got it right, bottom to top. And of course I remember, too, the magical moments when we would sing a piece we knew well, but which was dramatically adjusted by Peter to suit the mood and venue of the day. The choir was his instrument.

For me, there were three human qualities which I recall shining through in Peter's work with the National Youth Choir.

First, was his passion for New Zealand. This most quintessentially 'English' man was an early proponent of New Zealand choral music – at a time when championing it was still outside the norm. The early performances of works by John Ritchie, David Hamilton (while he was still a member of the choir), Jenny McLeod, Jack Body and others, helped set up a tradition that the choir has carried on and developed exponentially since then. He also revelled in the spontaneity of the New Zealand spirit (especially that of its young people) – something which even thirty years later should not be taken for granted. And, while he did not always feel he was the right individual to lead it, he was from the beginning a supporter of the choir's engagement with Māori music and music-making.

Secondly, there was what one could, I think, describe as a fragility. An unhappy choir, a poor performance, any tensions in the workings of the choir's structure, even Auckland's rain, could bring Peter's mood down. Perhaps this gave him an empathy with the racing speed of our emotions as seventeen to twenty-four-year-olds. I was involved in setting up choir forums, after which I sometimes needed to have very delicate discussions with Peter. It was important for him understand the concerns of the singers (rarely to do with him, personally, but which he always took to heart) and to find a path forward. I think these forums were very helpful in maintaining the wonderful 'chemistry' between choir and conductor.

The third quality was Peter's zest for life. The unbounded joy when a letter from Sheila, while we were on tour, told of the artichokes in the garden having sprung; the wicked delight in issuing quiet 'invitations' to a pre-dinner whiskey in his hotel room; the ability to make us all laugh at his complete inability to whistle in tune – these are the things that helped make his enthusiasm for music-making infectious.

The synthesis of all this, therefore, is that Peter is a motivator: he has helped many of us to enjoy ourselves while extending our limits. By touching the lives of a generation of young New Zealand singers and conductors in this way, he has been a seminal force in establishing choral music within the mainstream of New Zealand arts.

David Hamilton, foundation member of the National Youth Choir; composer, teacher and choral conductor. *Interviewed, January 2009.*

D   I first met Peter at university as a student in 1974 when he had just taken over as head of the department. Back then, everybody was expected to sing in one of the two choirs – the University Choral Society or the University Singers. I sang with the Choral Society all through my university days. After singing the Verdi Requiem, combined with the Dorians and the University Singers, I was hooked! The great thing about the University Choral Society was that anyone could sing in it, and people came from all over the university two lunchtimes a week just for the enjoyment of singing. There were about 200 people crammed into a fairly small space. Peter was great with that choir – just the right mix of good humour, bullying, cajoling and knowing how far he could push us, and where he could take us. We did Britten's *War Requiem!* We sang Fauré, Brahms, and the Verdi Requiem twice – the big, solid choral repertoire. It was fabulous. My last choral singing had been at primary school! And another great experience with Peter was singing

Left to right: Guy Jansen, Peter, and Sir David Willcocks.
Courtesy of New Zealand Choral Federation.

the Tallis forty-part motet, *Spem in Alium*, with an amalgamation of choirs. That was a marvellous experience.

E   *David, did you have Peter as a lecturer?*

D   Yes, he took stage one history of music which gave us a complete overview of music from Greek modes through to the end of the 20th century. I had taken sixth and seventh form music through the Correspondence School, and I found this course an excellent way of getting everything in context. It opened me up to other sorts of music. As one would expect, any time Peter touched on church or choral music a real sense of his passion came through.

E   *Did you sing with the University Singers?*

D   Unfortunately my very heavy workload meant I wasn't able to sing in that choir, apart from a short time in my second year which I thoroughly enjoyed. However, in my last year, 1979, the National Youth Choir was formed and, even though I'm not the world's greatest singer and was fairly close to the upper age limit, I applied and was accepted. I think they took anyone who said they were a second bass! I had four wonderful years in National Youth. I was over the age limit for the first tour, but they were fairly flexible at that stage and let foundation members stay on. We stopped at Los Angeles and sang at a number of cathedrals in England. That was a tremendous experience, especially as the choir commissioned a work from me to take on tour – *Stabat Mater*. It was wonderful to hear it performed in such great buildings.

E   *Did you have much input with the performance of your work?*

D   Oh yes. That's another great thing about Peter. He's always been happy to consult with composers about their works, so any comments I made were always accepted.

E   *What did that experience with National Youth Choir give to you, both as a singer and as a composer?*

D   As a singer it was an opportunity to sing in a more specialised group and to experience different repertoire – everything from Renaissance through to Jack Body and David Hamilton, and all sorts of interesting music in between. We sang an interesting work by Chris Norton in the first meeting of the choir. Naturally we were given a lot of sacred music as well. A very special time for me was the performance of Michael Tippett's *A Child of Our Time*, which Sir David Willcocks conducted. It's a wonderful work, but so expensive to mount with its full symphony orchestra accompaniment that I haven't had the chance to sing it again.

That wide breadth of repertoire was important, and something I have always aimed at with my school choirs. And it was an opportunity to perform first-class quality music to a very high standard.

As a composer, it was quite a heady experience to have two of my works performed on the first tour. Peter had already performed works of mine with both the University Singers and the University Choral Society – I wrote a 'Psalm 150' for them with strings. Not one of my greatest efforts, but he was prepared to work on it. The University Singers did *Lux Aeterna* and NYC took it on tour. We actually sang it in Coventry Cathedral in memory of those who had been lost in the Falkland Islands. What an incredible experience that was. So there was Peter's supportiveness for New Zealand music, especially with the Dorian Choir who did several pieces of mine.

E   *Perhaps that grew from the tours with the need to take representative music.*

D   Yes, there was the recognition that that's what the overseas audiences were interested in. But I think he also had an interest in exposing audiences to new and unusual music, as he would often do works from overseas shortly after they had been performed there. I must mention the first performance of *Lux Aeterna* in New Zealand. Peter actually repeated it in the second half. I have to say that it was almost like two different pieces!

E   *Oh dear! But, yes, he would often repeat a contemporary piece in the same concert. He felt that an audience wouldn't necessarily come to grips with such music in one hearing.*

D   That was borne out by another performance of *Lux Aeterna* a few nights later in Hastings, where the audience was very close to the conductor. At one point in the piece Peter heard an elderly woman whisper audibly to her companion, 'That can't possibly be right!' So, hopefully the second performance proved the point! Peter told the story for years after the event.

    All this was very helpful to me as a composer.

E   *There was some dissatisfaction in National Youth Choir that there wasn't enough light music or Māori music. Can you comment on that?*

D   I think many in the choir didn't like the lighter music we sang in the first couple of years. It didn't seem to sit well with that type of choir. We did sing some Māori music. There was a very clever arrangement by Sir William Southgate, which was a good balance of the Māori elements and European choral tradition. I don't think it is always a comfortable mix of cultures, musically speaking, but *The Love Song of Rangipouri*, written for the Dorian Choir by Dr Douglas Mews, presented both Māori and European cultures on their own terms in the same work very successfully. And the piece has lasted in the choral repertoire.

E   *How did Peter relate to the younger singers in National Youth Choir?*

D   Very well. Because he was from a university background he was used to dealing with young people of seventeen and eighteen. And he had young daughters of his own. The first NYC had members of about twelve and thirteen. The original intention of NYC in the early days was to include secondary school students but that changed.

There's a certain formality to Peter, and in some ways a distance, but there's also real genuine warmth once you get to know him. We had to get over that initial hurdle of thinking, 'Should I approach this rather formidable gentleman?'

That first NYC tour gave me many wonderful experiences, and I'm sure that time of singing such interesting repertoire, and watching a fine conductor in action, contributed towards my involvement with choral music in schools. The support that I've always felt from Peter has been very important to me, both at university as a student and later as a composer. Even when he left Auckland he was still interested in performing my pieces. He has a genuine concern that composers are supported, which is incredibly important, because choral music is often at the bottom of the pile for composers. So when he recognised that there was a genuine interest in writing choral music amongst some composers – David Griffiths, Jack Body, Anthony Ritchie, Chris Marshall, Gillian Whitehead and myself, for example – he was incredibly supportive.

E   *It's interesting to look at all these choral composers you have mentioned – they've all sung in one or other of Peter's choirs! How would you sum up Peter's gift to New Zealand music?*

D   It's almost impossible to quantify. It's huge. Not only choral music, but instrumental as well with the Auckland String Players and subsequently the Auckland Symphonia. In terms of choral music it's vast. So much can be traced back to Peter Godfrey. In fact, he has been labelled 'The Father of New Zealand Choral Music'. It's not strictly true, but very nearly! And through National Youth Choir and the Choral Federation, his influence has spread through the whole country. The latter was a really important thing.

Peter showed the world that there are high-class standards down here, and that there are composers worth hearing here as well. I think Peter needs to be recognised for his influence on choral composition in New Zealand as well as choral singing.

11

Wellington Cathedral, 1983–89

E   *Peter, why did you leave Auckland for Wellington? You were a professor of music at the university, you had the Dorian Choir, and you had many friends there. It was a huge shock to a large number of people.*

P   In 1982, after the morning service in Holy Trinity Cathedral, Sheila and I were invited to have coffee with our friends Philip and Trish Yates. I found myself saying, 'I miss church music so much!' Philip surprised me by saying, 'Well, I don't think they have found anyone yet for Wellington Cathedral. Would you be interested in that position? Let me phone my brother-in-law, Richard Prothero – he's acting director of music at the cathedral.' And he did, right then and there. Richard told me that they were to have a meeting with the dean on the following Thursday to discuss an appointment, and suggested that I talk with the dean.

     It just happened that I was going down to Wellington the next day for a National Youth Choir committee meeting. The idea of a move to Wellington became even more attractive as the administration of NYC was centred there, and I had just become director of that choir. So I went to see Dean Thomas. Halfway through the meeting I was offered the job!

E   *What did Sheila think of the move to Wellington?*

P   She didn't ever tell me! But, as always, she was supportive.

I couldn't make the move for some months, as I needed to complete the academic year at Auckland University, so we had eight or nine months to find a home. Every time I came down to Wellington for the monthly National Youth Choir meeting I went house-hunting. I didn't want to live in Wellington because of the wind and difficulty of gardening, so I would hire a car and come out to Waikanae – the best place for gardens, Richard had told me – and other nearby areas to see what I could find. Without success. By the beginning of December I still hadn't found anything. As we'd already decided to leave Auckland on 18 December it was quite frightening.

But … another stroke of good fortune! During the interval of a performance of *Messiah*, the music critic of the *New Zealand Herald*, dear old Lin Saunders, came up to show me an advertisement for a large property in Waikanae. It had an acre of garden and was to be auctioned in a week's time. My friend David Tudhope had a house in Waikanae, so he and my daughter and son-in-law Simon went to see it. They reported back that the garden was lovely but the house was far too small for us. They thought we shouldn't go ahead with the purchase. I had a meeting in Wellington on the following Monday, and was able to drive to Waikanae to see the property. Unfortunately Sheila was tied up with work and couldn't come down with me. I saw what they meant about the house, but I fell in love with the garden and had a strong feeling that it would all work out, somehow.

The next problem was that I just couldn't get down for the sale. Thank goodness David was able to bid on my behalf. Something made me phone him on the day of the auction, and say, 'I think you ought to go up a further $10,000.' The extra amount made the difference, and he was the successful bidder – against my next-door neighbour who was also very interested in the property. I was so lucky!

E   *And Sheila still hadn't seen the place?*

P   No! And she was worried about the house because Rachel didn't like it. But I said to her, 'Well, look, it's got a sweeping drive – and you've always said that you would like a sweeping drive.'

We had bought a property of someone who was deceased, so we were able to move in straight away. We left Auckland three or four days

Peter and Sheila's home in Waikanae, 2007.

after we'd bought it, driving down in our two cars. I must confess to feeling more and more worried about Sheila's reaction as I drove down!

Although she wasn't outspoken about the house when she first saw it, I know that Sheila was quite unhappy, and it seemed as though we couldn't do anything about it at that stage. It really was too small to take all our furniture. However, shortly after we moved, I was given a golden handshake by the university, which enabled us to enlarge the house. Now, who should be the architect but David Tudhope's son-in-law, Philip Porritt! He was a grandson of Sir Arthur Porritt, a recent governor general of New Zealand. Philip did a very good job with the house, creating a most elegant line with the outside appearance.

The cathedral gave us a charming cathedral cottage for our use, a townhouse just up from Wellington, so that I didn't have to travel in for each rehearsal and service (Waikanae was over three-quarters of an hour away). I spent most of my time there, but poor Sheila had to stay in Waikanae supervising the building process. I'm afraid her living conditions were very chaotic for quite some months.

E   *Going back to Auckland, briefly. It may have been quite easy for you to give up your university position and leave all that administrative work. But it must have been very hard for you to leave the Dorians, as it was for them.*

P   They were dreadfully shocked as there had been no warning. I was in a state of shock myself! We did have one last tour together, though,

Peter conducting Wellington Cathedral Choir sopranos.

in January 1983. We sang in various places in the North Island and ended up in Waikanae, where we gave what was to be the first of many concerts in the garden. These were to become very popular much later on. That was how we ended our long time together, the Dorians and me. We had experienced many wonderful things: winning the mixed · choir section of Let the Peoples Sing, several prestigious overseas tours, tours in New Zealand, many very fine concerts, and we made several very good recordings.

I started with the Cathedral Choir in Wellington in early 1983. It was most fortunate that Richard Prothero, the acting director of music, remained as organist, but he eventually left to take over the position of director of music at St James Church, Lower Hutt. And so the cathedral appointed an organ scholar, Katherine Dienes, who became my organ student. She was exceptionally talented and gradually became more and more involved with playing for services.

Incidentally, Katherine went on to make a most distinguished career for herself in England and is now director of music at Guildford Cathedral – the very first woman to be appointed to such a position in that country.

E *How well did the Cathedral Choir sing when you took over?*

P The choir was in pretty good shape although there were quite a few older voices that I felt didn't blend as well as they might. In spite of this, I didn't implement the age-limit rule that we had in Auckland – I really had been too tough there.

E *Did you audition the choir then?*

P I knew that the singers were feeling quite dismayed at the prospect of auditions, so I decided to leave things as they were for a year before holding them. I know how frightening auditions are for people, but they are absolutely essential in order to develop a good choir. They also give me an opportunity to advise people on what they needed to do to improve their contribution to the choir. My policy over auditions changed during the years. Perhaps I mellowed with age! I found myself giving some singers a chance to prove themselves further, by having voice lessons or working on their sight-reading, before presenting themselves for a further audition six months later. This was much more acceptable to them.

A number of Wellington's National Youth Choir singers joined the choir, and some of the older singers realised that it was time for them to leave. With the younger voices coming in, it wasn't long before we had a remarkably good choir, which grew to be quite large. There was also a junior choir, but as I was so busy my daughter Rachel Tipping conducted that. At one stage there were three Godfreys at Wellington Cathedral – four if you count Rachel. My grandsons Nicholas and James sang in the junior choir.

One thing surprised me when I arrived at the cathedral. Before the new building was erected the cathedral had been a 'pro-cathedral' and so was considered to be the parish church of the area. The choir had continued to sing more as a parish choir with the congregation joining in the responses and the psalm; and they also joined in the canticles, which were sung to chants. So the choir really only sang the anthem on its own. More recently they had introduced a weekly Choral Evensong, and once a month there was a Choral Eucharist on Sunday. I really couldn't accept this! We were a cathedral choir and I needed to take on the full cathedral tradition. Dean Thomas supported me in this, and so it wasn't long before we sang two fully choral services every Sunday, the Eucharist and Evensong, and Choral Evensong on

Thursday afternoons. Inevitably there was a little fuss about this at first, but the congregation became used to it, and I think they became quite proud of the choir.

After Thursday's Choral Evensong the choir met for an evening meal before a rehearsal. My dear Sheila was quite magnificent in the way she organised these meals, and even provided a lot of the food which she had cooked in Waikanae and transported to Wellington. On quite a few of these weekly occasions I was already in Wellington with the car, so she would actually walk from Waikanae to Paraparaumu, about nine kilometres, and come into Wellington by train, with a short walk from the station to the cathedral – carrying the food as well! Sheila loved walking but this was quite extraordinary.

I was dismayed to find that the Advent carol service was not being sung at the cathedral, and so introduced it in my first year there. Oh dear – this created an awful fuss because it was an annual service at St Peter's, Willis Street, where Geoffrey Coker conducted the choir, and he was very upset with me for starting it at the cathedral. He considered this special service to be his 'territory', and that I was treading where I had no right. But I considered that a cathedral should be doing this splendid service and that no one had any right to a specific service. I just had to go ahead, regardless. This is the sort of tough decision that has to be made from time to time, unfortunate though it is.

For both the choir and congregation each Advent carol service was a very special occasion, and they looked forward to it every year. With the choir's candle bearers being the only source of light in the cathedral for much of the service, it was very dramatic and quite inspirational.

The Cathedral Choir became a first-class choir, and my time at Wellington Cathedral was greatly rewarding. I was very moved when the Dean Michael Brown honoured me by appointing me director of music emeritus in 2002.

RECOLLECTIONS

Richard Prothero, assistant and acting director of music, Wellington Cathedral. *Interviewed, 6 January 2009.*

E   *Richard, I believe that you were involved in the appointment of the new director of music for Wellington Cathedral.*

R   Yes. I was on the vestry at the time and had been Stanley Jackson's assistant for many years. After his retirement we put together a programme of international advertisements, but were rather dismayed when it got a very limited response. The comment was made several times, 'If only we could find another Peter Godfrey.'

We were at the point of letting it all rest for a while when I received a phone call from Peter in Auckland asking if we had filled the position. I assumed that he was going to suggest a young protégé, only to hear him say that he had been to a morning service at Holy Trinity Cathedral with Sheila, and after it he had turned to Sheila and said, 'This is what I really want to do.' The next thing I heard Peter say was, 'Would you be interested in having me if I apply for the position?' Well, of course, I nearly dropped the phone in astonishment! However, I was in a slightly difficult position as we were looking for someone in their late twenties. So I went back to the vestry and, after talking about it at great length, we realised what a great thing it would be for music in Wellington if we had Peter Godfrey at the cathedral. And even if it was only for ten, even five years, it would be worth it.

I phoned Peter to discover that he had more or less changed his mind. He and Sheila loved Auckland. They had many friends there, they had a weekend home up at Whangaparāoa that they loved; they were great gardeners and had heard that Wellington was a terrible place for gardens. Clutching at straws, I found myself saying, 'Well, if you were to come to Wellington, all the gardeners live at Waikanae, because it's a gardener's paradise.'

That rather changed things! And then, when we were on the verge of making the appointment, Peter dropped in the small fact that he wouldn't be available for some months as he had to complete the academic year at Auckland University. The cathedral was so anxious to have Peter that they accepted the situation, and asked me to take over as acting director of music in the interim, which I did. Looking back on it, I don't know how I coped as I had a very big and responsible day job as well as a young family. However, I took it on and did the best I could. I enjoyed it immensely and the choir and I had a lot of fun.

E   *Was it difficult handing over when Peter eventually arrived?*

R   I knew that I was in an interim situation, but I was delighted to be appointed assistant director of music. For many years I did most of the organ playing. Occasionally Peter would play the last hymn and the concluding voluntary. He would do this for about three weeks until something intervened, such as a Youth Choir trip, where he would be away for weeks at a time, and I would be back playing again as well as rehearsing and conducting the choir from the console halfway up that high wall!

Peter's playing was immaculate, like everything he does, and he had quite a wide repertoire. But Peter didn't see himself as a concert organist – he was a choral man. Just before the Godfreys came to Wellington in 1981, Sheila took an opportunity to point out that we shouldn't expect a lot from his organ playing.

E   *What was the feeling in the choir when they knew that Peter had been appointed? His reputation is quite daunting and people are usually quite nervous of him!*

R   Generally speaking the choir was alarmed, and rightly so. The choir was in effect an all-comers choir at that time with no age restrictions, and we all knew that auditions and age restrictions were a large part of St Mary's Cathedral's great success all those years ago.

E   *How did Peter set about changing things when he arrived?*

R   It was only a year or two before his arrival that we had started singing cathedral-type services. The canticles were always sung to Anglican chants, and the responses were always ferial responses. There would be four hymns, and we would sing an anthem from the *Church Anthem Book*. The previous director of music, Stanley Jackson, had recently introduced some settings of the canticles – Stanford in B Flat and Walmisley in D Minor, for example. But it was something of a battle to introduce that type of music, both with the clergy and the congregation. The latter had always sung the Magnificat and the Nunc Dimittis, and rather endured the anthem! Someone made the comment that if the choir sang all three by itself you virtually had three anthems, and nobody wanted that. Stanley got over that problem to a certain extent, in the last two years or so, by introducing a mid-week Choral Evensong.

This all changed with Peter, though. I think his changes were accepted because of his background and his reputation, and he spoke with real authority. And I suppose the cathedral realised that he would still be in great demand elsewhere if they didn't accept what he wanted. Peter had the courage of his convictions, and was uncompromising in how he thought things ought to be. He had that magic way about him, which swept people along. So it wasn't long before all the services were cathedral-type services.

Peter arrived in time for the beginning of the academic year in 1981. Prior to this I had worked with him only at RSCM festivals, and at times when he had been invited as guest conductor for an Orpheus performance of *Messiah* and I was playing the organ for it. It wasn't enough for me to get a real taste for working with him on a regular basis. So I was anxious to establish for myself what his magic touch was. I discovered that it was a preoccupation with singing in tune.

Prior to that, none of us had really thought too much about intonation. Yes, you had to sing the right notes, but with Peter came the process of actually tuning a note and making leading notes and thirds a little sharper. At the beginning of choir practice, in the earlier days, he would sometimes spend an inordinate amount of time making us sing in tune, and listen to ourselves very carefully. If there was a secret to his magic, that was it – listening to yourself and to the whole choir. The other things were diction and the blending of voices.

I don't remember Peter paying much attention to breathing. Somehow it just happened. I'm not suggesting that the choir didn't breathe in the right places, but somehow he didn't need to spend a lot of time on that.

Peter wasn't a technical singing teacher in terms of voice production. He explained what he wanted, demonstrated it, and got it. But he didn't know how to teach it. His great asset was his own voice which was so beautiful – relaxed and utterly musical.

He was uncompromising about getting what he wanted, and lost some people as a result. The Wellington Cathedral Choir improved, though, to international standard, and it was Peter who achieved that, single-handed. He got the initial sound quite quickly – he always did, even if it was just an RSCM festival event – and he built up the repertoire quite quickly as well. He was horrified at the very few service settings in the choir library. Early on he went through the library and pulled out two copies – one for himself and one for me. He would tell me what we would be singing so that I knew what I had to learn. It was all part of lifting the standard. He wouldn't allow himself to relax – ever – even to the extent of making enemies of a few people who were, themselves, uncompromising, and who weren't prepared to put up with Peter's rehearsal style and demands, particularly over things like attendance and punctuality.

As the organist, I found that he would often put me in very demanding situations quite unexpectedly. In those days the choir was always played in by the organist. So after the bells finished ringing, I would improvise while the choir came in, and Peter would expect me to conclude in the key of the Introit. There was an intercom between Peter and the organ console, and sometimes Peter would arrive at his desk and say, 'Richard, we'll put this up a semitone.' And so, within just a few bars I would be expected to arrive in the new key. Not always easy! Or, as the hymn was being announced, he would say, 'I think we'll have this down a semitone.' I can remember complaining to him at the end of a service on one occasion, and his reaction was, 'Well – you're a cathedral organist!' Fair enough!

After that first year he brought in annual auditions. So at the end of the academic year the choir actually disbanded, and a chart went up on the noticeboard where people were to sign for an audition time.

E *That must have been very scary for them.*

R It was terrifying! I've seen people who were good musicians and could sing extremely well in the choir, but were not able to cope with sight-singing on their own. And yet there's no better way to do it. Peter tried to conduct the auditions very systematically so that everyone had to do the same things. And this included singing a song of their own choice.

E *Goodness – that never happened in my time!*

R He would set a strict time limit, and I was the scribe while he conducted the audition. It included a general interview, which gave the chorister the opportunity to discuss anything they wished to. That could be very revealing. All sorts of things emerged from the auditions, including some voices that Peter didn't know people actually had! It was quite amusing, really. Everyone would come in with some sort of excuse as to why they were not singing at their best – just getting over a cold, very tired, and so on. As a result of the audition a singer was either accepted, or accepted with tags – such as needing voice lessons, or sight-reading lessons – and you'd be re-auditioned in six months time.

E   *That, also, was quite different from my time – very fair.*

R   It was also quite expedient as the numbers of the choir had been reduced from something like thirty-five down to about twenty-five, and so those borderline people were still needed. Peter's work with the National Youth Choir meant that a number of them joined the Cathedral Choir, which gradually became quite large. We had a number of great singers, some of whom made singing their career at a very high level – Teddy Tahu Rhodes and Sarah Castle, for instance.

There was a junior choir at the cathedral, but Peter was reluctant to be involved with them because of the enormous pressure on his time with National Youth Choir. There were both boys and girls in the junior choir, which was trained by other people. His daughter Rachel Tipping was one of the conductors of the choir. At one stage Peter's two grandsons Nicholas and James Tipping both sang in it. Prior to his arrival the Cathedral Choir had consisted of men and women with about fifteen boys. The boys used to rehearse separately, and also with the adults before the morning service every Sunday.

The Cathedral Choir became quite a family affair. Sheila was a great supporter of Peter and the choir, and always present at the services. On Thursdays the choir would sing Choral Evensong followed by a bowl of soup and a roll. This was followed by choir practice. Sheila was very involved with producing the meal and, later, the meals became almost like banquets. Sheila was the co-ordinator of the roster.

E   *There were times when Peter was in Wellington with the car on a Thursday and Sheila would get to the cathedral walking and by train, while carrying the food!*

R   That's incredible. I was never aware of that. Everyone loved Sheila and Peter had a great ability to make the choir feel like a family. He and Sheila held an annual barbecue for the choir in their lovely garden. We'd all bring our barbecues and there'd be a huge crowd of choir members and their families. It was a great event, and Peter and Sheila both seemed in their element on these occasions.

Another thing Peter did was to take the choir away one January to Napier Cathedral, while their choir was on holiday. He thought it would be good for the choir to live and work together as a group for a week. We were accommodated in a girls boarding school and did our own cooking – there were some spouses who came and helped. We rehearsed every morning in the cathedral but the afternoons were free. We sang Choral Evensong every night, as well as an Epiphany carol service and Sunday choral services. That was a great bonding time. And the choir made several parish visits as well over the years.

Peter did a very lovely thing when I retired from the cathedral. Instead of a retirement gift, Peter decided to establish an organ scholarship in my name, getting people to subscribe to it.

E   *What a lovely idea!*

R   Yes, it really was. He did the same thing at Holy Trinity Cathedral in Auckland after his daughter Belinda died. And excellent organists have resulted from that scholarship. Anyway, in Wellington a sum of $12,000 was raised, adequate for funding a decent scholarship which was linked to a three-year executant organ course at the university. We advertised professionally throughout New Zealand. Katherine Dienes, still at school, was one of the applicants. She passed with flying colours, and was selected as the first recipient of the scholarship. And what an amazing career she has had since – now the first woman director of music in an English cathedral!

Eventually an invitation came to Peter to set up a choral foundation at Trinity College in Melbourne, similar to King's College, Cambridge. Peter was the perfect person to do that, and so his time at Wellington Cathedral came to an end.

I worked with Peter over many years in various capacities, and I have to acknowledge him as being one of the most significant contributors to my career in church music. We have remained good friends over many years.

Professor John Ritchie, composer, conductor and professor emeritus, Canterbury University. *Letter, 2 March 2009.*

Peter Godfrey added a touch of class to the New Zealand choral scene. Not only did he know his subject, but he set new standards of youth performance in the choral field through his musical directorship at the Anglican cathedral in Auckland, his conductorship of the Dorians and, subsequently, the Auckland University Singers. His choirs also sang New Zealand music!

He was a wonderful person to meet and talk to. His neatly clipped

Five generations of Wellington Cathedral directors of music.
Clockwise from back left: Peter Godfrey, Eric Copperwheat,
Richard Prothero, Stanley Jackson and Phil Walsh.

English accent, Cambridge rurality and military bearing were mixed up in a personality which was as engaging as it was self-effacing. What we had done to deserve having him among us I shan't ever work out.

Peter was involved with orchestras too. As a consequence he and I met frequently, exchanged podia on occasions, and had stints of conducting the New Zealand Symphony Orchestra.

Peter became my principal protagonist as a conductor of my choral music. It began when he conducted a stunning performance of *Lord, When the Sense of Thy Sweet Grace* with the Dorian Singers. It was as though he'd written it himself.

This led to other things. He asked for a piece for to be performed in Napier in 1986 at a Three Choirs Festival. It was to commemorate the centennial of the Napier Cathedral, and to recall the terrible earthquake of 1931. The music was laid out for three choirs and organ, and was not easy. Again, a masterful performance resulted.

And the following year, again at PDHG's (Peter's nickname) bidding, I wrote a cantata *Wings of the Morning* for the 50th Anniversary of the Royal New Zealand Air Force. The RNZAF Band and the Wellington Orpheus Choir were to be conducted by Peter with a young tenor soloist. I visited

Wellington to hear its final rehearsal, and the concert that night. Alas, the tenor was indisposed. It was decided at the rehearsal that Peter should sing the tenor's solo part, I should conduct and the show would go on! All I can say is that a minor miracle happened that night: the choir was totally responsive to what I wanted and the band cemented it together. Peter – who, of course, is a brilliant sight-reader – sang with conviction and I discovered it's a lot easier to compose an extended work than it is to conduct it, especially in a dull grey suit.

Peter and I have kept in touch as friends. We met as young men of very different backgrounds, both hyperactive and brimful of artistic energy. Now, as almost-twin octogenarians, we can extract from the past memories of times, places and multifarious musical sounds and occasions sufficient to prompt pleasurable recollection and nostalgic regret of our relative inabilities to hear, see or remember. And we laugh about it!

I can only say, and mean – I thank God for Peter Godfrey.

Judy Berryman, Wellington Cathedral Choir , Orpheus Choir; artistic adviser Orpheus Choir. *Interviewed, February 2009.*

E   *Judy, you are a great friend of Peter's and you've also been very much involved with him musically. When and how did you meet Peter?*

J   I first heard the name Peter Godfrey when I was living in San Diego. I discovered that every Saturday morning on public radio there was a programme called Let the Peoples Sing, which played recordings of the best choirs in the world. One morning we heard this wonderful choir singing the most fabulous music, the like of which I had never heard before – the Auckland Dorian Singers from New Zealand, conducted by Peter Godfrey. We ended up in Wellington for family reasons, so I joined the Cathedral Choir.

At the time, Richard Prothero was acting director of music after Stanley Jackson had left, so the cathedral was looking for a new director of music. One evening when we were rehearsing before an Evensong, we became aware of a man lurking among the pillars and peeking out while we were rehearsing. It was Peter Godfrey! It was obvious that he had been approached about the position. He took over the choir in late January 1983, and took rehearsals for at least a term without holding any auditions. These were held in May. Some people chose not to audition and others were not accepted. By that time he could draw on National Youth Choir, which contributed to the success of the choir.

Peter demanded the best, and homed in on intonation that was ever so slightly wrong. He would get us to do things over and over again. But somehow, in spite of all that, he commanded a great respect from all of us, and there was a great camaraderie in the choir. Every Thursday we'd have Choral Evensong at 5.30 and then we'd have a choir tea – of course we always sang 'Oculi Omnium' first – followed by a two-hour rehearsal. Those choir dinners were a wonderful way of cementing the group together, but Peter was the binding force.

E *The strange thing is that Peter is not really a social animal – he says repeatedly that he is not comfortable with people. But perhaps there are people and there are choir members! What was it that made him that binding force?*

J I think he knows how important the social and pastoral side of a choir is in order to get the best out of the singers. But there's something about Peter which makes you love him, in spite of the things that get on your nerves somewhat. I think every choir member felt special in a way that I've not experienced with any other choir director. You got personal contact with him. You could catch his eye and know that you gave him just what he wanted. And there was that back and forth relationship, individually, which was very important. You felt that your own personal contribution was valued.

Another gift of Peter's was to know exactly how much time should be spent on each thing in a rehearsal. At times he would leave something unfinished knowing that the problem would fix itself next time. He knew exactly how to pace a rehearsal. You weren't left rushing through things at the end that should have been rehearsed in more detail earlier. And in the Cathedral Choir where we were continually singing new repertoire, he would introduce us to a new work a few weeks earlier. His rehearsals were wonderfully well planned. We'd finish on the dot with something lovely that we enjoyed singing. Or he would leave a few minutes at the end to go over something that we hadn't got right, so that we went home feeling pleased with the rehearsal, no matter what had gone on before.

E *What were the main things that Peter gave to the Cathedral Choir?*

J Oh, goodness, there was so much. Stanley Jackson was very good, but we were really just a parish choir before Peter came. From Stanley, I learned about phrasing. But from Peter I learned about phrasing and intonation. Our repertoire increased hugely. And because the dean realised that there needed to be money made available for the choir, Peter was able to build up a large library of music.

E   *How did Peter's style compare with later conductors?*

J   Peter's communication with the choir was much more controlled. I think he felt the music as much as they did, but he didn't conduct with as much physical expression.

E   *Do you think the choir achieved the same level of expression?*

J   I think that, like his communication, the style of performance Peter achieved was pretty much controlled. His focus was on the pure, beautiful English type of sound. Phil Walsh, and later Andrew Cantrill, wanted something richer and warmer, more Italian in sound. Peter knew what he wanted as far as the sound was concerned, but he couldn't convey to the choir how to do it. He didn't know the techniques involved. Phil was not a singer, but conveyed what he wanted from his conducting gestures. Drew had much more voice training and knew how to explain things technically. He got an even better sound than Phil did, although Phil had the legacy of singers from Peter's time. It was interesting to sing with all three conductors.

E   *How would you describe Peter the man?*

J   Basically I think Peter the man is a very different person from Peter the choir trainer. In a choral situation, he's a leader, a commander. But it is never from ego – it comes from the music. In social situations, he is a modest, shy, self-effacing kind of person with not a lot of self-confidence, and he gets quite embarrassed if I say anything complimentary. There is a very soft core to Peter. He can be very kind and caring, and he's meticulous about writing letters or cards of thanks to people for even the tiniest thing – such as a card for his birthday. I wonder how many people know this side of him. Peter can only talk about music, really, because music has been his whole life.

Katherine Dienes-Williams, organ scholar, Wellington Cathedral; organist and master of the choristers, Guildford Cathedral.
Letter, 9 May 2009.

I first met Peter when he came to my school, Samuel Marsden Collegiate, to rehearse the Special Choir, as it was known in those days. We were to sing the ripieno in a performance of Bach's *St Matthew Passion* with the Wellington Orpheus Choir. Peter stood out as being very 'English' – his accent, and his rather formal way of speaking. We were all aware that we were privileged to be rehearsed by him, the director of the world-famous National Youth Choir.

Little did I realise then that I was soon to work closely with Peter as the recipient of the Richard Prothero Organ Scholarship at Wellington Cathedral. Peter became my organ teacher. He was very positive and encouraging, always full of enthusiasm, whilst having very clear and definite ideas – not only of the music he wished to do with the choir, but also what I, as organ scholar, ought to be doing and learning. All this was a life-changing time for me. Without the financial support of the Richard Prothero Scholarship, and Peter's tuition, my life would have been very different. Peter ensured that I 'learned my craft'. He insisted on the highest standards in everything I did.

He spent hours teaching me how to play hymns, psalms, the importance of memorising the texts and music, and to look ahead and watch the conductor. He insisted that I sing in the choir so that I would be aware of what it was like to be conducted as a singer, and so that I could be aware of the planning of rehearsals. He always had a clear idea of what needed to be worked on and how much could be achieved in a given time. One of his great assets was his sense of humour and he was always quick to laugh at his own mistakes.

Peter taught me the basics of conducting and encouraged me to compose for the choir by saying, 'I think you should write an anthem.' I asked him, 'To what text?' He gave me *Jesus, Dulcis Memoria*, which I duly composed, and which has become one of my most often performed compositions. He always made the best of a musical situation and turned it into a learning opportunity. An example of this was the occasion when I was feeling frustrated by the slow pace of a rehearsal taken by another conductor with a different choir, and Peter directed me to write down everything that could have improved the rehearsal.

My time with Peter in Wellington as a young musician was a tremendous preparation for my life as a professional conductor, organist, composer, teacher, and my present role of organist and master of the choristers at Guildford Cathedral. As the first woman to hold this post in the Church of England I am indebted to Peter for his early belief in me and his meticulous training.

An innate musician, Peter drew the best out of people while remaining courteous and God-fearing. People wanted to give of their best for him. He set everything in place for people to surpass themselves in musical performances that were always uplifting, sometimes magical.

12

Orpheus Choir, 1984–91

E   *Peter, you became director of music of the Orpheus Choir in 1984, a large choir of some 177 singers who'd had only one conductor since its foundation thirty-four years earlier – Malcolm Rickard, the person who had helped you come to New Zealand! How did you enjoy working with such a large choir?*

P   It wasn't the first time I had worked with a big choir. I'd had a large choral society at Marlborough when I taught there, and then in Auckland there was the all-comers choir at the university – there were over 200 singers in that choir. And, actually, one of the things I enjoyed most at Marlborough was taking the whole school for singing practice or 'congregaggers'.

If I could digress for a minute: I had been offered the job of director of music at Eton College many years earlier, but I had decided not to accept it because, when I went to a service, none of the boys were singing at all. Maybe it was just a sign of changing times, but I didn't think I could deal with that after Marlborough.

I had come down from Auckland before to conduct the Orpheus Choir, including the previous year when Malcolm was ill. I had no problems with them. But later on there were some difficulties in my relationship with the chairman of the choir. He arrived late for rehearsal one day, so I stopped the choir and waited for him to find his music and the place in it. He never forgave me for that!

E   *That was never a popular technique of yours! Things had become a little run down with Malcolm's illness – how did you find the Orpheus Choir when you took them over?*

P   Choir morale seemed rather low and there was quite a lot of absenteeism. Some singers took extended leave if they didn't like a programme! So I gave them a rehearsal schedule for each performance, which indicated any rehearsals that were compulsory, and made a firm rule that any singer who had missed three rehearsals was not allowed to sing in the following concert. That rule upset several long-standing singers when the rule was applied to them.

     Actually, one of them – Rosemary Collier – told me later that they sat together in the audience in the Old Town Hall, and when Malcolm saw them he said, 'So you're the naughty ones!'

E   *You had an enormous reputation at that stage for achieving superb results, but not always with, shall we say, comfortable methods! And there had always been a certain amount of rivalry between Wellington and Auckland. Did this make things difficult for you?*

P   It didn't worry me …

E   *I'm told that the choir was terrified! They thought that you would audition them as soon as you took over. And they really didn't enjoy having to sing unaccompanied in rehearsals.*

P   Perhaps I could quote from my son-in-law Simon Tipping's book about the Orpheus Choir, where he gives some interesting reactions from choir members. Alan Peart, the president, is recorded here as saying, 'It would have been nice to hear a difficult note occasionally.' And another singer, Janet Marshall remembers my comments from the rehearsals:

     'No, don't play it.'
     'Read it. Is it in your mind?'
     'Go back. Read it.'

     She added that I made them a much more professional choir. Simon's book also quotes a choir newsletter on the improvement in the sight-reading of the singers after eighteen months. 'We sang at sight the first four parts of the *Christmas Oratorio* and never completely came to grief.

Peter with the Orpheus Chamber Choir.

We have learned how to find our place again if we lose it, to re-pitch the notes and carry on. We no longer collapse in complete confusion.' You see, it does pay off in the long run, and they certainly did improve. It made the learning process so much easier and faster. To help with all this, I instigated a six-week-long course of basic theory, taken by Ivan Hill, the deputy conductor, and vocal training, which was taken by a foundation member of the choir, Peggy Roberts. Another thing I did was to introduce a 'singing day' that year – a whole day of singing on a Saturday at the beginning of February. This developed into an annual weekend workshop. There were two reasons for this – it was a very useful time for note-learning, and it served as a great socialising tool, giving people time to get to know each other.

As far as auditions were concerned, Malcolm Rickard had auditioned the choir just before he retired, so I decided to give them a whole year to settle in with me before holding further auditions. I've often wondered why he did go to the trouble of auditioning them then – perhaps he was trying to spare them the ordeal on my arrival! I auditioned 170 singers and accepted 140 back into the choir. It's never an easy thing to tell singers that they must leave, but it's absolutely essential and one just has to do it.

E *Did you miss the unaccompanied repertoire of the smaller choirs that you were used to?*

P Not altogether. National Youth Choir was singing that sort of repertoire, and I had the Wellington Cathedral Choir. The larger accompanied works were not new to me, as in Auckland the Dorians had combined with the University Singers to sing the *War Requiem*, the Verdi Requiem and also Stravinsky's *Symphony of Psalms*.

E *Did the choir continue to sing their usual works or did you introduce changes for them?*

P Yes and no. We had to keep the standard large works in our repertoire – the Beethoven Ninth and the Verdi Requiem, for example – so that they were on hand for national symphony orchestra programming, but one of the first things I decided to change was the almost annual performance of the *St Matthew Passion*. Instead, we did the *St John Passion,* which I always enjoy because of the more vivid action it portrays in the chorus parts. And it has glorious arias. I also introduced some changes in *Messiah* – some of the alternative versions of arias and the faster tempi. I was worried that this might not be received well by the audience, so I made sure that they were prepared for it in the programme notes.

I did tell the committee that it was no longer stylistically acceptable to perform baroque works and early classical period works with large choirs, and they really were off-limits to us. But I felt that the favourites with the audience, *Messiah*, the *St Matthew Passion* and the B Minor Mass in particular, could still stand up to performance by such choirs as Orpheus, and so we kept them in our repertoire.

One year we did Stainer's *Crucifixion* which drew a packed audience, but which didn't go down well with the press. I love the work but some find it rather syrupy. The choir did sing quite a few works in my time with them that they hadn't done before: Holst's *Hymn of Jesus*, Elgar's *Te Deum and Benedictus* and *The Music Makers*, Howells's *Hymnus Paradisi* and the Saint-Saëns Mass for Two Organs. We did Bach's *Christmas Oratorio*, Dvořák's *Requiem*, the Bruckner Mass in E Minor and some New Zealand works, amongst other things. So, yes, we did perform a lot of new repertoire.

Speaking of New Zealand works, there was one occasion when we sang the first performance of a commissioned work from John Ritchie,

Wings of the Morning. This was written for the 50th anniversary of the Royal New Zealand Air Force and we performed it in the Wellington Town Hall with the central band of the air force. Well, the most awful thing happened, the sort of thing one dreads! Poor Philip Hornblow, the tenor soloist, became ill just before the performance. Nobody else knew the music – except me! So I suddenly found myself singing the tenor solo with John Ritchie, who expected to be a member of the audience, conducting the work without rehearsal! It was tough on us both, but it came off remarkably well.

Recognition of Peter's impromptu performance in *Wings of the Morning.*

There was one other dramatic performance that I took part in with the Orpheus Choir during Philip Walsh's time with them. They had just begun a performance of the Brahms *Alto Rhapsody* – in the Wellington Town Hall with the New Zealand Symphony Orchestra and a fine group of soloists – when I noticed that Philip had changed his baton to the left hand and wasn't using his right hand. It was obvious that he was in agony, and he had to leave the stage before they reached the end of the work. I went round to see him in the interval, only to find him in the arms of a doctor. He had dislocated his shoulder! Poor Phil was taken off to hospital, which posed a huge dilemma for the second half performance of the Brahms Requiem. There was nothing for it – I offered to take over. There I was, brown suit and no reading glasses! All went well until I made a rather large gesture and caught my thumb on the music stand. Blood splattered everywhere – I'd gashed it quite badly. One well-equipped member of the orchestra passed me a sticking plaster and so things settled down, but I don't know I managed to put it on in the middle of conducting. What a night! I had ruined Phil's score with all the blood, so I bought him another one later.

E   *That story made its way into the news media all over the world! Management of a large choir with its reliance on orchestral accompaniment and good soloists several times a year is rather like running a small business. This must surely have been a constant pressure?*

P The finances of the Orpheus Choir had suffered considerably in the latter years of Malcolm Rickard, not because of his fault I must add. The choir had built up a very healthy amount of capital over the years, but it became more and more necessary to dip into this fund.

There were two main reasons for this. First, Wellington had several smaller choirs all vying for audiences – Cantoris, the Bach Choir, the Phoenix Choir and then the Tudor Consort. Inevitably, audience sizes dwindled. And perhaps some works became too familiar through repetition over the years – the *St Matthew Passion*, Beethoven's Ninth Symphony, and the Verdi and Brahms Requiems for example.

Secondly, the revenue that used to come from New Zealand Broadcasting had been cut back because of changes to their policy. For many years Broadcasting had allocated slots for regional programmes, but this had been cut and now there was only national programming. This meant that all choirs in the country were competing against each other for broadcast opportunities. So the choir could no longer depend on what had been a valuable source of funds.

And, inadvertently, I contributed to making things even more difficult for them.

Before I became director of Orpheus they had enjoyed a complete monopoly on annual performances of *Messiah*. The large audiences that this always attracted guaranteed them a large profit each year which either built up their capital reserves or compensated for any losses from earlier concerts in the year. The unfairness of this monopoly was made quite clear in a letter from Cantoris. Their conductor, Robert Oliver, was very keen to mount a performance of *Messiah* in baroque style with a small choir and period instruments. Robert had specialised in music from earlier periods and it was only right that he should have the opportunity to do this. Other conductors were adamant that the work should be available to them as well.

I was in rather a difficult position, as by then I was the president of the newly formed New Zealand Choral Federation and very much aware of my responsibilities to all choirs. I didn't believe it was right for any one choir to monopolise a work. There was a musical concern behind this as well. I felt that it was too easy for a work to become predictable and stale when performed every year by the same choir. I remember writing in a programme note for an audience, 'The annual performance of *Messiah* must be kept alive and interesting – even provocative.' That was the time when I introduced some of the alternative tempi, and arias with ornamentations that Handel himself had authorised. So I prevailed upon the Orpheus committee to change their long-standing policy and to perform *Messiah* on alternate years. They were not happy about this because of the financial implications, but eventually agreed somewhat unwillingly.

While I believed that this was only fair, it did result in unfortunate financial consequences for Orpheus. So we had to find other ways of compensating for this.

It became obvious that we needed to cut back on expenses in any way we could. So I suggested that we include some unaccompanied works into our repertoire, even though much of it is not suitable for a large choir. We also decided to try and sing at least two concerts a year with the New Zealand Symphony Orchestra, which didn't cost us anything and paid us for our services.

I was prevailed upon to do *Messiah* with organ accompaniment. Janet Gibbs, one of my first organ students in Auckland, provided us with many wonderful organ accompaniments and occasionally, solo items. However, it went against the grain not to have orchestral accompaniment for *Messiah*, so I actually contributed half my honorarium to help provide for this. Not something one does often!

The first thing we did was to look for sponsorship. This met with success and proved to be very beneficial for the first few years. A finance company, Leadenhall, agreed to become our first sponsors, guaranteeing us $15,000 a year for five years. This was an enormous help and we were most grateful to them.

Another thing I did was to form a chamber choir from members of the larger choir. Quite apart from the musical satisfaction of being able to do the repertoire that I loved so much, I saw it as an opportunity for the chamber choir to give concerts that were inexpensive to put on – no orchestral accompaniment or soloists – and which could help build up the reserves for Orpheus as a whole. I suppose it was rather unfair on the other choirs in the city, but there it was. The nature of the smaller choir attracted other singers in the city, including the local members of National Youth Choir.

The chamber choir gave its first concert in March the following year. They became a very good choir, although I remember them having rather a lot of trouble with one programme which, I have to admit, was very demanding – Schönberg's *Friede auf Erden*, a work by Douglas Mews and *The Christmas Story* by Distler. There was such a lot of chromaticism and dissonance, and so much German for them to learn, that I was not very popular, and in the end we abandoned it. The fact that we weren't able to have regular rehearsals with everyone present made it much more difficult. The concentration of 20th century music in the programme probably wouldn't have attracted much of an audience, anyway. Just one of those things.

E   *You would have become very busy with National Youth Choir once the tour for 1988 was in place. Did this impact on your work with Orpheus at all?*

P   I don't think so – except that I did take a term off in 1987 to prepare for the coming NYC tour. The choir had had a very good deputy conductor, Ivan Hill, but he retired in 1986. So I was very fortunate that my son-in-law Simon Tipping was available to conduct the choir while I was away – he was the conductor of the Phoenix Choir in Wellington. And Marie Brown, a singer in the University Singers from years ago in Auckland, took over as deputy conductor for two years. They both did very well.

What did impact on my conducting was a problem with my right shoulder which had been giving me trouble for quite some time and was getting worse and worse. It had got to the stage where surgery was necessary, and it was carried out after I arrived back from the exploratory tour. It was quite devastating when this was only partly successful. Here I was with all these choirs I loved working with, and I had the responsibility of the tour with NYC the following year. For quite some time I had to resort to just beating time with my left hand as I couldn't use my right shoulder at all. After that I could no longer use a baton as even that was too heavy for me. I learned to conduct with my left hand, and even now I have to alternate frequently between the two hands.

I decided to lighten my conducting load by asking the committee of the Orpheus Choir if they would accept my early retirement. I suggested to them that they appoint a permanent chorus master for the regular work and invite guest conductors. This would also be a help to them during the next year when I would be overseas on tour for some time.

That is what they did. The choir already had a marvellous musician in its ranks: Stuart Douglas, who had sung in the Huddersfield Choral Society, and who'd conducted both school choirs and adult choirs. He joined the choir in 1985 and became acting chorus master when I left with NYC in 1988, Marie Brown continuing as deputy conductor.

All this turned out to be very much for the good, as in 1989 I received an invitation from Melbourne in Australia that I didn't feel I could turn down. This was to help set up a choral foundation at Trinity College Chapel.

E   *I have never known you to say no, Peter!*

P   I had hoped that it would be possible for me to continue with Orpheus as guest conductor – that would have been marvellous as I enjoyed them so much, and it would have been something in place for me when I finally returned from Australia. I was able to keep it all going for a year or so, but it became obvious that it was too difficult for them to plan concerts and rehearsals around my returns to New Zealand, and so I resigned from Orpheus at the beginning of 1991.

However, Phil Walsh – such a brilliant young conductor and organist – had become director of music at the cathedral and he took over Orpheus. He was extremely good with the choir. I was the first person to have both conducting jobs, but it has become almost the status quo now. It's a good thing, actually, as it means that Orpheus knows there will always be an experienced person to take over when the need arises, and the director of music at the cathedral has another source of income.

13

Trinity College, Melbourne, 1989–91

E   *Peter, the two Wellington choirs were not to be your last big challenge. In 1990 you were headhunted to work with a choir outside New Zealand.*

P   I must say the invitation to start a choral foundation at Trinity College, part of the university in Melbourne, came as a complete surprise. The college has rather a lovely chapel and the warden of that time was very keen to be able to provide choral scholarships, one for each member of the choir along the lines of King's, but using women sopranos instead of boys. They would all be undergraduate students.

To set this up he was looking for someone who had been involved in something similar. It so happened that his secretary was Angela Mackie, who had been in the Auckland University Festival Choir that went overseas in 1974. She knew my background and suggested he invite me, which he did.

The idea was that Sheila and I would live in Melbourne during the terms, and return to New Zealand in the vacations, over a period of three years. They made a very generous offer which included paying for me to travel back and forth, Sheila too, and a good flat in the university grounds. It was a very hard decision to make because it meant resigning from the Wellington Cathedral position which had become so important to me.

Peter conducting Trinity College Chapel Choir.

E   *Why did you do it at that stage of your life?*

P   I realised it was time to hand over National Youth Choir to someone younger. Karen Grylls had taken over the Dorian Choir from me in Auckland and done brilliant things with them, so she seemed to be the right person for NYC. As it turned out, she took them to an even higher standard and has been with them until recently. And so one more challenge and the thought of establishing something like King's was very exciting. So there I was – ties cut with all New Zealand choirs except Orpheus, and a new job waiting in what was to me a new country. And at the age of 67!

E   *Was this a totally new choir that you had to start?*

P   They did have a choir, and there'd been one or two good people conducting them over the years. They weren't too bad but the standard did need lifting. It was necessary to start with simpler repertoire and build gradually from that. They still had a way to go when I left, though. We had a very talented organ scholar, Calvin Bowman, which was very helpful. He has gone on to have a wonderfully successful career in Australia. One thing happened in the choir that I have never come across before: people would ask to shift their position because the singer next to them sang sharp, or too loudly or … I found that quite difficult to deal with! I have to say that I found the musicality of Australian students was no match for New Zealanders. There was a lot of good singing, but their sight-reading and choral ingenuity did not compare.

E   *Did you have to spend a lot of your time in administrative work and organising finances?*

Sheila in the early 1990s.

P   No, not really. An immense amount of money was needed to set up a foundation of this nature but a board of trustees was set up to work on fundraising. One of them was Bishop Frank Wood, the former archbishop of Melbourne, whom I had met up with when we stopped over in Melbourne on our way to New Zealand all those years ago.

There was a considerable number of very wealthy people in Melbourne who were approached for financial help, as were graduates of the college. Gradually the funds were established for these scholarships, but not in my time.

E   *Did the choir have many services to sing each week at that stage?*

P   We sang two Sunday services and there was one other weekday service. They were quite popular, and people used to come from outside the university to attend them and to hear the choir. Interestingly, a neighbouring college was trying to do the same thing, which made for an element of healthy competition!

The master was very interested in what was happening and saw it all as being very worthwhile for the college. The choir did improve considerably in my two years with them, but they are a very good choir now. They tour all over the world.

I did become slightly more involved with the university by taking the University Choral Society. This was for students only, and had about 150 singers. I remember us performing the Verdi Requiem in Melbourne Cathedral, the first time I had ever conducted a performance of the work – formerly I had always prepared a choir for another conductor. And we performed other major choral works. Another enjoyable thing I did in Australia was to conduct a summer choral school in Adelaide for university choral societies from all over the country. Again I found that so many of the singers were not interested in sight-reading, expecting their notes to be played for them on the piano while they were learning the music. That was not the way I did things!

I had to cut my time short in Melbourne as Sheila became increasingly unwell. She had developed cancer which was beginning to taking over, and she was missing her home too much at that stage. We were both pleased to return to New Zealand and to our lovely home and garden.

Sadly, Sheila died in 1993.

Peter was devastated by Sheila's death. She had been a wonderful wife to him, supporting him in all his work and caring for all his needs. Not used to coping on his own, he was in a difficult position. Shortly after her death, Peter went to England where he visited family and friends. There he met up with Jane Barnett, a friend and former member of St Mary's Cathedral Choir and the Dorians. They married in the same year. It is sad to record that the marriage was not to last, and Peter and Jane separated in 2009.

14

New Zealand Choral Federation, 1981–2015

E   *Peter, perhaps your major contribution to choral music in this country was the formation of the Choral Federation. Where did the idea come from?*

P   In 1981 I went overseas to see what was going on in the way of choral conducting. I went first to Israel, Germany, and then I had a week in Sweden with the Swedish Radio Choir and their conductor, Eric Ericson. They were spending a week in a lovely castle to the west of Stockholm. He invited me to spend the time with them. I had a marvellous week listening to the rehearsals, and we sat and chatted quite a lot, talking about what was going on in Europe. After that week in Sweden, I returned to England and visited the Loughborough Summer Choral School in Leicestershire. At the same time there was a gathering of international choral conductors and administrators who were working to establish an International Choral Federation. They allowed me to attend their meetings. At the end of it all I realised that I must go back and organise a choral federation in New Zealand.

E   *What did they aim to achieve with the International Choral Federation?*

P   Well, connections between different countries and their music, and to find out what other countries are doing. That's proved to be very important and helpful. They have an annual meeting to which top choirs and their conductors are invited to give performances.

New Zealand Choral Federation's annual performance – Handel's *Israel in Egypt*, Wellington Town Hall, 1995.

E   *What a wonderful idea. So what did you do to start such an organisation in New Zealand?*

P   That was the time when our National Youth Choir had just started, and I was still at Auckland University but planning to shift down to Wellington. So I was terribly busy with very little time to do much about it on my return.

　　I'd like to digress a little here. During my time as professor of music, I became aware of students coming from the various choirs who were showing promise as choral conductors. So I decided to establish a choral conducting course at the university. And a most interesting experience came about as a result. I was away on study leave in 1981, collecting information to help establish this course, when I met and stayed with Eric Ericson, the great name in Swedish choral music. He told me about the course on choral conducting that he had established years ago with another person, when he was head of choral music at the

Swedish Royal Academy of Music.

And who was that person? None other than Mogens Wöldike. You'll remember that he was the man who asked Boris for conducting lessons. He had had to leave Denmark when Germany invaded because he was a Jew. So he went to Sweden and met up with Eric. Their conducting course was responsible for many gifted young choral conductors who went out into the schools, churches and the community and raised the standards of singing to a very high degree. I like to think that the university choral conducting course established something like this in New Zealand. Karen Grylls has taken it much further – choral conducting is now a degree course at Auckland University.

When I had settled in Wellington, I began to discuss the idea of a Choral Federation with various people – Guy Jansen, David Wood and others. It took some time to establish, partly because I was still busy with the National Youth Choir, the Cathedral Choir and the Orpheus Choir. However, the New Zealand Choral Federation started in 1985. There was a lot of enthusiasm for it in Auckland and Wellington, but strangely enough, not very much in Christchurch.

E   *What were the aims of the Choral Federation?*

P   The purpose of it all was to encourage more choral singing in the schools and the communities and to lift the standards of choirs. We held various schools and workshops for conductors and singers where people were taught how to improve their choral singing. An annual weekend workshop was established, which allowed people from smaller choirs to get together and sing larger works with the best conductors. These have been most successful and attract large numbers of singers.

E   *This would have involved a large amount of money, I imagine. How did you set this all up?*

P   In the early stages, through Guy Jansen's work with the Department of Education, we received government support, but this was withdrawn in 2006. By then we were largely self-supporting from subscriptions paid by the choirs. They were levied so much per member of the choir.

E   *Some of the large and older choirs in the country would have been well-established. Were there any problems in getting them to join? For example, the Orpheus Choir in Wellington was in financial trouble at one stage and decided to leave the Choral Federation because of the large annual subscription they were required to pay. What benefits would belonging to the Choral Federation have been for an established and successful choir such as the Orpheus?*

P Well, I think it should be seen that they were supporting other choirs to improve and to grow in numbers. I think that they should have felt responsible for helping to establish this.

E *What sort of choirs can belong to the Choral Federation?*

P Any choir can belong – school and university choirs, church choirs, community choirs. The Big Sing for secondary school choirs has now come under the umbrella of the Choral Federation that runs it annually. That's a huge success. Thousands of young people take part each year in a great number of choirs. The final concert is such an exciting event to attend with a very high standard of singing.

E *There are many students who have loved singing in their school choirs and who have done very well, but who do not go on to sing in choirs after they have left school. Do you think graduate choirs, like the one at Aorere College, might be the answer?*

P Yes, I think they could well be.

E *You are the patron of the NZ Choral Federation, Peter. Are you still actively involved?*

P Not really. Once the federation was firmly established I had to withdraw from involvement as I was so busy with other things. But I am always interested in what they do and try to attend the final concerts of the various activities – the final evening of The Big Sing is always a marvellous occasion.

It's been so interesting to see young choral conductors doing great things in New Zealand, after singing in the various choirs and coming from the conducting courses, not only the university course, but the various courses offered by the New Zealand Choral Federation.

On the occasion of his ninetieth birthday, Peter was celebrated in a special function by the governance board of the Choral Federation. Peter let it be known that he had to miss choir practice at St Michael's, Waikanae, in order to attend.

RECOLLECTIONS

John Rosser, immediate past chair of the New Zealand Choral Federation, founder and musical director of Viva Voce, associate conductor and chorus master of New Zealand Opera, deputy conductor of Auckland University Singers, founder member of National Youth Choir and member of Dorian Choir. *Interviewed, 26 January 2009.*

E   *John, what can you tell me of your experience with the NZ Choral Federation?*

J   Basically the Choral Federation started as an idea that Peter had, which was taken up by Graham Pollock and grew into NZCF. I wasn't really involved until fairly recently when the governance changed and I became chairperson.

My first experience of NZCF was in 1986, its second year. I was one of four young conductors invited to go down to Wellington for one of the first annual general meetings. During the weekend a masterclass for conductors was held with Rod Eichenberger, and we were the guinea pigs. And I took part in Sing Aotearoa on four occasions where singers from all over New Zealand get together with a guest conductor from overseas. One or two guest choirs are invited to perform as well.

Viva Voce became a member of NZCF fairly early on, although I have to confess that I couldn't see great value for chamber choirs to join NZCF back then. I could see why it was useful for choral societies.

E   *Why was that?*

J   It was the kinds of workshops that they ran for choirs then. They seemed to be directed at a fairly low common denominator rather than the more specialised choirs. And the issue of having to pay a fee, and not necessarily see themselves gaining anything from it, did cause resentment in some choirs.

E   *How has the Choral Federation grown to meet the needs of the wide range of singers in New Zealand?*

J   I can't comment on the preceding twenty years or so, but when the new board took over, all four of us were professional conductors – Karen Grylls, Guy Jansen, Richard Madden and myself – there are more now. We appointed an administrative officer, Grant Hutchinson, who was also a choral conductor and terribly passionate about music. He has been enormously helpful. With the knowledge that choirs can never be better than their conductors, we put a lot of effort into training and upskilling conductors. Last year we started choral clinics, which have been very successful.

E   *How do you run those?*

J   We have four international conductors coming out. Each of the four goes to a different area of the country where they give several workshops in weekends in different places. Twenty conductors and about fifty choristers came to the last one.

E   *What a wonderful opportunity for them. Now, tell me about The Big Sing.*

J   This was not originally an NZCF thing, but they took it over. It's a vastly popular and most successful event involving several thousand secondary school students throughout New Zealand. Regional finals are held where choirs are selected to sing in The Big Sing final, which is a major event for them. Their singing reaches an amazingly high standard. It's the next level down from our chamber choirs, and the future of choral singing in this country. As well, we have the Kids Sing for primary and intermediate school students, and the Classic Sing for adult choirs of all types. We are resurrecting Sing Aotearoa, too, by bringing out two international conductors.

E   *So all this wonderful work has developed from Peter's original idea. Amazing. How would you sum up Peter's gift to choral music in New Zealand?*

J   In a nutshell, he has made our choirs, almost single-handedly, a highly respected force in the international choral scene. There were pockets of fine choral work happening in New Zealand before Peter, but there's absolutely no doubt that Peter's influence in Auckland and subsequently Wellington, in National Youth Choir and Choral Federation has been massive. The Choral Federation could have been started by anyone but he had the mana to establish it. I think his real gift is the influence he's had on choral discipline and choir training, which is now flowing on into the next generation of choral conductors.

We take choirs seriously in New Zealand!

David Wood, inaugural national executive chair of the NZ Choral Federation, assistant director of music and concert manager of the National Youth Choir, member of Auckland Dorian Singers.
Email, 18 October 2014.

Peter Godfrey is a taonga of New Zealand academic and performance classical music. He is to New Zealand what Sir David Willcocks was to the United Kingdom: a giant kauri in the country's forest of choral music.

I have been fortunate to have known Peter since his arrival in the country in 1958. I was then a young student at Auckland University working towards a BA and BMus degree. I auditioned successfully for the Auckland Dorian Singers when Peter took over the choir in 1961, and was enriched by his direction for four most satisfying years. My working relationship with Peter began as a tutor and concert manager of the National Youth Choir, continuing until other employment caused my resignation in 1987. I was also involved with Peter in setting up the New Zealand Choral Federation in 1984. Peter was its president, and I was the chairman of the national committee and the Wellington-based executive until my retirement in 1988. My roles of tutor, conductor, administrator and colleague allowed me to observe Peter in all facets of his work.

CHORAL MUSIC: Today, New Zealand is regarded as a foremost choir-performing and choir-promoting country in the world of choral music. Many have contributed to this reputation, but I am in no doubt that Peter is the person primarily responsible through his work with the Auckland Dorian Choir, the University Singers and the New Zealand National Youth Choir. Through his enthusiastic and able leadership he has enriched the lives of thousands of ordinary New Zealanders – who either sang in his choirs or attended their concerts. To the nation he demonstrated that well-trained choirs of amateur musicians – under energetic, skilled conductors – could achieve standards of performance comparable to those by professional musicians. Furthermore, he has encouraged able students and choristers to specialise in choir conducting and singing and arts management.

ADMINISTRATION: Peter firmly believed that choral music in New Zealand must be supported by sound administration and financial systems. He took personal responsibility for ensuring that those who had the administrative and financial direction of his choral groups were given responsibility, authority and acknowledgement. He insisted that all aspects of management, not just musical, were to be carried out properly. The success of such groups as the National Youth Choir of New Zealand and the Orpheus Choir of Wellington under his direction was as much to do with the soundness of the administration and financial systems he had helped to set up, as it was with their quality music performances. Much of this was due to Peter's own leadership.

NEW ZEALAND CHORAL FEDERATION: Peter established the Choral Federation specifically to foster the development of choral music in this country. As a member of the international federation it was his mission do so. NZCF was among the first of its kind in the world of choral music. In spite of his busy work schedule Peter travelled the country widely as its president, to form regional choral bodies and plan conferences and various activities. He conducted sessions, spoke at workshops, attended key meetings and encouraged others to help the new organisation.

Within the space of just a few years the NZCF became arguably the country's strongest and most active and influential nationwide organisation in New Zealand's National Amateur Arts Assembly. Its executive in Wellington met monthly, supporting several regional committees, its own paid administrator, own newsletter, own library, and holding national and regional conferences annually, including the now highly regarded annual Big Sing competitions for secondary school students.

CHORAL COMPOSITION: To my knowledge, more than any other musician of his generation, Peter advanced composition of serious choral music by New Zealand composers, such as David Griffiths, David Hamilton, John and Anthony Ritchie, Douglas Mews, Jack Body and Jenny McLeod. He made sure that wherever possible New Zealand works were included in the programme of the many performances he conducted. One of the strengths of New Zealand choirs taking part in international competitions and concerts overseas is their selection and performance of New Zealand pieces – by Māori and Pacific Islanders as well as pākehā writers. As a consequence, New Zealand choral works feature regularly today throughout the country, including in our schools.

MUSIC EDUCATION: Peter regards singing as a foundational activity and skill in the general curriculum, alongside literacy and numeracy. He sees singing as of immeasurable benefit to a person's mental, physical, emotional, and aesthetic development. 'Singing is good for the lungs, is good for the soul, is good for the development of the ear, is good for social collaboration and society in general, and is good for the development of musicians'.

As head of the faculty of music at the University of Auckland, he made it compulsory for all music performance students to join one or more of the university choirs as part of their course. Research and experience, he argued, showed that choral singing developed a high degree of aural and singing skills. Peter was also the first professor to insist that all instrumental performers under his jurisdiction sing their lines as well as play them.

In addition, he was the first choral conductor in New Zealand to make it desirable, even mandatory in some cases, for members to undertake voice training from a professional singing coach. He became increasingly aware that the formal training of the voice strengthened vocal agility, dynamic range and tonal strength, as well as the vocal ability to sustain demanding rehearsals and performances.

As president, Peter ensured that the NZCF gave priority to The Big Sing, where thousands of teenage students of all ethnicities experienced the discipline of training for many weeks to reach as high a standard as possible. Furthermore, they enjoyed the benefits of working in a team and performing before their singing peers from other schools. Today the regional and national competitions have become for many schools the key musical quality event of the year. These competitions have boosted the quality and quantity of choral music-making in New Zealand secondary school choirs, seen today in the very high standard of the world-ranking New Zealand Secondary Schools Choir.

CHORAL CONDUCTING: Peter was the first head of music at a New Zealand university to offer courses on choral conducting as part of the music degree qualification. As a result of these courses, and the conducting courses he helped organise and run at national and regional choral conferences, a bevy of young, able choral conductors has been trained and motivated to lead the choirs of New Zealand – in primary, intermediate, and secondary schools; tertiary institutions; and community choirs. Some are current leaders in our New Zealand choral scene. Others have made a mark as directors of community musicals and shows. Some have gone on to become well-rounded musicians in other fields – as composers, performers or administrators. All this has been accomplished in the past half century, significantly after the arrival of Peter Godfrey to our country. Much is the outcome of his dedication and quality of his leadership.

15

Retirement and the Kāpiti Choirs, 1992–2012

P Here I was, back in Waikanae, enjoying my home and garden again and … retired!

E *Sheila said quite frequently that she dreaded the time when you retired, as your only interest outside music was the garden.*

P It did seem rather a dismal prospect. I'd never been used to having time on my hands and even though we had an acre of lovely garden, that certainly wasn't going to fill up all my time! The prospect of no more music-making with choirs was really quite unbearable. But, as it happened, it was not to be for long.

By another quirk of fate, my old friend, Paddy Nash, had moved to the area. She knew that life would be impossible for me without a choir of some sort and said, 'Well, we can't have you sitting around all day with nothing to do.' So she discussed this with a friend, Pat Barry, a baritone soloist, and together they told me of their idea to form a choir in the Kāpiti area. The region encompasses three towns, Waikanae, Raumati and Paraparaumu, with a population back then of just under 40,000 people to draw from.

We had a meeting to discuss the feasibility of this and decided to audition people to form a chamber choir of about twenty-five

Peter conducting the Kapiti Chamber Choir in his garden, 2006.

to thirty people. Initially we were looking for good musicians who were competent readers with well-produced voices, but I found that, with the male voices in particular, the people who auditioned were somewhat older than I had envisaged, and I just had to accept that the choir's sound would probably not be what I was used to. In fact, the choir had an age range of twenty to eighty!

E   *It's one thing to form a choir but there are other things to consider. Rehearsal venues, administration, music and financial considerations, for example. How did you manage that?*

P   As far as administration went, Paddy, the obvious person, took on the role of administrator. She was an incredible help to me all the years we worked with the Kapiti Chamber Choir. We decided that rehearsals should be in the geographical middle of the Kāpiti area. Paraparaumu College with its music suite and auditorium seemed a logical place. So we approached Merick Stein, the head of music there, who was pleased to have us use the facilities. That was one problem solved. Then he and the head of community classes, Julie Parsons, suggested that we be considered as a school evening class. And that is what happened. It gave us free use of the hall and remuneration for me. It was an ideal solution at the time.

E   *What was it like for you, conducting a local choir after a lifetime of working at the highest level?*

P   Well, it was rather a shock, I have to confess – very basic stuff for me at first! We started with twenty-one singers with varying degrees of experience and ability. I chose to start with Byrd's four-part Mass, which was perhaps a little unkind of me, and some unaccompanied part songs. I remember one singer confessing to me that in 'Shenandoah' he noticed he was turning from page two to page three when other more competent singers were up to page eight! But they coped, and the Kapiti Chamber Choir quickly became a marvellous team of about thirty-five auditioned singers. The choir developed a great spirit and it wasn't long before we achieved a high standard of performance. For example, we were able to do Mozart's Requiem in 1996 – only four years after the choir began.

Most of our concerts were held in St Paul's Anglican Church, Paraparaumu, where the acoustics were reasonably good, and there was a useful Allen digital organ. But some of the most popular concerts were held in our garden at Waikanae, where people would bring their own garden seats and gather around the choir. After one such concert we were able to donate a considerable sum of money to the National Youth Choir for its tour to Australia.

Our repertoire over the years grew to be very wide with a mixture of shorter unaccompanied music and larger works. I was very fortunate to have such excellent musicians as Ellen Barrett and Barbara King as our rehearsal pianists and accompanists, while Peter Averi provided superb organ accompaniments. From time to time we really required an orchestral to accompany us, so a group of players would be put together, many of them from the Wellington Chamber Orchestra but some of them local. Fauré's and Mozart's Requiems, Bach's Magnificat and the *St John Passion*, were such occasions amongst other great works.

Really, the choir became a fine choral instrument remarkably quickly.

E   *You also conducted the Kapiti Chorale.*

P   Yes. This was a choir that had begun in 1983 as a small chamber choir with Lois McNeill as their conductor. When I 'retired' to Waikanae in 1992, Lois and I worked together to form a community choir to sing *Messiah*. The Kapiti Chamber Choir and the Kapiti Chorale were the mainstay of the large choir but it attracted a lot of other singers as well. It was a great success. As a result I organised a community choir every two years or so to sing the large choral works, such as Bach's *St Matthew Passion* and Verdi's *Requiem*. These were always popular.

When Lois's health failed in 1994, I was asked to attend a meeting with the committee of the Kapiti Chorale, following which I was appointed as their new conductor. I decided that the nature of the choir should be quite different from the chamber choir. So it became an all-comers un-auditioned choir of up to a hundred singers, some of whom came from as far away as Wellington! This choir allowed people who loved listening to the great choral works the opportunity to sing them. A lot of the singers didn't read music, so it was quite amazing what they coped with. They were very enthusiastic and dedicated to doing their best. I found myself rehearsing them in a different manner – more light-hearted, making them laugh, and trying to keep things fun for them so that they enjoyed their singing. Singers who moved from the chorale to the chamber choir say that I didn't encourage them in the same sort of way. I suppose they were right. I feel that the chamber choir was working in a more professional way – getting things really right, singing in tune, watching the beat and all the important things of good choir singing – whereas I wouldn't fuss too much about that with the big choir. From time to time for large works, both choirs would sing together, requiring a larger auditorium, especially when we had orchestral accompaniment. We were fortunate in being able to use the auditorium at El Rancho, the Christian holiday camp in Waikanae, where we had some marvellous performances.

These two choirs were very satisfying for me and gave me plenty to do with rehearsals, programmes to plan, soloists to organise and sometimes an orchestra to rehearse. But inevitably, when I noticed that I was beginning to make some mistakes, the time came for me to retire from conducting them. I left the chorale in 2004 and the chamber choir in 2006. It was a terrific wrench but I still had the St Michael's Anglican Choir in Waikanae to keep me going. I was delighted when the Kapiti Chorale asked me to be the choir's patron, and then made me a life member in 2008. I still go to both choirs' concerts and look forward to them.

E   *You mentioned the choir at St Michael's, Waikanae. After all your work with cathedral choirs this seemed to be an unusual step for you to take.*

Kapiti Chorale performing *Elijah* at El Rancho, Waikanae, 1997.

P It was sometime in the late 1990s that I was approached by Norman
Purdie to start a choir at St Michael's Anglican Church to sing
Evensong there once a month. I said that I would be interested if I
could audition all the singers. That was not acceptable to Norman as
he knew of several people who were keen to join who had little singing
experience. Richard Prothero accepted the project and worked with
the choir for two years. When he decided to leave, Norman asked me
if I could help find someone to take over. I had no success with this, so
I offered to help them out for the rest of the year. This was in 2002. I
enjoyed working with them and getting back to church music so much
that I decided I would continue with them. When I took over, the
choir had difficulty with sight-reading and had not had much variety
of music. With persistence, they improved little by little and soon sang
different music at each month's service – a full cathedral Evensong with
an Introit, a setting of the responses, a psalm, the canticles, an anthem
and hymns. It was a lot of music for them to learn. But they became
sufficiently good to sing occasional services at Wellington Cathedral
when the Cathedral Choir was away. Those were very special occasions
for us all. I remained as their conductor until 2012, when I knew it was
time to give up – I was ninety and ready for a rest. I had really enjoyed
working with the choir, although I know I was a bit tough on them

at times, especially the poor sopranos! And I loved selecting the music each month. It was marvellous to be involved with church music once again. The choir has been most generous in keeping me on as a second tenor – so here I am, still with a choir at the age of ninety-three!

I didn't 'retire' to the Kāpiti Coast quite as planned, but it has been a rich and fulfilling time here, and I have made a huge number of friends.

And he never stops. When Peter moved to a retirement village in Waikanae at the age of eighty-seven, he established the Parkwood Singers, which he still conducts. In Anthony Dreaver's book on the Kapiti Chamber Choir, Ten Years' Singing, *Peter sums up what it is about choirs that he loves.*

I have been involved with choirs for over seventy years. That makes me wonder how many people have passed through my hands. I have made so many hundreds of friends … nothing else could have done this. As time has passed I have become more aware of the social aspect of belonging to a choir, and being involved with you all in the Kapiti Chamber Choir has made me even more aware of this aspect.

Most of us know from involvement in sports how much we rely on each other's support – and the very same thing happens in a choir, but the reliance can last for a considerably longer period. However, singing in a choir does not need the competitive element, although the challenge of not letting the side down is always with us. We may not compete against another choir, but we do have an audience whom we have to win over. Therefore, each choir member plays a very important part, singing the right notes, in tune, with the correct words at the precise moment. Discipline is a highly important feature – without it you so easily let the side down. Personal responsibility is therefore a strong feature of being in a choir if it is to be a good one. Each of us needs to realise how important each of us is and how much everyone else in the choir relies on you…

… I really appreciate the continued opportunity of working with choirs on the Kāpiti Coast. Many times I have set off from home on a Monday or Thursday evening, feeling too stressed or depressed, but once I am with you all, sampling the joys of making music again, I soon become elated and full of vigour. So long as you are dedicated and show your dedication then I am truly happy.

Many of us have had ten years singing together … years of struggle, frustration, but also of the very greatest satisfaction. We are very lucky to be able to sample all of this, young and old. Don't let it stop.

St Michael's Church Choir at Wellington Cathedral.

Ten Years' Singing also records the criteria Peter used on choosing programmes for the choir. As audiences, and most likely singers as well, probably never stop to think of the enormous amount of thought and work that goes into a programme, it is worth recording Peter's words here.

Fundamentally, I must choose music which the choir can sing. At the same time, it must be music which our audiences will like. Some music takes time to be fully appreciated, and singers must be encouraged to stick it out.

A plan for the whole year requires a variety of styles and level of difficulty. Both secular and sacred music are needed, with a balance between them. Having said that, it must be admitted that there is more sacred than secular music in the choral field.

The length of pieces must be gauged and balanced. A programme can be committed to just one work – an oratorio or a passion – or may consist of short secular pieces.

The matter of accompaniment must be considered by making use of local players, and by using some accompanists as soloists for variety. A complete programme of choral music would bore some audiences.

You need to find out what other choirs and other musical organisations are planning. The New Zealand Choral Federation has gatherings of conductors and administrators in Wellington in April and October to discuss openly their ideas and plans.

Programmes need a central message, or a group of messages. Inevitably there will be some repeats. From time to time special events may control the selection of music. The Kapiti Chamber Choir has given several concerts in our garden in autumn where I chose works centred on flowers, birds and bees, weather and so on. ...

It is important to promote music by New Zealand. It was not until I was invited in 1972 to take the University of Auckland Festival Choir to the International Universities' Festival in New York that I really began to seek out works by composers from all around this country. This was an eye-opener and, indeed, helped to stimulate our composers to write more. The choir now rarely presents a concert without some music by New Zealanders, and has also commissioned new works.

It is essential for the choir to break new ground. I seek out composers associated with a particular year – their birth or death – and this can stimulate us to try works that may not have been performed before, or

Peter holding his Kapiti Chorale life membership, with Ellen Barrett & Peter Averi.

for some time. Another factor governing a choir's repertoire is the availability of scores. Contact with other choirs is one way to locate scores. But New Zealand is one of the few countries with a national lending library scheme, centred at the National Library in Wellington. In England I remember that each singer bought their own music for a programme.

RECOLLECTIONS

Gordon Dickson, chair of Kapiti Chamber Choir.
Letter, March 2002.

When the Kapiti Chamber Choir was formed in the early 1990s I seem to remember that there was a debate in the community about the role of excellence. Some felt that it was more important to encourage participation. I know this was debated in schools, where some said that it was more important to have children simply participating in sport rather than have them competing against each other.

Right from the first moments of our first rehearsal, held in a prefabricated building at the far end of Paraparaumu College, it was obvious that, although we were a bunch of raw recruits, Peter was in pursuit of excellence. He must have wondered at times whether it was all worth it. But he persevered.

My abiding memories of our more than ten years together are: his mastery of the choral repertoire (particularly European sacred music and the Anglican tradition), his unparalleled musicianship, and that drive for excellence. This was characterised by such dry statements as, 'Getting better', and the occasional, 'Quite good', which we learned was high praise!

While I suspect that he is uncomfortable with accolades, there is no doubt that we were in awe of him. We were very aware that Peter was the doyen of choral conductors in New Zealand and that he had an international reputation. We knew that he had conducted some of New Zealand's finest choirs, including the National Youth Choir, the Dorians and, of course, King's College, Cambridge, during an exchange visit.

A vivid memory remains with me from an earlier occasion when I sang in a choir in Wanganui in the mid 1970s. We were invited to sing Bach's *St Matthew Passion* with the Orpheus Choir. It was to be recorded in Wellington for Radio New Zealand's Concert Programme. We were pretty nervous about this and, indeed, close to shock when we arrived at the final rehearsal and found that the conductor of the Orpheus Choir, Malcolm Rickard, had been taken ill and Peter Godfrey had been flown down from Auckland to take his place, for both the rehearsal and the performance.

I will always remember the first notes of the orchestral introduction and the look on Peter's face. The orchestra began with a series of very discordant notes, which after some time resolved into 'Happy Birthday' – somebody in the orchestra knew that it was his birthday! There was a round of applause and everyone had a good laugh which helped to relieve our nerves. Later in the rehearsal I was astonished when Peter looked across at someone in the orchestra and shouted, 'You're playing E flat – it should be E natural!' That was the beginning of my acquaintance with that remarkable ear of his.

Adrian Aldridge, St Michael's Church Choir.
Letter, November 2008.

I will never forget a telephone conversation Peter and I had a couple of years ago. He would always insist on my sending him a draft of the new service sheet before it was printed. He would phone me the following morning and tell me all the places where I had made mistakes. On this particular morning he phoned me up and in a rather loud voice said: 'I can't find anything wrong!' To which I quietly replied, 'You sound rather disappointed, Peter.' 'I am!' he retorted.

Belinda, my wife, and I have enjoyed our time in the choir. It is hard

A standing ovation at the end of Peter's last concert
with the Kapiti Chamber Choir, 2006.

work and one has to put up with quite a bit of hassle, but one realises that Peter is only striving for improvement, and his heart is in the right place, even if his methods seem rather tough at times. We have certainly made tremendous advances since the early days of the choir, and the great fellowship, together with the personal satisfaction that one gets from taking part in great services – such as the ones in Wellington Cathedral – make it all worthwhile. Recently I was in the bank when Peter came in. I noticed that after talking to me, he wandered around the bank talking to all the young tellers. Later in the day when we spoke by phone he mentioned that we had met earlier, but could not remember where. When I mentioned the bank, he said: 'Ah! All those lovely ladies'. Peter must be one of the only people who goes to the bank purely to admire and talk to the ladies!

Pam Sinclair, St Michael's Church Choir.
Letter, March 2009.

I first met Peter when I was looking for people who would be willing to show their gardens to the public. We were raising money to pay off the final debt on a small Anglican church – St Michael's and All Angels at Waikanae Beach – where Peter now plays the organ each Sunday morning, and where he conducts weekly practices and monthly Choral Evensongs with the parish choir.

I saw this man on his knees, weeding. He wore gardening clothes and a rather battered old hat. Was this Professor Godfrey? Or was it someone working in his garden?

It was Peter. One of the great loves of his life has been gardening. There are beautiful, long-established trees in Peter's garden – amongst them an enormous copper beech and an equally large native rimu – walnut trees, glorious rhododendrons, and a vast number of fruit trees. Peter once told me he grew twenty-four different fruits – grapefruit and lemons, tomatoes, apples, tamarillos, olives, currants, and some not found commonly in New Zealand gardens, such as papaya, loquat (originally from China and Japan), babaco (originally from Ecuador) and two beautiful, small mulberry trees. He has a great love of roses, which he tends with great care, and which reward him with wonderful blooms for much of the year. One small circular rose garden is in memory of his daughter Belinda, who died after a car accident many years ago.

Most choir members have sampled fruits and vegetables from his garden – there is often a box of lettuces to 'help ourselves' from as members leave choir practice. Some of us have been invited to pick beans, grapefruit or mulberries from his garden too.

Wonderful choir concerts have been held in Peter's garden over the years. And choirs, including our own church choir, have held pot-luck lunches at his home at the end of each year, always with the sung grace 'Oculi Omnium' accompanied by birdsong.

Peter has introduced our parish choir members to the most beautiful church music, and even though one section has often earned the term 'ruddy altos' – I'm one of them – we've greatly appreciated his perseverance. It has been a unique experience, which has given us and the congregation an enormous amount of enjoyment over the many years.

Laury Sinclair, chair of St Michael's Church Choir.
Letter, March 2009.

The enigma of Peter Godfrey might be summed up as follows:

As music director he always chooses beautiful music, and expects his choir to sing it exactly as the composer intended. He is driven to excel. Indeed, all he ever wants is perfection, which leads to vigorous, challenging rehearsals in order to achieve the required standard of performance. The air can be punctuated with:

'Why do I have to bully you?'

'You're flat!'

'Stop! I won't show you how. Look at it and work it out yourselves.'

'It's the ruddy altos (or sopranos) again!'

'Get rid of those agricultural vowels. It's tooooo, not tew!'

'Look at me. How else can you know when to come in (or slow down).'

And this on psalm chanting: 'Is the important word *and* or *the?* No! Then sing it as you would say it!'

Of course, the advice is always sound, but it depends on how it is conveyed at times! However, his winning smile reappears quickly to smooth things down. Afterwards, away from the podium, he becomes the 'other' Peter – charming, generous-hearted, sharing walnuts, silver beet and lettuces from his garden, and caring deeply about his choir members, even if he can't always remember their names these days. It's no wonder that he generates total loyalty and admiration from his choristers.

From *Ten Years' Singing*, more of Peter's rehearsal comments:

ON THE CHOIR'S INITIAL RENDITION OF A GODFREY WORK:
'One or two notes crept in without the composer's permission.'

ON PERFORMING A PARRY WORK (OR MENDELSSOHN, OR GIBBONS)
'I want you to do it this way. I called Parry earlier, and he says it's okay.'

A RARE MOMENT OF PRAISE:
'That's better – well done! I just have to be rude to you and then you get it right.'

ON BREATHING FOR LONG PHRASES:
'You may take a breath – at the beginning.'

ON 'CLEARING' NOTES:
'You've got to come off. You can't just go on dribbling.'

ON A MISSED ENTRY:
'Ah, hmm! Are there any tenors here tonight?'

SOPRANOS:
'Sopranos, that top A was terrible. Everybody will just get up and walk out.'

'You got a beat ahead – you fast women!'

ALTOS:
'Too many and too bossy.'
'Altos, your F sharp is flat – again …'

TENORS:
'Dear tenors. They are beyond criticism because they are so few and therefore so valuable.'

BASSES:
'Gentlemen and the basses …'

16

Peter Averi

Peter Averi ONZM has a musical career that spans more than sixty years as an organist, broadcaster, adjudicator, concert manager of the New Zealand Symphony Orchestra, artistic director of Wellington City Opera and music director of the television programme *Praise Be*. *Interviewed, 3 December 2008.*

E   *Do you remember when you first met or became aware of Peter Godfrey? And what were your impressions of this new man from England?*

PA   I first became aware of him when I worked for New Zealand Broadcasting. I knew about this man Godfrey, who'd recently come out to Auckland from England, as his reputation had been very quickly established. I can still remember hearing a live church broadcast of Matins in early 1959. I was bowled over by the sound of this choir without knowing which one it was. I became aware that it was St Mary's Cathedral Choir, Auckland, and that Peter had brought about this amazing change in the very short time he had been with the choir. It was quite electrifying, as prior to Peter it had been more like an average parish choir. So my first acquaintance with him was at a distance.

I met with him some time later in the recording studio. In those days various university lecturers who were conductors of some standing in this country would be invited to conduct a studio broadcast with the National Orchestra, as it was called in those days. They would be given two days to rehearse before the recording session. Peter was one of them. I do remember that orchestras were not all that happy with choral conductors because the discipline is totally different. Choral conductors seem to need to shout and roar at their singers, and when Peter did that, he ran up against them. So I think that from an orchestral point of view, he was not a conductor they looked forward to working with – but he was not alone in that respect.

People who conduct choirs need to work with an orchestra using a different approach.

I have a letter from Peter, written after he came down to conduct the National Orchestra in December 1975, in which he says, 'I think that there was a definite "end of term" feeling amongst the members, and although their attitude was terrific in performance and recording, I felt now and then that I wasn't in complete control. This may well have been my fault. As it happens I was tired at the time, and I have found so often that this is reflected in both choirs and orchestras when one is working under pressure. However, it was a great experience for me and one which was a considerable challenge, the sort of thing I need from time to time.' I wrote back to assure him that this was typical of that time of year when the orchestra was a bit jaded, anyway.

E   *This is interesting, but hardly surprising. He was always on the verge of exhaustion and would have been back from the first Dorian tour only a relatively short time. You have an enormous connection with Peter as an organ accompanist. When did that start?*

PA   My first engagement with him was a concert with the Dorian Singers in 1967, when they performed a Bach cantata with the Auckland Symphonia. I played continuo on a small chamber organ. And I played for him again early in 1969 in Holy Trinity – by then the new organ was installed.

Rehearsals with Peter were always interesting, although, I have to say it, somewhat exhausting! I very quickly became aware of his focus on perfect intonation. He would stop a thousand times to get a chord right. I have learned in more recent years that he has a loss of hearing in his right ear from his rifle shooting days. I'm always amazed at his acuteness of perception of pitch – it is so remarkably good. He might rant and rave at the sopranos or the altos (the sopranos came in for the most flak!) but it was always the vertical structure of the chord that he was so insistent on.

E   *Those bright thirds and leading notes!*

PA   Yes! His insistence on the highest standards of intonation, tone and diction raised the Dorian Choir to an unprecedented level.

E   *How do you think he achieved those standards so quickly?*

PA   To a large extent it was from his own exceptional abilities as a musician. But he came at a time when, with a few notable exceptions,the standard of choral music in this country was not very high. New Zealanders were in considerable awe of overseas musicians as there was not the same level of training available here. So a highly skilled musician from England was held in very high regard.

E   *So the choral scene was rather like a parched desert ready to soak up all that it could?*

PA   Exactly. I think Peter was the pioneer for getting New Zealand choral music on a higher plane. Of course there was Maxwell Fernie in Wellington, who established his own strong choral style after some years at Westminster Cathedral in London. Interestingly enough, he returned to New Zealand almost at the same time Peter arrived here. But Max was a more private person, and although he was very highly regarded, especially in Wellington, he didn't have as wide-reaching an influence. Max would never schedule a concert; he would say, 'We'll give a concert when we are ready', and so his choir gave relatively few performances. Peter's choirs worked to a schedule of concerts for which they had to be ready, and they gave concerts throughout the North Island, and even in Christchurch.

     One important thing that I learned from Peter, and which has stood me in good stead all my accompanying life, was: Be Ready. He instilled in his singers that once they finished one thing, they got their music ready for the next. I enjoyed that organisation and discipline.

E   *How did you find his rehearsals as an accompanist?*

PA   You couldn't rest in a rehearsal with Peter because of his focus and drive. There was no time wasted. I had to be thinking ahead of him all the time so as to be ready after a stop. He was his own taskmaster – he set standards and didn't compromise. Relating to more recent times, I found it rather unnerving in rehearsals when he would stop and go back. An organist has to find the stops used previously and Peter would not always give time for this! I thought 'Peter, you're an organist yourself – I thought you'd know better!'

E   *Your next involvement with Peter was in Wellington Cathedral. You were manager of the New Zealand Symphony Orchestra then, and well established in Wellington. What was the standard of the Wellington Cathedral Choir before he took it over?*

PA   It was in better shape than Auckland had been. Stanley Jackson had built the choir up to a very good level, but it was a great coup to get Peter for the position.

I played for services at the cathedral quite regularly from 1982 on. I remember one occasion, not too long after Peter had arrived there, when another conductor stood in for him. Things were not going well as choirs don't often like having different conductors, and can give them a hard time. Finally it got too much for him and he stormed out, arriving up at the organ loft exclaiming (not to me, but to God, I think), 'I'm sick and tired of this Godfrey worship!' So it obviously hadn't taken long for Peter's magic to have woven its spell on the choir!

I loved my times with him at the cathedral because we did all the great repertoire and he took such wonderful care over the psalms, often doing them unaccompanied. And I remember being so impressed by Sheila's devoted support of Peter. At this time they were living in Waikanae, nearly an hour's drive from Wellington in those days, but they did also have the cathedral cottage. Sheila would spend some time in Waikanae, but would go into the cottage with supplies of food, baking and cooking utensils.

I'm sure Peter would acknowledge that she probably made some sacrifice to her own career and accepted a lesser role in order to enable him to fulfil his.

E   *He was a lucky man. Sheila was an exceptionally supportive wife. Peter's reputation is quite daunting for many singers and they can be in fear and trembling before he arrives. Would the Cathedral Choir have felt this way?*

PA   Probably so, I think. But I'll tell you where the fear and trembling really was – it was with the Orpheus Choir. When Malcolm Rickard retired, remember that he was the one who was responsible for bringing Peter out to New Zealand in the first place, it was logical to suggest that Peter took over. Peter's reputation for demanding exactness in all aspects of singing in a choir had gone before him, and there were some who thought that the position should have been advertised.

My association with Peter continued, because I became the artistic manager for Orpheus for five years after I retired. I would find soloists, arrange orchestras and such things. We developed quite a close relationship at that time.

E   *What are your observations of the reactions of singers in Orpheus to his style of rehearsing?*

PA I've seen two quite distinct reactions. One, when people are in absolute awe of him and very apprehensive of making a mistake, the other, when people get a bit ruffled and somewhat hurt by his cutting remarks. But his bark was worse than his bite. He would never insult anyone personally – he was too much of an English gentleman for that. And he had the humility to apologise if he had gone too far. But he was merciless when it came to people being a bit slack.

To my huge surprise, after achieving such high levels of choral singing, Peter took on the Kapiti Chorale when he retired to Waikanae. This was a rather low-key ad hoc group of enthusiasts, and nothing like what he had been used to working with at that stage. It was quite remarkable to see that he was prepared to be patient enough with non-readers, and his chivvying was always couched with a bit of laughter. He would literally attack the sopranos – they always got the worst of it – for singing flat in those descending passages and on those repeated notes. He would go on and on about it. But what happened when he said, 'You b— sopranos' was that the other sections would laugh, which took the heat out of it.

E   *Peter has an amazing missionary zeal for a musician who has worked with outstanding choirs of international calibre. He did a similar thing with the all-comers choir at Auckland University and was very proud of it. There were no auditions and many of the singers were non-readers. It is the same with the church choir of St Michael's in Waikanae to this day. It's a part of Peter that is quite remarkable, isn't it?*

PA   Yes, he's enabled people to be participants in a way in which perhaps they would never otherwise have had a chance. The Kapiti Chorale grew from a little group up to a hundred people who wanted to sing with him. It probably would be 200 except that such a large number of people was prohibited by fire regulations. I did admire his patience with this choir.

It was a different thing with the Kapiti Chamber Choir. They were auditioned and he was pretty choosy about members.

The extent of repertoire that he achieved with the Kāpiti choirs was quite amazing! He did Elgar's *The Music Makers*, which was no mean feat. And the Verdi Requiem which was highly successful. There was Britten's *Rejoice in the Lamb*, the Duruflé Requiem, Dvořák's Mass in D, the Fauré Requiem, *Messiah*, of course, the Haydn *Nelson Mass* and *The Seasons*, Constant Lambert's *The Rio Grande*, the Mozart Requiem, the Rheinberger *Stabat Mater*, Rubbra's *Missa in Honorem Sancti Dominici*, to name just some of the larger works. And there were many concerts of a wide variety of the short choral pieces, many of them unaccompanied.

One of the highlights for me was a performance of the Brahms *German Requiem*, which did not involve the organ at all. We knew that the venue was difficult, and didn't have an organ. Peter heard that Brahms had arranged the accompaniment for two pianos and managed to get copies. The score was quite beautiful because the piano parts were typically Brahmsian, and Judith Wheeler and I thoroughly enjoyed playing it. It really was a great performance.

My time with Peter and the two Kāpiti choirs was an absolute delight. We did so much of the cathedral repertoire – *Harwood in A Flat*, the Stanford settings of the canticles, Parry's *I was Glad* – all those wonderful pieces which are an organist's joy to play. One thing in particular I will always treasure. After every performance Peter would always send me a card of thanks. It reflects his refined English qualities and etiquette.

E   *What do you think the 'X' factor is with Peter?*

PA   That's an interesting question. I think that the name of Peter Godfrey stands for quality of performance. Nothing is left to chance, not even processions in and out, which are always rehearsed. He was meticulous about detail. You dared not show up at a rehearsal without your 2B pencil. There was never any doubt that scores should be marked efficiently to prevent the same mistake from happening again.

E   *Did you know that Peter went to a local shop and bought several packets of 2B pencils? When a choir member went to buy a pencil the reply was, 'I'm sorry, we've run out of them. Professor Godfrey has bought them all.'*

PA   What a character. Another thing in a Godfrey rehearsal was putting up your hand if you made a mistake. That was to show that you knew what you'd done wrong and he wouldn't have to stop the choir. It became such a habit that it wasn't unknown for someone to put their hand up in a performance! His rehearsals were amazingly well organised. Everything was covered efficiently, there was no waste of time and the rehearsal would finish exactly on time.

Peter has extraordinary energy. The other day he told me that he had been mowing his lawns at 7.30 in the morning before coming to take part in a rehearsal with the Kapiti Chorale for their twentieth-anniversary concert! At the age of eighty-six! This means that if a man of his age pushes himself to such an extent then we've got to push ourselves, too!

There's something intangible about some great conductors that just makes things work. Peter is one of those. And people trust him – they feel that they are in safe hands. He has a special charisma. As well there were those little things that showed the human side of him – the parcelled up lettuces from his garden, the bags of lemons from his tree, and so on.

Peter has always been most supportive of me and encouraged me in my playing. My experience with him has always been fun. I regard him as a close friend.

17

Family: the Tippings

PETER AND SHEILA HAD FOUR CHILDREN: BELINDA (DECEASED), RACHEL, Diana and Patricia, and three grandsons. Rachel Tipping was interviewed on their behalf, along with her husband, Simon Tipping. Both are steeped in music: Rachel is a former music teacher and organiser of The Big Sing, and Simon was conductor of the Phoenix Choir and associate professor of music at Massey University, Wellington. *Interviewed, 21 May 2009.*

E *What are your earliest memories of your father, Rachel?*

R To be honest, I don't have many. I remember Dad conducting services in Marlborough College Chapel, and concerts in Marlborough. I was aware that he was involved in a lot of music and, because he had an important position as director of music at the college, we didn't see much of him. The only memory I have of him at home was him building crates in preparation for our journey to New Zealand when I was nine.

S I find that quite amazing, as Peter totally disavows any practical ability and insists that he cannot follow instructions!

R I think he had some fairly practical college boys working with him. Anyway, the crates all held together, even the one he built for his grand piano. And when we settled in Auckland, he built kitset beds and bedroom furniture for us four girls. So he had to be able to read and follow instructions for that!

E *You were nine when you came to Auckland, Rachel. How did this great change in your life affect you?*

R I don't remember having any particular emotional reaction. It was all a bit of an adventure for us children, really. But I do remember looking up into my mother's face as we left Southampton and seeing a look of utter grief, which I have never forgotten. She knew that she might never see her parents again. In fact, her mother died before she returned to England in 1963.

   Mum always put Dad and his career first, at great cost to her own life and career as a doctor. We children came second, and her career third. I think a great many successful men must owe their careers to the loyal support of their wives.

S I'm sure it is possible for a balanced family life to be maintained when a parent is a highly successful person, but it must depend on the focus of the individual parent. I think that, even where high-achieving people are able to achieve a happy and stable family life, there is a price to pay, and it is somebody else who pays it.

R In Dad's case, his career was his focus, and consequently ours as well. Everything revolved round that. But Mum was a dedicated mother and, even though she would be working all day and usually out taking a clinic in the evening, she would be up at five, baking to fill the tins, sewing clothes, getting the housework done, and getting us all breakfasted and off to school. I really don't know how she did it.

E *How did having a prominent father impact on you as a child?*

R I felt quite proud of being Peter Godfrey's daughter, and I think that I basked in a little bit of reflected glory. I used to be given the job of selling programmes for the String Players' concerts, and at the end I would present the flowers. There's a funny story that I must tell here. At one Sunday afternoon concert Lin Saunders, the critic for the *New Zealand Herald*, arrived and held out his hand saying, '*Herald.*' I replied to him, 'I'm sorry, but we don't sell the paper here.' I was so embarrassed later on when I realised what he meant!

E *Did he get his free programme?*

R I don't think so! As it isn't in Dad's nature to give praise, we girls tended to feel that we weren't doing well enough. It rather undermined our confidence. And because Dad was so busy, we really didn't see much of him. He was out lecturing during the day, conducting just about every night and busy with cathedral services on Sundays.

E *Peter's quick rise to success in Auckland was quite phenomenal with the Cathedral Choir, String Players and the Dorian Singers. Why do you think he took on so many things, and what made him so successful?*

R Dad's a high achiever, and he has always had amazing energy. But I think the main reason is that he has an obsessive nature. He is compelled to take up whatever challenge is offering. In fact, he thrives on and needs constant challenges.

Dad always takes a very efficient rehearsal – with orchestras as well as choirs. I'm sure this comes from his preoccupation with time. Everybody has to be on time. And he likes to organise each day to a schedule. His rehearsals were always meticulously planned. I remember in the cathedral days that Matins had to start on the dot of 10am when the choir would process out from the choir vestry. And throughout his life he's always looked at his watch – it's turned to the inside of his wrist, and he's always looking at it, even when staying with us on holiday at Akaroa!

S I have a story about Peter's utter dislike of anyone being late. It was when National Youth Choir was rehearsing in Christchurch. The four tutors went off to the Botanical Gardens for a lunch and returned a little late. Peter stopped the rehearsal and said, 'And where have you people been?' We tutors didn't have any work to do – we just had to sit in on the rehearsal and listen. But it wasn't good enough for Peter! And it went on all afternoon. If anyone was late for an entry it was, 'You're late, so-and-so – don't be like those people over there.' The joke did wear thin as the afternoon went on!

E *I suppose, when you think of it, his working life has been fragmented between lectures, rehearsals, organ lessons, concerts, meals … and he would always have to be mindful of time. So what was it like for you, Simon, to marry into the Godfrey family?*

S It was stimulating in that there was a lot going on and a lot of music, which was wonderful for me. Sheila was always very kind and thoughtful and Peter seemed to approve of me –

R   Well, you were a musician!

S   – so there weren't any difficulties at all.

E   *Was your own style of choral conducting and training influenced by Peter?*

S   No, my choral experiences came from my time as a chorister in England, in Christchurch singing under Bob Field-Dodgson, and then later I had some professional conducting lessons in Christchurch and London. So I really only had occasional times to observe him from behind.

E   *Was it difficult for you when Peter came to live and work in Wellington?*

S   Yes! I was quite established in Wellington and recognised as a choral conductor with my own choir, the Phoenix Choir. It was doing quite well – and would have continued to get better – but having someone like that who was at the top of the profession was quite disconcerting for me, especially as Peter tended not to comment on any of our concerts. In fact at that stage I gave up the choir, started to do a lot more orchestral conducting, and threw myself into the development of the Wellington Polytechnic Conservatorium.

On the other hand, looking on the positive side, Peter did quite consciously involve me in several professional things of some standing. He asked me to be on the committee to set up the Choral Federation, which was interesting. And he asked me to conduct the Orpheus Choir for four or five months when he went overseas. I was very pleased to be asked. But my main problem was that he is a very hard act to follow. I always tried to avoid any comparison with him – you always come off second best when compared to the top person! Later Peter did involve me in writing reviews of his Kāpiti choir concerts, which I always found a bit of a balancing act, I have to admit! I didn't whitewash the concerts, and whatever I wrote, Peter was always fine with it. He said, 'Just say what you think – they need to hear how it was.'

E   *What are the qualities you most admire in Peter?*

R   I admire his choral skills and his energy. I can't imagine how he keeps going. And I admire the way he works with amateurs. He's just as happy working with amateurs as he is with more professional singers, and I think that that is a really good side of him. But he still expects very high standards from them. I remember his criteria for auditioning people for his choirs. The number one thing was enthusiasm. His singers had to have enthusiasm. The ability to read music came next, together with intelligence, but having a good voice wasn't the most important thing.

S   I have to say that sometimes, when I've watched Peter conducting, I've wondered how he achieves what he does. I've sung in his amateur choirs a few times, and as I watch him I find myself thinking, 'Well there's not actually a lot going on here.' There's that constant emphasis on perfect intonation, and his conducting conveys the beat but not the shape of the music.

E   *So how does he get those wonderful results with all his choirs?*

S   I think it is a combined thing. Peter loves the music and he loves what he does – the choirs love him and the music – and these things, together with his unique charisma, unlock the music and allow it to flow.

RECOLLECTIONS

Nicholas Tipping, Peter's eldest grandson, is a jazz musician and former head of the jazz department of the New Zealand School of Music.
Email, 2009.

One of my earliest memories of Grandpa is him telling me that your tummy button is where you put in your salt and pepper when you have dinner! And whenever I was up at their bach with him he made me toddle down to the garden every evening to get the mint for his evening drink!

I think that I must have pleased him very much by being a chorister at Wellington Cathedral while he was director of music. I sang there for five years. Grandpa was obviously very proud of having me in the choir, and photos were taken of me, one with Grandpa and one with the retiring Bishop. I sang the 'Once in Royal David's

Peter with chorister grandsons James and Nicholas.

229

City' solo at my last two Nine Lessons services, the first time in Grandpa's last year and the second in Phil Walsh's first year. By accident, Grandpa gave me a note a semitone too high to start on, and responded to signals from members of the senior choir who had perfect pitch (which he didn't have) by signing to me that I needed to bring the melody down a semitone – it sounded terrible! Phil Walsh gave me the right note next year.

Grandpa would always say 'Amen' very loudly at the appropriate moments during the services, and he would give me a little wink when I walked past him in the services in the cathedral.

Dad and I went to a concert once when the Orpheus Choir was performing *Wings of the Morning* by John Ritchie, accompanied by the Air Force Brass Band. Grandpa was supposed to be conducting it, but the tenor soloist (Phil Hornblow) was sick, so Grandpa sang his part while John Ritchie conducted it. Dad and I were on the edges of our seats – the tenor part went very high, and Grandpa is not a tenor!

As children we used to love climbing the trees and playing cricket in the Waikanae garden, though Grandpa used to complain about the damage we did to his garden! We always used to go up there on Christmas Day and Granny would cook a huge Christmas dinner for the family – and then we would stay the night, and she would look after us on Boxing Day so that Mum and Dad could get our house and car packed up ready to go down to Akaroa.

Grandpa and Granny used to record all *The Muppets* programmes for us so that we could watch them when we went to stay there. They also had a big collection of *Dad's Army*, *The Good Life*, and *Open All Hours* programmes, which led to my love of British comedy.

That was where the family tradition started of singing 'Oculi Omnium' every Christmas. We boys started off singing the treble part, but I later learnt to sing any of the parts that were needed. Our family has carried on the tradition of singing it at all family occasions, and we can even do it without Grandpa's help now!

Once when I was singing in the Wellington Youth Choir, we did a combined concert with the Kapiti Chorale (it may have been the chamber choir). Grandpa was conducting, and I knew he was going to try to catch me out for not watching for an entry. So I memorised the entire piece and watched him every second, and he said afterwards 'There was only one person in the entire choir who was watching me for every entry, and that was my grandson.' I got a sympathetic round of applause!

Grandpa used to include me as a very inexperienced percussionist to play timpani in various performances, such as *Messiah* in Kauri Hall with the Kapiti Chorale. He loved my vocal quartet Face Value, and included us as a guest item in one of his Kāpiti choir concerts. He sent me a card afterwards thanking us for our 'magnificent artistry'.

He has always been very supportive of my career, although I am a jazz musician. He came to my final Bachelor's recital, and managed to fall asleep during the fastest and loudest piece! But I really appreciated him coming. Even now he always listens when I'm presenting programmes on Radio NZ Concert, which is very touching. I often write them with him in mind, as someone who doesn't understand anything about jazz.

I have always admired Grandpa as being an amazing musician, both in a practical way (for example being able to hear individual singers getting things wrong), and in a more general way in terms of winning international competitions, and for his dedication to and expertise in choral music.

James Tipping, grandson. *Email, 2009.*

Kym, my wife, and I began our OE and backpacking tour of Europe in 2006 with a trip to Cambridge, where we met up with Grandpa who was there on his last trip. We met him out at the front of King's College before Evensong, where he looked me up and down and made a disparaging comment about my shorts – he was in a jacket and tie. I made some reference to it being a very hot summer's day and I didn't have anything smarter in my rucksack, not realising the significance of his comment until the Provost arrived. We were introduced to her and sat next to her in the service, after which we went back to her garden with Grandpa for a drinks party. How I wished I'd been the one in the jacket and tie!

Later that evening he came back with us for dinner at our cousin Pam's house, where we ended up watching the 2006 World Cup football final. He really enjoyed the whole evening and the game, but managed to fall asleep in front of the TV just as the penalty shoot-out started. One time at Akaroa I really wanted to take him out on the speedboat to show him my water-skiing skills. Not doing a lot of music myself, I wanted him to feel that I was actually capable of something. There didn't seem to be any way to get him from the rocky beach into the boat easily, however, so in the end I tried to piggyback him from the beach through the shallows and into the boat. I only made it about a metre before I had to stop, so in the end he just rolled up his trousers and waded out to the boat. To his credit he came with us for a whole lap of skiing, but I don't think he enjoyed it one bit.

We have lots of lovely memories of Waikanae as we were growing up. It was such a lovely big space for us boys to play cricket in, and one of the best things was that we knew we didn't have to hunt too long for any balls we lost in the garden, as he would have found them while weeding by the next time we came up.

He and Granny used to look after us every Boxing Day for a night or two while Mum and Dad packed for our summer holiday, which was always a highlight. They gave me a red tractor one year for Christmas which was later passed on to Andrew, and Nick his first bike, which I inherited.

One of the highlights of a Waikanae trip was driving to the tip in (or on the tray of) his ute. He always had a tin of hard-boiled sweets in the glove box, which used to disappear rapidly when we were around, particularly while he was out of the ute emptying the tray of its garden rubbish!

In 1987 when I was six, I took part in a school science fair, growing some cabbages and polyanthus from seed. I'm not sure what I was meant to be measuring! After the science fair Grandpa took the plants off our hands and planted them in his fantastic vege garden. At the end of the year he brought down three enormous cabbages to give to the head teacher and my teacher! That was amazing.

Latterly I loved having a tour of his garden with him and discussing things like compost, fruit trees and the different veges that went in at different times of the year. One year when he came down to visit us in Akaroa, where Kym and I had been living for the year, I was proudly able to show him my vege garden, which I had faithfully weeded for the occasion. The poor plants hadn't exactly flourished in the clay soil, and having being buffeted by the coastal winds all spring, but nevertheless he was very tactful in telling me how well I'd done!

Andrew Tipping, grandson. *Email, 2009.*

Grandpa would often ask if I was singing in a choir, and if not, why not! Although I've had only one or two experiences of singing in Grandpa's choirs, I did sing for a year in the Wellington Youth Choir in 1998. One experience during that year was memorable. The choir gave a concert in Paraparaumu, near Waikanae. Nick and I were both singing and Grandpa came to listen. We went to talk to him after the concert. Grandpa didn't recognise me for a few seconds, and didn't even realise that I'd just sung in the concert. I'd had my head shaved, not something he appreciated.

One occasion, when I was studying at Auckland University, I popped in to see him in Waikanae on my way home for a holiday. Grandpa asked me about my lecture timetable. Strange question, I thought, but I told him it was fine, not too busy.

'How about Monday and Wednesday, around lunchtime?' he asked.

'Both free,' I told him.

'That's when the choir rehearses!' I'd been tricked. He had started the choir, and still knew when it rehearsed.

So I decided to go and see Karen Grylls and audition for her choir. As it turned out, the choir was great fun and singing under Karen for the next two and a half years was a fantastic experience. In fact, it sparked my interest in singing again, so I do have Grandpa to thank for that. I joined the chamber choir at my church in London – Holy Trinity, Brompton – where we sang wonderful sacred music.

After our conductor expressed an interest in seeing music from other countries I emailed Grandpa. I was delighted when two large envelopes of New Zealand music, including some of his own compositions, arrived for me in London.

At Christmas 2007, I went with Grandpa to the service of Nine Lessons and Carols at Wellington Cathedral. We sat together in his 'seat' in the choir stalls, next to the choir. It was special for me as I was moving to the United Kingdom a few months later, and I know it was special for him. But there was an embarrassing moment in 'While Shepherds Watched Their Flocks by Night' when he turned to me in one verse, conducting me to make sure I didn't take a breath from one particular line to the next!

As a family, we sing 'Oculi Omnium' at Christmas, and have sung it at each of my brothers' weddings. On one occasion Mum gave us the starting note as usual. I noticed Grandpa pointing upwards. I didn't know what he was meaning until I realised that the bass notes were lower than usual. Grandpa knew that Mum had started us a semitone flat.

I used to see Grandpa at least every six months from 2005–08, while I was living in Wellington after finishing university. I know this for one reason: I would be summoned every time daylight saving either began or ended to change all the clocks in his house! And when I did visit there was usually a short list of technical requests to look into, mostly related to his computer. His requests weren't limited to my visits, though. I would recognise his number on my caller display at work. One time I answered, 'Hello, old boy' – as we call each other. On hearing a long sigh, I asked, 'What's wrong with that bloody machine now?' It was always 'that bloody machine' causing him problems.

One summer, Grandpa asked me to come up to Waikanae to do some waterblasting behind his house, an area of not much more than a metre. I turned on the waterblaster and was saturated in seconds. It was all I could do to stop myself being thrown backwards into the bushes with the power of the water pressure. He had hired an industrial strength machine for a tiny area. Grandpa and technology did not mix well!

The difference between generations was highlighted when my family attended one of Grandpa's garden concerts in 2005. Nick and I had a good chuckle when we read about the 'contemporary' composers in the programme. Only one of these composers was alive at the time and some died back in the 1950s and 60s. But Grandpa has done a great deal to promote and encourage genuine contemporary New Zealand music.

As children we loved going to the beach in the back of Grandpa's ute, trips to the tip, raking leaves and gathering walnuts, climbing the trees in Grandpa's garden – even though we were told off for it, playing cricket using the walnut tree as stumps, hitting balls into his flowers – then trying hard not to stand on them when retrieving the balls, games of 'Kick the Bucket' which would destroy Grandpa's plastic buckets, and watching videos of *The Muppets* and *Dad's Army*.

In more recent years, my visits to Waikanae were spent wandering around his garden, being told about all his flowers and vegetables and when to plant and pick them, and usually fixing the 'bloody machine'. Over lunch we'd talk of my study, work, church and, invariably … singing.

18

Honoured by the Queen and Others, 1978–2008

E   *Peter, you had a surprise phone call from Buckingham Palace in 1978. Would you tell us about that?*

P   Oh yes, that occurred when I was in England as acting director of music at King's College, Cambridge, for a term. Philip Ledger and I exchanged choirs. At first I was sure it was a hoax. A voice on the other end of the phone said, 'This is the Master of the Queen's Household. The Queen would be very pleased if you could come and have lunch with her on Wednesday week.' However, it was no hoax and, along with eight others, I had lunch with the Queen and the Duke of Edinburgh at Buckingham Palace. That was in mid-February 1978.

Peter and Sheila at Buckingham Palace.

I haven't a clue why the Queen asked me to go along, but I understand these lunches are a regular thing now. The Queen and the Duke had obviously been well briefed, and the lunch was a relaxed and informal affair. It was also very highly organised, although not obviously so. For example, during the first two courses the Queen and the Duke spoke to those on their right, and for the third and fourth courses, to those on their left. I sat on the Queen's left. Coffee was later served in the drawing room, and we were discreetly manoeuvred so that some of us spoke to the Duke and some to the Queen.

In March 1978, I returned to the Palace to receive my MBE from the Queen. They really were very special occasions.

OTHER HONOURS

ROYAL SCHOOL OF CHURCH MUSIC

Peter was a special commissioner for the Royal School of Church Music and conducted various courses for the RSCM. In recognition of his work Peter was made a Fellow of the RSCM (FRSCM) in 1973.

AUCKLAND UNIVERSITY

After Peter's resignation from his position as head of the music faculty at Auckland University, he was made professor emeritus in 1982.

THE QUEEN

In 1988 Peter received a CBE award for his services to choral music. This was presented at Government House, Wellington.

LET THE PEOPLES SING

In 1995 Peter was invited to be a member of the panel of the prestigious international competition Let the Peoples Sing, in Canada.

WELLINGTON CATHEDRAL

Peter was appointed director of music emeritus by Dean Michael Brown in March 2002.

NEW ZEALAND ARTS FOUNDATION

In 2005 Peter was honoured with a New Zealand Arts Foundation Icon Award for his services to choral music in New Zealand. This is the highest

The panel for Let the Peoples Sing.

honour that can be awarded outside the New Zealand Government honours system. An Arts Foundation media release said that '... all Icon recipients had one thing in common: their humility and delight in being so honoured by the arts community', and quoted Peter Godfrey: 'I'm aghast. Amazed. I can't believe I've been singled out.'

UPPINGHAM VETERANS RIFLE CLUB

As has been recalled, Peter had a great love of rifle shooting as a young man and passed this on to students at both Uppingham School and Marlborough College. In 2006, during one of his many return visits to England Peter was presented with the following letter from Chris Kelsey of the Uppingham Veterans' Rifle Club.

> It was brought to the attention of the committee at the UVRC AGM at Bisley that without your coaching talents, post-war shooting at Uppingham School could well not have seen any of the successes that it did. Whilst coaching the school team and leading them to their first Bisley success with the Marling in 1948, enthusiasm for the sport was nurtured and still survives

today with the school having produced Ashburton wins, Queen's Prize winners, Great Britain Rifle Team captains and Commonwealth medallists.

Whilst the school team now has to travel significantly further afield than the old full-bore range just outside the boundaries of Uppingham, and the 500 yard firing points used may no longer be on top of old buildings, the attributes of an excellent coach remain the same. From all that has been said I am certain that your organisation, temperament, kind yet enthusiastic approach would yield as much success today as it did when you were guiding the Uppingham School Shooting Team.

You have been described to me as 'The Father of Post-War Uppingham Shooting' and your efforts have shaped the sport in the school, in turn affecting the adult lives of all those in the Uppingham Veterans Rifle Club as we continue to enjoy the sport.

KAPITI CHORALE

At the Kapiti Chorale's 25th anniversary gala concert in November 2008, Peter was honoured with life membership. He had been the music director from 1994 to 2004 and, following that, he became patron and occasional guest conductor. These were the first life memberships awarded by the Kapiti Chorale. At the award presentation Norma McCallum, president of the choir at that time, said: 'We are honoured and delighted to have the encouragement of such eminent musicians who call the Kāpiti Coast home.'

THE DIOCESE OF WELLINGTON

It was the evening of the service of Nine Lessons and Carols at St Michael's Church in Waikanae, Sunday 14 December 2008. The choir had been rehearsed thoroughly and the service had followed the usual pattern until the end of the final collect when the vicar, Rev Henry Resink, changed the usual order of the service, breaking with tradition. Instead of saying the blessing, his words were, 'Peter Godfrey, would you please come up to the altar.' The look on Peter's face was one of complete puzzlement, but he did as he was requested.

Then followed a most moving occasion. Henry took up an official looking document and began to read from it in a solemn voice:

It is my pleasure to commemorate the dedicated service of Professor Peter Godfrey to the Anglican Diocese of Wellington, and indeed the

Province of New Zealand, over many years.

Peter Godfrey is renowned for the vast contribution that he has made to music, particularly church music, since coming to New Zealand in 1958. As lecturer in Music at Auckland University he was, at the same time, Director of Music for Auckland Cathedral from 1958–74, before he became Professor of Music until 1982.

The choirs he has conducted have performed some of the greatest religious works the world has known, such as Handel's *Messiah* and the Requiems of Verdi and Brahms, to New Zealand and international audiences.

Peter's outstanding contribution has been to establish new standards for choral singing in this country, thereby lifting choirs such as the Dorian, the Orpheus, the National Youth Choir and Wellington Cathedral's choir (of which he was Director of Music from 1983–89) to higher performance and status. Part of his legend has been built on making his choirs among the best in the world, and their music – much of it religious – greatly loved, and brought to a wider audience than ever before.

Reaching beyond the elite singers, Peter has also coached all-comers choirs into excellence. His style of coaching, while vigorous and challenging, always aimed at as near to perfection as he could manage. As a result, individual singers pushed their limits to something better than anything they had achieved before in choral teamwork, and they responded with total loyalty and admiration.

An illustration of this may be seen in his work over the past six years with the forty-member Waikanae Parish Choir, which sings Choral Evensong on the third Sunday each month at St Michael and all Angels, and on other special occasions, including services for The Way of the Cross, Easter, Advent and the Nine Lessons and Carols. The choir has also sung, by invitation, at other churches, notably Wellington Cathedral for two services, and the Waikanae Presbyterian Church in 2008. Peter regularly plays the organ at St Michael and all Angels for services including funerals.

With the people of Waikanae Parish, and the many others throughout the Diocese and Province, I celebrate Peter's unique skills, leadership and achievements, and the faithful service he continues to give through his remarkable music ministry.

Henry congratulated Peter and pinned the Bishop's medal on his lapel. The congregation and choir rose to their feet and broke into long and loud applause. Peter stood absolutely still.

As soon as the applause died down, Peter said, 'Can I go now?'

A typical Peter Godfrey response! That was not the end of it. After the organist had concluded the voluntary and Peter was receiving congratulations, he was heard to say, 'It's not good enough. It should never have happened in the Nine Lessons and Carols. Eric Milner-White would be turning in his grave.' A gentle suggestion came that perhaps Eric Milner-White was joining in the celebration (in heaven).

19

Those Who Follow: Rosser, Maskell, Grylls

JOHN ROSSER IS FOUNDER AND MUSICAL DIRECTOR OF VIVA VOCE, associate conductor and chorus master of New Zealand Opera, past chair of the New Zealand Choral Federation and deputy conductor of the Auckland University Singers, a founder member of the National Youth Choir and former member of Dorian Choir. *Interviewed, 26 January 2009.*

E   *John, when did you first meet Peter, and how did he influence you?*

J   I was in the Auckland University Singers for four years from 1979 to 1982. It was a watershed in my life, as I realised I was having more fun than pretty much anything I'd ever done before. I think by this time Peter had come to regard the Singers as his 'baby' – it was a choir he had a special fondness for, and he very much relaxed with us, so it was a wonderful and exciting group to be part of. Peter was away for quite a bit one year and would ask me to take the odd rehearsal for him. He must have seen me waving my arms around in front of smaller groups on tours, essentially mimicking him!

It was the first conducting I'd ever done, but it seemed to go all right.

Around that time a holiday work scheme for tertiary students (similar to the PEP scheme for the unemployed) had been set up by the Labour Department, whereby you could submit a work proposal and, if it was

241

approved, you'd be paid as if doing any normal job. A tremendous initiative and a wonderful way to earn much-needed income during the summer break. Hence a few of us in the Singers devised the idea of forming a small choir to sing a cappella choral music in rest homes and malls through December and January, and in schools during February. It was accepted, and The Summer Singers were born.

For two summers in a row, we assembled at 9 o'clock each morning to warm up and rehearse before giving four half-hour concerts a day over those three months. In a sense, we were possibly New Zealand's first professional choir. Peter helped us choose the fifteen or so singers and put the conductor in place (James Tibbles for the first year and me for the second). It was a wonderful introduction to serious choral singing, and conducting.

E *You were also involved with National Youth Choir. Can we talk about that?*

J I'd only just joined the University Singers in 1979, when brochures appeared around the music department and Peter started talking about this new National Youth Choir. I auditioned and became one of the foundation members. To be there at the beginning of this choir was very exciting. I didn't know the founder, Guy Jansen, at that stage, but thought it a very good decision of his to invite Peter to be principal guest conductor. It was wonderful to meet all these young singers from round the country, and there's no doubt we felt chuffed to have made it into the choir.

E *What were the outstanding things for you in National Youth Choir?*

J The tours – internal and then overseas – were great fun because Peter loved touring. I don't think the NYC came fully into its own until the next 'generation' – the 1988 tour choir that had Teddy Tahu Rhodes, Martin Snell and Paul Whelan in its second basses! When I last counted, about three-quarters of the foundation choir were still involved in music today, either professionally or in some other way.

E *It was a brave thing to create a national choir that could rehearse for only three weeks a year. How did Peter cope with those time restraints?*

J The singers were expected to come knowing their music, so very little time was allotted to note-learning. And there were four tutors who took sectional rehearsals to go over anything that required more detailed attention.

E   *A change in the soprano sound of Peter's choirs seemed to develop over the years. What encouraged him to move away from the treble sound to a more full-blooded tone?*

J   It may have come from hearing choirs overseas when he was on sabbatical, and also from conducting young women at the university who were having singing lessons and had developing solo voices. No doubt he came to enjoy the beauty and fullness of sound they could produce. But even then, although it was mandatory for singers to have singing lessons, the women were reined in somewhat to achieve the blend he wanted. Vibrato was not really encouraged.

E   *You sang in the Dorians, too, didn't you?*

J   Yes, I joined Dorians in 1980 and sang with them for four years. It was a less social choir than the University Singers. We worked hard, had only a five-minute break in the middle and then went home – no meeting together over coffee. The younger ones of us felt a generation gap, and perhaps didn't get the full, immersive experience we'd come to expect from our singing. But it was a great musical education.

I was in Dorians when Peter announced he was leaving. He'd been conducting rather listlessly and looked very out of sorts. Halfway through the rehearsal he made the announcement that he'd decided to retire from Auckland University and take up the position of director of music at Wellington Cathedral. There were several sobs from the first and second rows – sops and altos of course! Peter couldn't handle it and walked away for several minutes.

E   *Yes, I witnessed that reaction on both sides when he had to resign from Holy Trinity Cathedral Choir. How did you find Peter as a conductor?*

J   He had a beautiful style of conducting, and the way he achieved the musical result he wanted was superb. Perhaps his greatest skill was his rehearsal technique. He really made me aware of the importance of preparing and pacing rehearsals – having an awareness of which bars needed real attention, how much time to put into a piece, when to push singers, when to pull back and move on. I never felt bored, but rather constantly challenged as we moved from one piece of music to the next. He had the ability to make every work interesting, and to make you want to sing for him, regardless of the repertoire.

E   *You talk about his beautiful style of conducting. But conducting style has changed quite radically, and in comparison Peter's style is quite metrical with little movement of the arms and hands. He would rely on small movements of the hand and expressions in rehearsal such as 'put it across, chaps' and 'think of the words'.*

J   The more we've become aware of the American style of choral conducting and its teaching, the more we're asked to question the limitations of the 'British' style. But on the whole, Peter's beat produced beautiful singing and line. I do remember, though, that on one occasion when the Singers were on tour in Australia, Peter had been invited to give a lecture on choral conducting at a college. On the way there, obviously a little nervous, he called me up to his seat in the bus and said, 'Tell me what it is that I do. I've never really studied conducting – I just learned at the feet of others.' He had just picked it up from observation. And to a certain extent I did the same, by watching him avidly for several years.

E   *It was like that for us all then – conducting wasn't taught in our formative days. It's interesting that Boris Ord didn't believe in teaching choral conducting, neither did David Willcocks. But Peter now does. And his establishment of the choral conducting course at Auckland University was a brilliant move, wasn't it?*

J   Indeed, even if he wasn't always sure how to teach it! And of course it's vital to be open to other input. A year after Peter left Dorians, UK conductor and composer Andrew Carter came out here for a year and it was fascinating to observe a very different kind of influence on the local choral scene. Andrew taught me the great importance of the choir as an entertainment vehicle. Peter's attitude towards choral music, while immensely passionate, always felt semi-religious, and there was the sense that audiences should want to go to Dorian concerts 'for the good of their souls'.

By the end of Peter's time with Dorians, there were often, despite the very high standard, fewer than a hundred people in the audience. I was by now a complete choral obsessive and steeped in 'Godfrey' (singing in four of his choirs at once), but I could see that something was missing, that the audience was feeling excluded. Andrew taught me that choirs can attract, entertain and retain an audience through arresting and varied programming, but without being lowbrow. Both men saw choral music as a sublime vehicle of human expression; they just drove it in different ways.

E   *What was your philosophy when you started your own choir?*

J   Right from the beginning of Viva Voce twenty-five years ago, I wanted to make choral singing entertaining and approachable – to build up an audience while performing the music we loved to a high standard. We managed to get 1,100 people along to the Auckland Town Hall at the end of last year, to hear a largely a cappella concert, so our themed-programme approach seems to have worked very well. I believe that concerts of a lot of short works need to be linked, with a theme and often a (light-hearted) commentary, or even the most dedicated listeners become bored. Peter used to talk to the audience, and very urbanely, but could err on the academic side. Nothing I do, though, has arisen out of a criticism of Peter's style; it's just that we live in a more visual and less formal age now, and Viva Voce needed to respond to that. Peter's legacy is a whole, integrated choral philosophy of discipline, quality and enjoyment, and I'm immensely glad I was brought up in it.

TERENCE MASKELL IS THE CONDUCTOR OF THE GRADUATE CHOIR NZ and a number of Auckland school choirs, a former conductor of the Auckland Youth Choir and a former member of the Holy Trinity Cathedral Choir, Auckland University Singers, University Festival Choir and Dorian Choir. *Interviewed, 18 January 2009.*

E   *Your work with choirs has been recognised for many years as being of the highest order, culminating now with the Graduate Choir, which is one of New Zealand's finest. What influence has Peter had on your music life?*

T   Immense. Absolutely immense. Peter was responsible for my discovery of choral music. Joining the all-comers choir at university as a student was a real revelation. Suddenly I was singing Haydn, Palestrina and Brahms. And I discovered that I could sight-read it all. I just soaked everything up like blotting paper. Peter was my lecturer for stage one History of Music, a potted coverage of music from nought AD to the present day. A mammoth amount to study in a year! He'd say, 'I apologise to those of you who are not Christian, but the history of

Western music is tied up inextricably with the history of the Christian church.' And I became acquainted with what became known as the 'Godfrey sniff' – his way of disarming what could be sticky situations.

I was fortunate to sing with the Festival Choir, my first experience of performing at such a high standard and touring overseas. I must tell you a funny story. When the Festival Choir became the Auckland University Singers and it was my turn for an audition, Peter said, 'Ah, Terence, sing this note.' He went to the piano, played a note, which I sang, and then said, 'Thank you, goodbye.' Peter was a reserved sort of person, but he could be excruciatingly funny.

I joined the Dorian Choir and the Cathedral Choir – in its last days at St Mary's Cathedral – some ten years after Peter's arrival in Auckland. Both choirs were well-established by then and very good. I admire Peter hugely because he chose to come to a young country where choral music was quite raw in comparison with England, and then lifted the standard of choral singing throughout the country to an incredibly high degree. Several of his choirs became recognised internationally. If he had stayed in England his career would probably have been quite different. He would either have remained a school teacher or he would have needed to get onto the 'cathedral ladder', working with choirs that were already established.

E   *What did Peter do to shape the sound and the music?*

T   I think he was an instinctive choir trainer. Choral training is very different these days. We have to be able to diagnose and fix the problem, otherwise our singers don't trust us. But what Peter did was to say, 'You're too loud' or 'Altos, you're bloody flat' or 'Sopranos, that top A was terrible' or 'Basses, those vowels are agricultural'. He would tell the choir what he wanted, and demonstrate it with his own beautiful singing, but he didn't tell the choir how to do it. And that was typical of his time, especially in his younger days.

Choir trainers can now get doctorates in conducting and phonation – forming the sound. Conductors are very much more aware of voice production. Things have become very, very specialised. So the sounds that choirs make with these sorts of conductors are very different from the sounds made by the Dorians in those years gone by.

E   *Peter says that as a chorister and choral scholar he received no vocal tuition. They sang scales with Boris Ord for warm-ups, where he would say things like 'no wobbles', but gave them no training in technique. So Peter must have just absorbed and imitated the sound made by the older choristers. And that sound would be passed down through the ranks, as it were, from year to year.*

T I think that's right. We listened to the recordings of choirs conducted by people like Boris Ord and David Willcocks, and simply copied the sound. The women in Peter's choirs sang with a very heady, pure sound. Their voices became de-sexed, and these days there is a lot of criticism of that sort of sound – women are expected to sound like women. Actually, it's quite difficult to sing in tune if the whole body is not being used.

Choral conducting can be said to be derivative. We learn from those who give us our experiences. But that will stagnate unless we can grow ourselves. I and others have benefited from the growth of choral music in this country, and Peter has been hugely responsible for that. But equally important, for me, has been my exposure to other choirs and conductors. We have seen and heard the work of many overseas conductors and their choirs through courses and tours – largely through the efforts of the New Zealand Choral Federation. And so, many of us are now quite eclectic in the way we conduct our choirs. For example, I expect my choir to have a different sound for different genres. In Peter's time we'd sing a spiritual in the same way as we sang Palestrina.

E *There is a different attitude towards balance of voice parts in choirs these days too, isn't there?*

T Absolutely. It used to be a top-heavy sound where the sopranos were basically accompanied by the rest of the choir. This put a lot of pressure on the sopranos! My personal preference is the other way round – a heavy bass line for a strong foundation, then the tenors, followed by the altos or counter tenors, with the sopranos as the icing on the cake. Of course, the high voices will carry more, anyway. My philosophy is that if the basses have a cutting edge to their sound, not just a 'wuffle', they provide the harmonic basis and support for the tuning of the rest of the choir.

Peter's style of conducting was quite restrained, quite controlled. He achieved musical phrasing and the balance of voices in polyphony from his rehearsals. But any gestures would be small and mostly contained within the beat. And he would mouth the words, as most choral conductors do, which made a connection with the singers.

Singers who have sung a lot together develop an ability to feel the music and to shape the phrases intuitively. And this happened with both the Dorians and the Cathedral Choir. Peter's main focus was on intonation, almost to the point of being obsessive about it. If singers are nervous of singing out of tune they can become inhibited. And so a choir of forty to sixty people under Peter wouldn't make as robust a sound as under somebody else.

As a result of the early music movement, attitudes towards tuning have changed. In Peter's time, everything was based on equal temperament tuning. He insisted on really bright thirds and leading notes – almost certainly a hangover from his days at King's, and something perpetuated later by Sir David Willcocks. But in natural tuning they are actually flatter than those from the keyboard. And so, in unaccompanied singing, the awareness is now that the choir should tune to the harmonics coming up from the bass line. This means that the thirds and sevenths will be flatter than those on the equal temperament keyboard instrument. But when accompanied, the choir then needs to tune differently – in fact, sing out of tune. This demands a high level of listening acuity.

E   *What were the most memorable times for you in Peter's choirs?*

T   The overseas tours. Although I toured with the Cathedral Choir in Australia, and with the Dorians on their first tour, the Festival Choir tour, which was the first of the tours, is the most memorable for me. Singing in the Lincoln Centre, New York, with the University Festival Choir in 1972 was a major highlight. You could have heard a pin drop during the entire concert. I think Peter was enormously proud of us. We sang at the Kennedy Centre in Washington, and went to the White House where we met the president's wife, Mrs Nixon.

Our tour was originally to be three weeks in the Eastern seaboard of the United States. But it was discovered that it would cost not very much more to go on to England, and so that is what we did – as well as parts of the Continent. It is difficult to describe the emotional impact of singing a service in King's College Chapel. These were heady experiences for us all.

E   *How would you sum up Peter's contribution to New Zealand choral music?*

T   Huge! It is true that he came to a choral backwater that was ripe and ready for something to happen, and who better than someone of his pedigree. What we've seen in subsequent years, by and large, are the fruits of that. I'm also a self-taught person, and my many experiences in Peter's choirs gave me my love of choral music and desire to be a conductor. But I keep watching people and gleaning things from their differing techniques and styles. My style is eclectic because I have absorbed a great deal from other conductors and choirs.

It was a brilliant move of Peter's to set up the New Zealand Choral Federation. It has done an incredible amount to foster choral music in this country. No one can dispute the fact that Peter is the father of choral music in New Zealand. There were others before him and during his time – Victor Galway from Dunedin and Max Fernie in Wellington, for example, to name just a few – but they worked in a small area, without the national influence that Peter had. And Peter brought with him a wealth of new and exciting repertoire from England and Europe that had not been performed here before – particularly 16th century music. The Graduate Choir NZ borrowed from the Dorian library a set of a motet by Peter Phillips recently, and to my amazement, it was handwritten by Peter. And King John of Portugal's *Crux Fidelis* was always sung from another of his handwritten copies. Peter must have worked indefatigably to produce these manuscripts – and there were others – because they are so time-consuming, especially if they are to be easily read by the choir.

E   *Let's sum those Auckland days up for Peter: university lecturer, St Mary's Cathedral Choir, Auckland String Players/Symphonia, Auckland Festival Choir/University Singers, Dorian Choir, all those overseas tours, a garden and a wife and family. Plus the organisation of it all: rehearsals, planning the music, keeping thorough records including an amazingly detailed account of his life in scrapbooks, albums and on the computer. When I asked Peter how on earth he found the time to keep records, he replied, 'I do them in January, in the holidays, when there is nothing much else to do.'*

T   Conductors are so lucky now. Many things would have been so much more time-consuming for Peter in those days. Sets of music that he ordered would probably have had to come by ship, whereas we only have to log on to the internet to see texts and specimen pages and listen to samples of them – and copies are in our hands in a matter of days. Our computers, photocopy machines and email make administration so easy and immediate, whereas Peter had handwriting, his typewriter and 'snail mail'. I don't know how he did it all! An extraordinary man.

D R KAREN GRYLLS ONZM IS ASSOCIATE PROFESSOR IN CONDUCTING AND head of choral studies at the University of Auckland, conducts the Auckland University Chamber Choir, is musical director of New Zealand Youth Choir, founder and musical director of Voices New Zealand, artistic director of Choirs Aotearoa New Zealand, and former musical director of the Dorian Choir. *Letter, 25 October 2014.*

In the late seventies, I made my way from Invercargill to Auckland. I left my teaching position at Southland Girls High School to begin study for a Master's degree at the University of Auckland. My choral experience until that time had been variable: I sang in the a cappella ensemble and in the Knox Church Choir as a student at Otago University; prepared the university choir for a performance of Fauré's Requiem; directed the choir at First Church, Invercargill, during my teaching days, and conducted the premiere performance of Philip Norman's opera *Stiff Luck for the Undertaker* at the Ngaio Marsh Theatre in Christchurch. Looking back, I guess I was fortunate to have had some conducting experience, but I'd had no conducting lessons and no opportunity to sing in excellent choirs.

I arrived in Auckland at the start of the academic year in 1977. There were wonderful musicians on the staff, including Professor Douglas Mews, Professor Thomas Rive and other such luminaries. I was earnestly encouraged by my peers to audition for the Auckland University Singers and the Dorian Choir – I had no prior knowledge of these choirs, nor had I any clue who Professor Peter Godfrey actually was. I'd simply never heard of him!

Life changed very quickly. I successfully auditioned for both choirs, and remember well my first class in choral music given by Peter in the old Princes Street music department. Later, on the Auckland University Singers' Australian Tour in 1980, I was given the honour of conducting Samuel Barber's *Reincarnations* in one of the concerts. I later discovered this was a rare occurrence that an assistant conductor was given the chance to conduct in a public recital.

By the end of my postgraduate time in Auckland, Peter had made it very clear to me that I should study conducting overseas. Through his continued encouragement and support, and after four years of study in America, I found myself invited to apply for the position of director of the Dorian

Choir (in 1985 after Peter's departure to Wellington), and for musical director of the National Youth Choir of NZ in 1989, after Peter retired.

The decision to study in America was really a pragmatic one: I was able to study at the University of Washington, Seattle, for a PhD in Theory, and a Master's in Choral Conducting. I had intentions of returning to New Zealand to teach at the university, and an academic – rather than a performance – doctorate would be required.

During my study abroad, I lived through the various versions of American choral sound. I had earlier experienced the best of the English choral tradition first hand with Peter. It was, however, the Swedish choral sound that fired my imagination then, and still does today. It came as no surprise to me that all Eric Ericson's singers in the Royal College of Music Choir in Stockholm took singing lessons. I worked hard to understand the components of vocal technique: in particular, I listened to fine pedagogues such as Isabel Cunningham, Beatrice Webster and Marvin Keenze (Philadelphia) teach in their studios. I wanted to know what they listened for and how they instructed their singers. It became immediately clear to me that vowel colour and resonance defined intonation, and that it was possible to sing with a healthy, well-produced vocal colour in an ensemble. The inclusion of kapa haka items in the repertoire also brought with it the possibility for a more connected and robust vocal quality.

As time went on, I found it no longer acceptable to say to singers in rehearsal that they were 'flat' or 'sharp' without giving them some idea of a solution. Young singers by the end of the 90s were beginning to take performance singing as part of their school curriculum, and could engage with the language used in their voice studio lessons. If there were gains in vocal skills, sight-reading and musicianship didn't always keep up. In my own Dorian audition, years before, I was asked to sight-read Bax's *Mater Ora Filium*! With such sight-reading examples, young singers may fare less well today. There is no replacement for rehearsing a cappella and singing regularly in a good choir to develop these skills.

Without doubt, at critical steps in my career, Peter gave me enthusiastic encouragement. He attended my choral concerts wherever and whenever he could, and I am indeed very grateful for his keen support of my early life on the podium. Peter gave his singers a wonderful choral discipline, good humour and a love of singing at the highest level of excellence. In his own inimitable way, he gave all who sang with him this great gift.

20

Nostalgia Choir, 2004–15

E   *Peter, a very special choir – the Nostalgia Choir – was formed relatively recently, and has given great joy to some of the former singers from your Auckland choirs. Whose idea was that?*

P   In mid-2003 dear Ray Monteith, the 'mini Bish' as we called him, died. He was in his hundredth year. As his final illness began to take charge, he kept in touch with me about music for his funeral, all of which was decided upon a few weeks before he died. I was unable to get up to Auckland for the day originally chosen, so the funeral was put off to suit me! We had a magnificent choir of over sixty singers from past cathedral and Dorian choirs – Ray had been a member of the Dorians before I came out here and was later patron. We had a wonderful rehearsal and service.

     My time in Auckland was very limited on that occasion, and because I had to catch a flight back the same afternoon, I was unable to get to the 'party' in the hall afterwards, and so I didn't meet up with all the lovely friends I had in the choir. When I got home the idea came to me that they might form a choir the following January to sing services at the cathedral when the Cathedral Choir was on holiday. A marvellous committee, led by Margery Charlton, was soon established which resulted in a choir of about fifty singers, which would sing for eight days in the middle of January. We started with a Saturday rehearsal and continued for the following week, with two services on both Sundays, and mid-week Evensongs as well. We had a great time and it was amazing how well they all sang in spite of advancing age. I loved being back in the cathedral again with a choir. So it's continued each year, but with recent changes to make allowances for my own advancing age! Quite a few of the Nostalgia Singers have formed the St Mary's Singers who provide services at the cathedral when required. They are conducted by Anita Banbury and form the core of Nostalgia Choir, which meets for only a weekend in January now, not a week. I sing bass but am allowed to do a little conducting as well! I'm so lucky at my age to be able to work with singers from so long ago.

Margery Charlton had a large part to play as a committee member in organising the Nostalgia weeks at Holy Trinity Cathedral, Auckland. It is not the first time she has contributed to the success of a choir that Peter was involved with. He paid a wonderful tribute to Margery in one of his autobiographical writings, and a slightly abridged form of that tribute is recorded here.

When the invitation came to take a choir to the USA, it became obvious that we would need a secretary/administrator, and it soon became obvious that Margery's keen interest and very efficient administrative skills would fit the bill for such a position. We worked closely in the preparations for the tour, and she was such an enormous help in every conceivable way on the tour – except from a musical point of view, although she always had interesting comments to make on our singing. Once the choir settled back in New Zealand, she continued to act as secretary, and was very important in the preparations for the tour to the ISME Conference in Perth in 1974. However, when I was appointed professor at the beginning of that year, I very much needed an administrator for the School of Music, and Margery was the obvious choice. She continued in that position until after I left Auckland at the end of 1982. However, when the Dorians decided to do a European tour in 1975, it seemed the sensible thing to do to have Margery as our main organiser and administrator for that, as well. When I moved to Wellington for the beginning of 1983, and worked more closely with the National Youth Choir, she would often come to our training camps to help in whatever way was possible.

Margery provided the most important initiative in attracting

Nostalgia Choir rehearsing in Holy Trinity Cathedral.

me back to Auckland whenever it was possible. She organised my seventieth birthday celebrations there, and then did the same for my eightieth, when a massive concert was given in Holy Trinity Cathedral (many people were turned away, including a past Governor General!) with combined choirs as well as single choirs from the Auckland area.

After the tragedy of Bishop Monteith's death in 2003, I came up with the idea of having a 'get-together' with past members of the Cathedral and Dorian choirs during the summer holiday of 2004 (January), and inevitably asked Margery if she could organise this. I will always be blessed by the enormous enthusiastic support which Margery has given me since I arrived in New Zealand. She even came over to England to attend Jane's and my wedding in 1994.

RECOLLECTION

Janet Irwin, Dorian Choir.
Letter, 23 February 2009.

Dear Peter,

Sometime during this year's Nostalgia Choir reunion, I decided that I wanted to write you a letter. My next birthday is my eightieth – and you are well on the way to your next milestone! I don't want either of us to fade away into the wild blue yonder before I have thanked you for the wealth of wonderful, Dorian-related memories which inhabit my mind. You have, quite simply, enriched my life. A few of these memories …

… Coming to my first audition in December 1960, the first of about twenty auditions) and leaving a two-month old baby in his carrycot on the verandah of your house when I went inside to sing …

… New Caledonia in 1966. I know you weren't there, but you chose me and seven other Dorian women to spend ten days in Noumea – and join in singing *Messiah* in French with a local choir at the opening of a new 'Conservatoire de Musique'. It was the first time in my life that I had left New Zealand, and the whole enterprise seemed completely surreal. Monsieur B (I've forgotten his name) was quite eccentric. There was no Conservatoire – but he had pots of money. He had imported a mini orchestra from Sydney, and some ballet dancers from Melbourne, as well as us eight ladies from Auckland. We were all accommodated in a luxury hotel on Anse Vata beach. There was a *Messiah* performance in French, in a musty old movie theatre. And we had a cocktail party hosted by the Mayor of Noumea. Luckily I had packed a cocktail dress …

… Fiji in 1972 for the South Pacific Festival, memorable for being able to take John and my three teenage children with me. They still remember a lazy trip down the river by canoe …

… 1975: flying low over London and seeing places I had known only from photographs and newsreels – the Thames, Big Ben and the Houses of Parliament, St Paul's – for real! …

… Singing Bach in German to a German university audience in Munster, and being given a standing ovation. I stood there with tears streaming down my face. I think that a small part of my mind was still stuck in my wartime adolescence, when all things German were to be despised, or feared or hated. In that moment a barrier was shattered …

… A trip down the Rhine Gorge, with castles and vineyards and the Rock of the Lorelei, a day trip by train to Heidelberg, Cologne Cathedral, Beethoven's house in Bonn, walking the streets of Paris, a group of us spontaneously singing *Locus Iste* under the dome in Chartres Cathedral, drinking cherry brandy at the Mayor's reception in Copenhagen after that ghastly overnight train journey, seeing original Rembrandts in the Hague …

… 1977, when my husband, John, and our sixteen-year-old son

accompanied me on the second Dorian tour. The joy and privilege of singing in Canterbury Cathedral, Salisbury, Gloucester, Chichester, St Paul's, King's College, Cambridge; York Minster, etc, etc. The excitement of the Maltings, and *Death in Venice* with Peter Pears – seeing Benjamin Britten 'lit up' in his box as we applauded. And the thrill of bumping into Janet Baker backstage …

… My two-bar solo in one of David Griffiths's compositions in Gloucester Cathedral during the Three Choirs Festival – the highlight of my singing days …

The more I write the more I remember. I haven't started on the trips to Sydney and Christchurch, or the many blessings of my Dorian years in Auckland, and the many lifelong friendships I have made and cherish. Just one blessing that I must mention – the overwhelming joy and privilege or singing Bach's B Minor Mass – not once, but twice.

All these things happened, and my life has been enriched beyond measure, because of your inspired leadership, brilliant talent, all-encompassing love of choral music and patient (almost always!) nurturing of choristers. Peter, thank you.

21

That Remarkable Ear: A Conclusion

THE ACUTENESS OF PETER'S EAR IS LEGENDARY. HE CANNOT TOLERATE bad intonation, and mistakes of any kind are anathema to him. I once asked Peter if poor intonation actually hurt him physically, as he reacts so strongly to thirds, sixths and sevenths that he considers to be flat. He said yes. When I asked where it hurt him, he pointed to the side of his head and said, 'In here, somewhere.' Peter's ability to know which singer is out of tune or singing a wrong note – no matter how large the choir – is close to superhuman.

It is a fact that Peter's attention was always more on the soprano section than any other, and his habit of walking up and down in front of sopranos to find out who was singing flat or sharp was terrifying for them. Humiliating, really, as no other section received that treatment. One by one the singers would fade out from nervousness. The altos were growled at for flat thirds and leading notes, but that was all. Tenors had a relatively easy time of it because their rarity made them precious, and therefore they were treated more carefully. The basses were often just left to get on with things. By contrast, every note the sopranos sang was under close scrutiny. Top notes were gone over again and again, usually with a stressed, screwed-up look on Peter's face even before the note was sung – not conducive to relaxed vocal chords!

Peter discussing a score with Elizabeth Salmon c. 1974.

I drove Peter up to the Nostalgia weekends in Auckland a few times. We stayed overnight with his old friend Pat Moore, and Pat's wife, Heather. They were really happy occasions – except for one, which saw me wanting to get back into my car and drive home again. Pat had been given a CD of The Three Tenors for Christmas, which he was enjoying greatly. He played it for us, and he and Heather began singing along. I thought I should join in as well, and did so, aware that I was sitting right next to Peter and that his legendary ear would be picking up every sound I made. That had not worried me much in the past, but I was older and hadn't sung for a while. All went well until there it was … a high note. Should I sing it or leave it? Courage prevailed. I wish it hadn't. My throat tightened and I made a hash of it. Peter's reaction? 'What gives you the right to sing out of tune and spoil it for everyone else?' he said. I don't think he meant to be so hurtful. It was just his instinctive reaction to a sound less than beautiful. He simply couldn't bear it.

I experienced the warm and caring side to Peter's nature too. I sat LRSM Performers some eighteen months after starting to play the organ – daunting, to say the least. A week or so before the examination I dreamt that I had passed with excellent marks and saw my name in the paper. I was shattered to discover on waking that it was a dream. My confidence lessened to the point that I wrote a note to Peter to say I was withdrawing from the exam. Apparently he went striding up his drive to find me over at the cathedral and dissuade me. 'That bloody woman', he was heard to mutter. But he invited the 'bloody woman' to go for a weekend holiday with the family, which restored me to sanity. I sat the exam and passed.

And of course Peter could be very funny. An incident comes to mind when I was waiting for the green light to record a programme of organ music for the concert programme of Radio New Zealand. I was very nervous! I need to explain the joke before I share it with you. Sometimes the pedal stops on an organ include a Contra Fagotto – a 16-foot stop. And on larger organs there is usually a 32-foot pedal stop. The red light was about to change to green when Peter, who was to turn pages for me, leaned forward and whispered in my ear: 'Have you heard the one about the 32-foot contraceptive?' It's difficult to concentrate on playing after such a joke, but my nervousness dissipated quickly!

Peter had a fixation about his singers coming equipped with a 2B pencil. Later it became, 'Always come with *three* 2B pencils. One for yourself and one for each of your neighbours.' This was important, though, as it made for efficient learning – singers noting what Peter said as well as circling personal problem areas. I was sad to hear that at a recent St Michael's rehearsal Peter had sidled up to the librarian and asked, 'Do you have a spare pencil? I forgot mine.' It seems that in his old age he has indeed become one of us.

Peter used to say, 'I don't give praise.' And he didn't. We always knew when we had sung well, though, and somehow that was sufficient. These days, Peter has mellowed to the point of saying to me after a service, 'You played very well. You played very, very well.' It's so special!

Blend, intonation, a beautiful straight tone and good vowel sounds were Peter's focus. He made a telling comment in one Nostalgia Choir rehearsal – 'Sopranos, don't you realise you are the stars of the show? And all you are doing is burying your heads in your copies!' – and another as he and I listened to recordings of the St Mary's, Holy Trinity Cathedral and Dorian choirs on one of our journeys to Auckland. Peter was quite entranced with the singing on the whole, but at one point asked, 'Why are the sopranos always so prominent in my choirs?' His sopranos knew the answer to that – we all did. They were the ones who were given most of his attention!

The sensitivity of Peter's ear was fantastic, but he didn't have perfect pitch – exquisitely tuned relative pitch was his gift. Peter would dearly have liked perfect pitch, although I think he could have become demented by the ways that pitch shifts through tiredness, stress, hot or cold weather, inattention and so on. On one of the two Dorian tours Peter bought a new watch tuned to the note of A. He would put it to his ear constantly, trying to develop perfect pitch. He did develop quite a keen sense of pitch as a result, but it wasn't perfect. In later years if he knew someone had the gift, he would sometimes ask them to give the choir their starting notes. Peter suffered quite dreadfully following an inner ear problem – vertigo or similar. For a while he complained that one ear heard a semitone higher than the other, which must have been sheer torment.

Modern trends encourage a more equal balance between the voice parts and a more telling resonance, but Peter's focus on sopranos produced a different weighting of voice parts. His sopranos produced a very pure, boy-like, almost ethereal sound, especially in the earlier days – the white head-tone of his ever-beloved Kings. We sopranos tried so hard to emulate that sound in St Mary's Cathedral Choir and were discouraged from having singing lessons in case the dreaded vibrato would develop.

Much has been said about auditions and the terror that they provoked. Some singers took to the sherry bottle to calm nerves, and one or two admitted to having gone on tranquillisers to help. Alec Loretto, lecturer in music at Auckland Teacher's Training College, was auditioned for the Dorian Singers in 1967, with Peter as chief auditioner. Alec's witty response to the audition report he received shows Peter's rigorous approach:

> Three main points. First, until October 23rd, the date of my audition, I believed I could sing major scales in tune. Your presence and that of your three colleagues with their pitiful looks and cynical glances soon convinced me of my error. It might interest you to know that between the hours of 7.00 and 7.30 a.m. each day, when I take my daily bath, I sing major scales and, sometimes, tonus peregrinus. You are all invited to listen to the former. The men may, if they wish, listen from inside the bathroom door. The ladies, I suggest, may listen discreetly from without. I extend this invitation because I believe my major bathroom scales are more in tune than my Choral Hall variety. You say my voice is light. Alas, my heart was heavy.
>
> Your second comment – 'Ear good' – is even more disturbing. Which ear is good? My left? Or my right? And even more worrying, what is wrong with the other? Is it musically deficient? Does it require medical attention? If 'Ear good' means that I know how to solve the ear tests perpetuated by the Associated Board, Trinity College, Auckland University, and, dare I add, Dorian Auditions, you are wrong. Sir. I do not. I hate them. I seriously question their value when played on a keyboard instrument. I refuse to work at them and am resigned to failing them, as I'm sure I did on the night.
>
> Your comment under the heading, 'Sight Reading', is the giddy limit. It requires not words or mine to expose the comment 'Can be improved' as the very acme of sick humour.

Peter Godfrey has been under close scrutiny throughout these pages, and now is the time to share how this book came about. During dinner with us on the evening of Friday, 31 October 2008, Peter announced that a few days prior, it had been fifty years since he and his family had arrived in New Zealand. How could I have forgotten! I first met Peter a month after his arrival – late November 1958. He was on the adjudicating panel for six music bursaries awarded by the University of Auckland for the Executant Diploma Course, and I was auditioning as a candidate for one of them. That evening fifty years later, Peter lent me a copy of the recently published book by William Owen on Sir David Willcocks. I was riveted by it. It was the first oral history I had read, and I relished the living quality of the style.

The next morning an arrow of certainty shot into my mind that this was the way to create a much-needed biography of Peter. Having been his first organ student in New Zealand, lectured by him at university, a member of St Mary's Cathedral Choir and the Auckland Dorian Singers, assistant conductor of the Dorian Choir and soprano soloist, continuo player with the Auckland String Players, a tutor with the National Youth Choir in its first two years of existence, Peter's assistant and organist for the parish choir of St Michael's Anglican Church, Waikanae, and a close friend of the family's for fifty years, I also realised that I was probably an appropriate person to organise such a biography.

So I set to work sending out letters and emails inviting Peter's family and friends, colleagues and former members of his choirs to share their memories, as well as recording interviews and transcribing them, editing and so forth. I am indebted to the many people who responded, in many cases giving a substantial amount of time to the task, delighting in the opportunity to pay tribute. The resulting book focuses on the extraordinary gift Peter gave to choral music in New Zealand and the people who were part of that. He also contributed enormously to Auckland University, and to Auckland orchestral music by developing the Auckland String Players into an excellent string and then full symphony orchestra, but those are subjects for another book.

What comes through is the picture of a man who arrived in this country imbued with what he had learned as a young chorister at King's College, Cambridge, and who remained true to the 'King's tradition' of choral singing throughout his life here. A man who shared his passion with hundreds of singers and the thousands who came to listen, and succeeded in transforming our choirs into world-class performers on the international stage. There is no doubt that my musical life and those of many others would have been the poorer had Peter Godfrey not come to New Zealand.

Opposite: Peter with Dottie in Mahara Place, Waikanae.

Postscript

ONE EVENING IN 2009, PETER JOINED MY HUSBAND AND ME FOR A MEAL, and we talked a little about Peter's life. I have recorded part of the conversation here as a fascinating last word from the man himself.

E   *Peter, you say repeatedly that you are not comfortable in social situations.*

P   No, I'm not! I haven't anything interesting to say. I'm just a bore.

E   *And yet you've amassed the most amazing number of friends and acquaintances. Perhaps you feel limited in conversation because your life has been focused on only two main areas.*

P   Really? What are they?

E   *Well, what would you say?*

P   Women?

E   *I hadn't thought of that. That makes it three things!*

P   Walnuts?

E   *Not what I was thinking of. That's four things.*

P   Gardening?

E   *We're getting there!*

P   Oh – and music.

Acknowledgements

Many people have contributed to the making of this book. My grateful thanks must be expressed to the following:

Peter Godfrey for the time shared with me recording interviews, and for allowing me complete access to his own autobiographical material, records, reports and photographs.

The late Sir David Willcocks for his foreword, and the many people who contributed interviews or written material. The response to my letters of request for participation in the book was overwhelming in its generosity.

Simon Tipping for his permission to use *Orpheus: Portrait of a Choir* and *Choir of the World: The New Zealand National Youth Choir* as reference material. 'Use anything you need,' he said. This was helpful when it came to creating questions and fleshing out material as Peter's memory failed.

Anthony Dreaver for permission to use material from his book *Ten Years' Singing: The Story of the Kapiti Chamber Choir*, especially Peter's amusing expressions recorded faithfully by Anthony over many rehearsals.

New Zealand Choral Federation publications, Kapiti Chorale, Kapiti Chamber Choir, New Zealand Arts Foundation, New Zealand National Youth Choir, SOUNZ and Ritmico for all their help.

Hilary Monteith and Noni Kenny who responded immediately to the queries that were emailed quite frequently in the last stages of writing the book. Peggy Haworth for sharing Alec Loretto's amusing letter. Peggy was most helpful in providing a wealth of written and taped material for research.

Peter Averi for reading the manuscript, making corrections and endorsing the book. Thank you, Peter.

Kapiti Chorale member Norma McCallum for telling her daughter about the book I was writing, and Mary McCallum of Mākaro Press for accepting it for publication with such enthusiasm and friendly support that helped greatly with the completion of the project. Not many authors have the luxury of a publisher finding them rather than the other way round. And to Mākaro's Paul Stewart for his fine contribution to the edits and design of the book.

My husband, Tom, for his long-suffering patience and loving support.

Index

Z